p 85 clearly a question
of what one deems authoritative -
whether it's verifiable or ancient -
on what basis.

What role do practices have in the
Theo school

Athens

paideia p 161
       p 228
       p 236
       238

       259
64 Schooling, culturing, character formation
66 deep foundation- knowledge of the divine.
6 Teacher, midwife, involves conversion
   shape persons identity, not to fit a
particular social role.
   to form persons with habits that
enable them as agents in to apprehend God
Christianly.
   formation of people - does so indirectly, by
focusing on somet

73

Rituals — since God can only be understood
indirectly, we need rituals. 109

Craig Dykstra on practice 118.
⭐ see definition of practice 118.
121-123

170 = mediating response to God.

To Understand
God Truly

To Understand God Truly

What's Theological About a Theological School

David H. Kelsey

Westminster/John Knox Press
Louisville, Kentucky

Book design by Joni Weingarten

First edition

Published by Westminster/John Knox Press
Louisville, Kentucky

This book is printed on acid-free paper that meets the American National Standards Institute Z39.48 standard. ∞

PRINTED IN THE UNITED STATES OF AMERICA
9   8   7   6   5   4   3   2   1

Library of Congress Cataloging-in-Publication Data

Kelsey, David H.
  To understand God truly : what's theological about a theological school /
David H. Kelsey. — 1st ed.
      p.   cm.
  Includes bibliographical references and index.
  ISBN 0-664-25397-0 (pbk. : alk. paper)

  1. Theology—Study and teaching.   2. Theological seminaries.   I. Title.
BV4020.K45 1992
230'.71'1—dc20   92-4359

in memoriam

Hans W. Frei

Contents

Acknowledgments

Far more than many books, this one grew out of conversations that still continue; it owes large debts to my conversation partners. Central among these partners have been the members of the Issues Research Advisory Committee of the Association of Theological Schools and the participants in several symposia, conferences, and summer seminars the Committee sponsored, funded by generous grants from the Eli Lilly Endowment, Inc. At one of the conferences Rebecca Chopp, Craig Dykstra, Edward Farley, Barbara Wheeler, and Charles Wood discussed with me an early draft of the first four chapters in pointed and helpful ways, as did Kathryn Tanner, later, on an early draft of the entire book.

I want to record my thanks to four people in particular without whom this book would never have been finished: Robert Wood Lynn, who, having first proposed the project, persisted in encouraging and supporting it; Julie Kelsey, whose unsentimental view of theological education from the perspective of parish ministry kept me honest as we discussed what I struggled to write; Barbara Wheeler, whose acute critical judgment of two drafts of the manuscript saved it from innumerable incoherences, unclarities, and stylistic gaffes; and Maggi Despot, splendid copy editor and typist, whose ability to decipher my illegible handwriting revealed abundant native talent for a brilliant career in cryptography should she ever weary of religious studies.

This book is dedicated to Hans W. Frei, friend and colleague, whose sudden death at the height of his powers deprived us all of an extraordinary theological educator.

D.H.K.

Yale Divinity School

Part One

Locating a
Theological School

1

Orientation:
Or, After the Fall

Every year on the weekend before the start of the fall term of the theological school where I teach, the student organization offers a retreat as part of the orientation for new students. New faculty members have also found it helpful. For years it was held at a lovely little conference center on a rocky neck projecting into Long Island Sound. It is an opportunity to reflect on one's own expectations of theological education and to begin to get a sense of the nature and overarching purposes of this particular school in which one has invested those expectations. The retreat has always been called "Before the Fall."

Inevitably, a fall does come. Innocent idealizations of theological education give way before concrete realities of the particular theological school whose ethos is the medium in which one now largely lives and whose polity constrains one's life in powerful but often elusive ways. At some point virtually everyone involved in the enterprise feels the pinch of a misfit between yearnings and expectations that are important (and vulnerable) parts of one's personal identity, on one side, and on the other a set of unexpected, often unintelligible, frequently frustrating "givens" that appear to be important (and invulnerable?) parts of the identity of the school. The pinch gives rise to questions. What are the purposes and priorities that really govern and structure this school? What is realistic to expect of theological education, whether done in this school or in some other? If institutional reality could be remade to heart's desire, what would the ideal theological school be like? Most basic of all, since it is theological

13

schools and theological education we are questioning, what is *theological* about them? Theologically speaking, what ought to be the purposes and nature of theological education? What theological commitments ought to be decisive criteria for assessing and reshaping the ethos and polity of a theological school?

Those are the types of questions this book addresses. I have five hopes for it. First, I hope for the book to be accessible. I have not tried to achieve this by simplifying complex issues or by avoiding serious theological analysis, critique, and argument. Of course, I hope to achieve accessibility partly by explaining what I mean, and what I take others to mean, as clearly as possible in plain English! But I also hope to achieve it by constantly supposing that I am addressing someone who has entered the world of a theological school fairly recently—perhaps a student starting her second year of study, or an academic who has just joined a theological school faculty and has never herself been previously involved in theological education, or a person newly appointed to the board of trustees of a theological school. This is a book addressed to those who have felt the pinch of a misfit between their expectations of theological education and the realities of a theological school. It is addressed to questions that arise after the fall—usually in the dreary February of the second year one is in the school.

Second, I hope the book will succeed at being a collegial partner in an ongoing conversation. For nearly a decade now a lively but fragile, potentially important theological conversation has been going on among theological educators about the basic nature and purpose of theological education. It has been nurtured in many ways: by research into basic issues in theological education underwritten by competitive grants offered by the Association of Theological Schools (ATS) and funded by the Lilly Endowment, Inc.; by the work of some theological educators commissioned by the Endowment to think about these questions; and by a series of seminars and conferences convened by the ATS to discuss some of the results of this research and reflection. I have had the opportunity to observe this conversation from a privileged vantage point.[1] I have become deeply impressed by the importance of this conversation to the health of theological education in North America.

The conversation is nonetheless fragile because hitherto there has never been a lively tradition of discussion of theological education by those who are engaged in doing it. Fortunately, theological education is not itself a scholarly specialization. It has no academic guild. Consequently, no faculty member is promoted or awarded tenure for research and writing on this topic. There is little literature on the matter. There is not even the shared vocabulary that would make discussion easy. Nor has there been a clear knowledge of which assumptions are widely enough shared to make it possible to state disagreements as genuine engagements and not as exercises in talking past one another. The conversation could easily break down because it has so little standing in the world of theological education, has no well-established tradition to nurture it, no reward system to encourage it, no institutional home to give it enduring structure. At the same time the liveliness and potential importance of this conversation are shown by the remarkable number of significant articles and books it has generated over the past half dozen years. I intend this book to be a contribution to the conversation, moving it along in new directions, perhaps, but only in dialogue with other voices from whom I have learned a great deal.

My third and fourth hopes for this book are closely connected but are quite distinct. I hope to make suggestions about the most helpful *way* to think about these issues—suggestions about the differences between more useful and less useful ways to *pose* the issues—as a contribution to making others' discussions of these topics more fruitful. I consider these suggestions to be largely formal. They are not designed to support one side of a disagreement about the nature and purposes of theological schools against the other side. Rather they are designed to help disagreements be posed in ways that are as productive as possible in generating further conversation and new insights.

My fourth hope is to make a cogent case for a sketch of the particular theological view that the purpose of a theological school is to seek to understand God more truly, and that a school's "nature" follows from this "purpose." I consider this to be a material theological proposal. In a discussion of his book *Theologia: The Fragmentation and Unity of Theological Education,*[2] Edward Farley once ruefully observed that any essay on the nature and purposes of theological education is inescapably a contribution to utopian literature. This book will be no exception.

It will be utopian both in the sense that I make no attempt to explain how we can get from here to there—how to actualize my proposal—and in the sense that, given human nature and the state of the world, it is probably a quite "unrealistic" proposal. In these ways utopian essays are "useless." However, at its best a utopian essay provides both unusual distance from the world as it is and a view of the world from an unusual angle. It sketches its city—or, in this case, its crossroads hamlet—in ideal terms with ironic intent. Despite its straight face, it is not so much a proposal seriously to be believed to be the best of all possible practical arrangements as it is a critique of present arrangements that is pointed enough to provoke significant conversation. A manifesto is flatfooted advocacy of a blueprint for reform; it's the irony that makes a proposal utopian. I hope for this book to be useful precisely because it is ironically utopian.

My ways of realizing these two hopes will be deeply intertwined in this book. Formal suggestions are terribly abstract. Without some illustrative material it is often very difficult to grasp and hang on to the point of the suggestion. Accordingly, the *way* I develop my own theological sketch of the idea of a theological school and the way I argue for it in preference to alternative theological views is meant as a series of illustrations of some suggestions about fruitful ways in which to pose these issues. Of course, I hope to persuade you that my material theological view of the theological school is the most compelling one. If I fail to do so, however, I hope that by that very failure I will have commended to you the fruitfulness of my suggestions about how to pose some of the central issues. The two are quite distinct hopes.

My final hope for this book is to bring into the center of the conversation the importance of the public and concrete character of theological education and the importance of attending to all the factors that make for that concreteness. It is for that reason that I propose to shift the name of the topic from "theological education" to "the theological school." "Education" is a very abstract term. It is used to designate a process. But the educational process always takes place in some particular institutional setting located in a particular socioeconomic context, has a particular ethos of its own that amounts to a "culture" open to ethnographic study, has its own structure of power, is offered by a particular group of faculty members themselves socialized in various ways as academic professionals, and is undergone by a particular student body. The phrase "theological education" misleadingly invites us to consider our topic in abstraction from much or all of that. In ordinary English, the word "school" seems more readily to connote the concrete institutional dimensions of the enterprise than does "education." I hope to make the case that it is *theologically* necessary to attend to the concreteness of theological education. A genuinely theological answer to the question "What is theological about theological education?" will keep these sociological, political, and economic dimensions of the enterprise at the center of the discussion.

WHAT HAVE WE GOT INTO?

The most obvious characteristic of the world of theological schools is the enormous diversity among its citizens. It is a deeply pluralistic world. Oddly, much discussion of what is theological about theological education ignores the diversity among theological schools. It may well be that theological education, if it deserves the name, is a process whose governing purposes are the same in all theological schools. It is also true, however, that the process never takes place in the abstract. It always takes place in some concrete location, in some particular school whose unique identity is rooted in its history, in some tradition of piety and theology, in its local culture, its ways of being financed, its ways of governing itself, its relations to a denomination, and its relation to the academic disciplines' "guilds."

The relation of this concrete location of education to the process of education is not like the relation of a husk to a kernel of wheat. It should not be assumed, for example, that the differences between theological education at Denver Seminary and at Harvard Divinity School are merely marked variations on "essentially" the same process simply because they are both genuinely places of theological education. "Theological school" should not be contrasted to "theological education" as "container" and "contained." Because the two interpenetrate so deeply, conceptual contrasts like "form/content" and "structure/content" are not helpful in trying to understand theologically the nature and purpose of theological schools.

The diversity among theological schools is partly rooted in differences among their deepest theological commitments and it is partly rooted in historical and sociocultural factors. I shall argue that any theological "idea" of a theological school must take the "non-theological" factors shaping a school as seriously as it takes the "truly" theological issues. This is my first formal suggestion about the most helpful way to pose questions covering theological education: Keep reflection tied to concrete social reality by keeping the concrete particularities of theological schools central to the discussion. To that end it will be useful to sketch the "location" of theological schools on the map of North American academic and religious institutions.

For purposes of this book we shall identify the world of theological schools in North America as all accredited graduate schools of theology in the United States and Canada. That is, we shall identify the boundaries of the world of theological schools with the membership of the Association of Theological Schools. Admittedly, this is somewhat arbitrary. There are many schools that are not members of the ATS calling themselves "theological schools" or "seminaries" that train leaders for churches. However, it can be justified as the least problematic way of tracing the boundaries of the world of theological schools. The Association of Theological Schools is an agency that accredits Protestant and Roman Catholic theological schools in Canada and the United States. Its criteria for accreditation give us the most formal description of what all these schools have in common. Among those standards, for example, is the requirement that usually degree recipients from accredited undergraduate colleges and universities may be admitted as students: thus theological schools are "graduate" schools. Despite the extreme pluralism marking this world, all 179 of the association's accredited member schools (as of 1990) have in common that they have met ATS standards. (In addition to its accredited members, the ATS in 1990 included eight "Candidate" schools involved in the two-year process of accreditation, and eighteen nonaccredited "Associate" members, for a total membership of 205 schools.)

If a theological sketch of the idea of a theological school is a utopian exercise, the community it describes is less an ideal city than a crossroads hamlet with an overwhelmingly white male population. In the larger world of academic institutions, theological schools are lilliputian. Twenty years ago Warren Deem, a professional consultant to the ATS, remarked that "the average Protestant seminary today— with its 15 faculty and 170 students—has resources which are more analogous to a neighborhood primary school than to a modern graduate professional institution."[3]

Modest changes in the relative statistics during the past twenty years have not undercut the force of the analogy. In 1989, enrollment in the M.A. and M.Div. programs of 202 reporting theological schools averaged 278 students per school if one simply did a head count of students (or 188 if one calculated on the basis of "full-time equivalence" [FTE]), and they averaged a faculty of 17 full-time faculty members per school (on an FTE basis).[4] About 46 percent of the students were enrolled in M.Div. degree programs requiring three or more years and designed to prepare persons for ordained leadership roles in the churches. Almost 37 percent of the total student population were enrolled in one- and two-year master's programs (M.A.R., M.R.E., M.T.S.)[5] or in nondegree certificate programs. The rest were enrolled in other, more advanced degree programs.

On average, they are still overwhelmingly white and male communities. As of 1989, there were more than twice as many men as women in M.Div. programs.[6] African American students, men and women combined, amounted to less than 7.3 percent of the total student population.[7] In size, theological schools are still more like primary schools in white neighborhoods that discourage the education of women than they are like modern graduate professional institutions in an open and pluralistic society.

Within this world of hamlets there is nonetheless a good deal of variety. For one thing, despite their small size on average, there is a great range of size among theological schools. Moreover, there has been a twenty-year trend toward relatively larger student bodies. In 1989 there were twenty-nine schools with fifty or fewer students. The smallest had a student body of eight. At the other end of the spectrum there were three schools with student bodies of a thousand or more in 1989. The largest reported 3814 students.[8] For another thing, there has been a steady drop in the number of students engaged in theological education full-time. Only a little more than two-thirds of the total enrollment of theological schools (68 percent) were full-time students in 1986 (the last year for which this figure was available); by contrast, well over three-quarters (78 percent) were full-time in 1978.

The financial resources of these academic hamlets are as relatively small as are their populations.[9] Theological schools accredited in the United States by the ATS in 1988–89 averaged expenses of $15,226 per FTE student out of average revenues of $15,560 per student. Almost a third of all expenditures (32.1 percent) went on average to pay instructional costs. Another 20.4 percent was spent on administrative costs and 6.2 percent for library expenses. On average only 9.5 percent of total expenses was reported devoted to the costs of operation and maintenance of the schools' plants.

The greatest part of revenues (36 percent) came on average from annual gifts and grants from religious organizations, individuals, and government contracts. This is "soft" money that cannot be relied on to repeat itself yearly. On average, roughly a quarter of the revenue (24 percent) came from student tuition (excluding tuition covered by financial aid) and another fifth (20.5 percent) from endowment funds. Only the latter is relatively "hard" money, a source of income providing a reliable basis for long-range planning.

It is important to note that none of these figures, whether for expenditures or for revenues, covers what the ATS calls "auxiliary enterprises," food, housing, books, and so forth (12.4 percent). This area is a net drain on theological schools. Between 1983–84 and 1985–86 theological schools reported that their deficits in auxiliary enterprise expenditures grew on average by 73 percent.[10] Presumably much of the apparent surplus of revenue over expenditures went to cover this deficit.

Within this financially constrained world there is nonetheless a striking variation of revenue and expenditure per student from one denomination to another. In 1987, the last year for which these figures are available, the continuum ranged from revenues of $15,727 and expenditures of $14,501 per student in schools affiliated with the Protestant Episcopal Church to revenues of $3,950 and expenditures of $3,536 per student in schools affiliated with the Southern Baptist Convention. In the same period Roman Catholic theological schools reported average revenues of $9,137 and average expenditures of $8,613 per student; nondenominational and interdenominational schools reported average revenues of $5,664 and expenditures of $5,673 per student.[11]

Clearly, the average theological school is not awash in funds available for discretionary spending, for covering the start-up costs of major new academic "experiments," for providing new student services, or even for providing adequate support services for administration and faculty. Nor has the average school likely sources in industry, government, or organized religion to which it can turn for major grants to fund such projects—or even to fund research with a high enough surcharge for "administrative costs" to help release other funds for innovative projects. Financially, the average theological school is like a primary school in a small town with a very limited tax base that is not likely to grow much in the foreseeable future.

In the cosmos of higher education, theological schools are in other respects like crossroads hamlets. Their small scale invites certain kinds of expectations. Clear recognition of their small size, however, imposes important reality checks on just those expectations. Compared to theological schools, most institutions of higher education in the United States and Canada seem to range in size from large to gigantic societies. After several years spent earning a degree in such contexts one understandably comes to yearn for an educational experience in a more intimate community, not just advanced seminar by advanced seminar, but as a total academic environment. A theological school's relatively small size fosters the expectation that it might provide just that kind of setting for learning. Moreover, the religious needs and commitments that often interest people in theological schools tend to place a high value on experiences of "community." Again, the school's small size encourages the expectation that sharing the common life of a theological school ought to provide just such experience. Furthermore, when one begins to see ways in which the theological school one has entered might be improved, its relatively small size can invite the thought that, compared to much more massive institutions, it ought to be relatively easy to change.

Further reflection suggests, however, that it is precisely the small-ness of theological schools which requires that such expectations be checked for realism. This does not mean that we should abandon such expectations. It means, rather, that expectations should be kept concrete. That is, they should be carefully nuanced so that they are expectations of *these* schools in their concrete particularity. "Smallness" is an abstraction; it is theological *schools* that are (relatively) small. For one thing, as we have seen, they are very limited financially. Hence, one's picture of an ideally intimate community as the context for learning must involve a "small-ness" a theological school can afford. The picture's implications regarding ratio of students to instructors or to supervisors, its implications regarding support services for students personally, support services for students' work in the library or in the "field," for housing arrangements, and so forth, must be manageable in a financial setting with few discretionary funds. If realization of the picture requires changes in the school's faculty or overall deployment of resources, they may need to be changes that can be introduced incrementally. Most schools' budgets do not allow for massive start-up costs for new programs.

For another thing, as we have seen, the average theological school is not a very pluralistic hamlet. It includes far fewer women and people of color than does American Christianity at large. That is another feature of the present concrete reality of theological schools. The absence of internal pluralism in a theological school can significantly inhibit change. That is especially true if the changes one has in view are responses to perceived theological and cultural pluralism within the churches, or responses to religious and cultural pluralism in the host cultures into which the churches are sent in mission. If pluralism outside the theological school is not reflected inside it, the school as a community may itself be too invested in institutional patterns appro-priate to a less pluralistic church and world to be easily changeable. Small, intimate but homogeneous villages are not necessarily easier to change than large, pluralistic, and impersonal cities.

GRUMBLING

The citizens of these crossroads hamlets grumble. It is not too much to say that they complain vigorously about their common lot, sometimes loudly. About what, specifically? It depends a bit on one's role and status in the hamlet.

Anyone who has lived for a time in student dormitories or apartment buildings or has eaten in their dining halls can recall endless student complaints about the theological school's curriculum. The complaint may be that the curriculum is too "academic" and insufficiently "professional"; too "theoretical" and insufficiently "practical"; or, conversely, that it is too single-mindedly focused on producing "professional ministers" in a certain model and too inflexible to allow individual students to pursue their own intellectual interests; and, above all, that the curriculum consists of too many small pieces of information that are not adequately "integrated," that it provides not so much a course of study as—in H. Richard Niebuhr's wonderfully wry phrase—"a series of studious jumps in various directions."[12] One will also recall equally frequent complaints about the lack of "real community" within the theological school. Increasingly during the past two decades one could also have heard complaints that there are insufficient numbers of women and persons of color within the student body and faculty, that the school is insufficiently "pluralistic."

If one had spent time with faculty at coffee hour or lunch or weekend socializing, one might have heard these complaints and, in addition, grumbles of a different sort: that the teaching load is so large as to leave no time for research and writing; that local church and denominational demands on faculty leave insufficient time to keep up with new literature in the field, let alone contribute to it; that committee responsibilities cut inappropriately into time required for academic matters; that responsibilities to provide pastoral care and spiritual direction to students erode time needed to prepare for teaching and to contribute to scholarship;[13] that sabbatical leave policies are nonexistent or inadequate to help resolve these conflicting demands on faculty time. Faculty characteristically complain about inadequate resources as well: insufficient library resources, inadequate secretarial and other "support" services, too little power in the school's governance structure to help shape the context of their work, and the like.

Administrators grumble about these same matters and in addition have complaints peculiar to their roles. A recent survey, whose confidentiality was guaranteed, asked deans of Protestant and Roman Catholic theological schools belonging to the Association of Theological Schools what the major problems or issues are that their schools face.[14] Their responses included familiar problems: the need for curricular reform to integrate "theoretical" and "practical" sides of ministerial education more adequately, or to make the course of study more truly "professional"; the need to make theological schooling more adequate to ecumenical and global "pluralism"; the need to improve the quality of theological school teaching; the need to make theological schooling more truly a "spiritual formation." Their answers, however, included another range of problems rooted in administrators' specific roles and responsibilities. As one respondent wrote, "I need basic help [regarding]: Board governance and development, administrative structuring, and dealing with a diverse student body. . . ." The complaints from this quarter are that theological schools have been badly organized, inadequately managed, insufficiently prepared to raise needed funds; they face a shrinking pool of candidates for admission and an ever smaller pool of appropriately prepared future faculty members. Newly appointed administrators complain of being inadequately supported by their own schools to deal with this legacy. Genuinely *basic* help would be help that addresses this sort of problem. At this point administrators' grumbles even extend to the recent literature addressed (like this book) to basic issues in theological schooling. "Too often," one respondent wrote, the literature "fails to move beyond the hermeneutics of the issue or problem, leaving the person who must 'do something with the problem' frustrated!"

Clearly, there are certain problems in theological schooling today that keep reappearing in this grumbling. They have to do, notably, with

- The *goal* of theological schooling—how to prepare genuinely "professional" church leaders, or how to "form" future church leaders "spiritually";
- The *curriculum* of theological schooling—how to integrate the "theoretical" and the "practical" sides of the curriculum, or how to overcome the fragmentation of the curriculum;
- The adequacy of theological schooling to its social and cultural

context—how to make it adequate to the pluralism of its immediate and worldwide settings, or how to "globalize" it, or how to make it "inclusive";

- The *human resources* of theological schooling—how to cope with the apparently shrinking national pool of candidates for admission, or how to find appropriately prepared younger faculty;
- The *financial resources* of theological schooling—how to be most effective at "development";
- The *governance* of theological schooling—how most effectively to provide leadership in a theological school, or how most effectively to engage a board of trustees in the enterprise, or how most fruitfully to involve faculty in governance of a school.

These are all crucial problems confronting theological schools today. For some schools they are critical. The survival of some schools depends on the solution of one or more of these problems in the near future. More broadly speaking, the future of all theological schools obviously depends on the ways they solve these and other such problems. Indeed, they are often cited as cumulative evidence that theological schooling is, as such, in a state of crisis today.

Note, however, that grumbling in theological schools gives expression to another type of issue that cuts across these problems. It is not accidental that the grumbles listed above can all be formulated in the "how to" form. They are all problems in the strict sense that at least in principle they admit of solutions. Of course, in many concrete cases circumstances may be such that they cannot be solved in actuality. The needed resources, imagination, or skill may simply not be available. Nonetheless, they invite a problem-solving approach. In many theological schools it is urgent that the problems be addressed. If they aren't, the schools' futures will be seriously compromised. Grumbles about theological schooling expressed as problems calling for solutions must not be denigrated as though they were a relatively superficial nuts-and-bolts approach to challenges faced by theological schooling. They signal real difficulties, and deep ones.

However, complaints about theological schooling can give rise to another kind of question. Indeed, many of the expressions of theological school grumbling as "problems" to be "solved" also give indirect expression to this second type of question. This second type of question raises issues, notably:

- Should we think of the goal of theological schooling as the preparing of "professional" church leadership; if not, how should we characterize its goal;
- Should we organize our thinking about theological schooling by using such contrast terms as "theoretical/practical," "academic/professional," "head/heart"; if not, how should we think of it;
- Should we think of theological diversity as a "pluralism" or as a "variety," or think of ethnic, racial, sexual, and class diversity as "pluralism" or as "variety";
- Should we think of theological schooling as "character formation" or "spiritual formation" or "personal formation" or "intellectual formation"; and if more than one of these, how are we to understand their interrelation?

It is not accidental that grumbles about theological schooling are expressed here in questions taking a "should we" form. They raise conceptual issues. They do not pose a problem; rather, they challenge the very terms in which conventional wisdom has posed the problems. They do not solicit workable "solutions"; rather, they solicit conceptual "resolution" of basic conceptual disagreements about how best to describe theological schools' (problematic) reality. They arise at the point of conflict between differing perspectives on the nature and purpose of theological schooling and force the basic issue: "What's this enterprise all about, anyway?" "What's theological about a theological school?"

This book addresses grumbles about theological schooling insofar as they are expressed in the second, the "should we," form. That in no way discounts the importance, nor minimizes the urgency, of grumbles expressed in the "how to" form. At least partial remedies, it should be noted, are available for some of the "how to" complaints. Some graduate business schools offer summer institutes for academic administrators. Workshops are available to help boards of trustees and their presidents clarify their goals and responsibilities. Institutes are available to assist theological schools to develop more effective "development offices." Moreover, many of the "how to" problems can only be solved in ways unique to a particular school's concrete situation; generalized advice and abstract recommendations are of little use. By focusing on issues in the "should we" form, this book, like a number of other recent studies of theological schooling, raises questions that must be asked constantly *while* we are attempting to solve the real problems of any particular theological school. It challenges conventional wisdom about how most helpfully to describe what the problems are. It asks whether some of the most widely perceived problems in theological schooling are not in fact made more obscure and intractable simply because of the concepts we conventionally employ to pose them in the first place. This book urges that it is of utmost importance to think critically about *how* we are thinking about theological schooling precisely while we are in the midst of the process of "doing something with the problems" that most certainly do threaten theological schooling.

The first step in that direction is to get clearer about the types of factors that make each theological school the concrete reality it is. That involves clarifying where our theological school hamlets have been located by history and how very diverse these locations are. The next chapter offers a sketch of those matters.

Notes

1. Cf. David H. Kelsey and Barbara G. Wheeler, "Mind-Reading: Notes on the Basic Issues Program," *Theological Education* (Spring 1984), pp. 8–14. Representative articles generated by this discussion have appeared frequently in *Theological Education* since 1983, notably in the issues for Autumn 1983; Spring 1984; Spring 1985; Supplement, 1987; and Supplements I and II, 1988.

2. Edward Farley, *Theologia: The Fragmentation and Unity of Theological Education* (Philadelphia: Fortress Press, 1983).

3. Warren Deem, *Theological Education in the 1970's: A report of the Resources Planning Commission* (Dayton, Ohio: ATS, 1968), p. 779.

4. Gail Buchwalter King, ed., *ATS Fact Book on Theological Education for the Academic Years 1988–89 and 1989–90* (Pittsburgh: ATS, 1990), pp. 4–10, 25, 26, tables 1.01, 2.04, and 2.04b.

5. Ibid., p. 25, table 2.04a.

6. Ibid., p. 36.

7. Ibid.

8. Ibid., p. 14, table 1.04a; and pp. 4–10, table 1.01.

9. See ibid., pp. 86–91, for documentation of this paragraph and the next.

The figures used are the most recent audited figures available at the time of writing. The figures are calculated on a "per head" basis.

10. It grew from $60 per FTE in 1983–84 to $104 per FTE in 1985–86; cf. ibid.; cf. William L. Baumgaertner, ed., *ATS Fact Book* (Vandalia, Ohio: ATS, 1987), p. 47.

11. Baumgaertner, ed., *ATS Fact Book* (1987), pp. 132, 142.

12. H. Richard Niebuhr et al., *The Purpose of the Church and Its Ministry* (New York: Harper & Brothers, 1956), p. viii.

13. For an account of the severity of this particular time-bind in Roman Catholic theological schools, see Robert J. Wister, "The Teaching of Theology 1950–1990: The American Catholic Experience," *America* (Feb. 3, 1990), pp. 90–91.

14. The survey was conducted in 1989 by Auburn Theological Seminary as part of research leading to an evaluation of a variety of projects in theological education sponsored by the Lilly Endowment.

2

Crossroads Hamlets

Where may we locate these crossroads hamlets? At what crossroads do North American theological schools develop? The piously conventional answer has been, "At the crossing of Athens Highway and Jerusalem Road." Perhaps in a dismal February after the fall, a frustrated and disillusioned contemporary answer is likely to be, "At the intersection of Snare and Delusion." A more helpful and, at any rate, historically more accurate answer would provide a multiple choice: Theological schools grow up at the intersection of the Berlin Turnpike and (pick one or more) Trent Road, Augsburg Road, Geneva Road, Canterbury Road, Northampton Road or Azusa Street. That is to say, the factors that shape the concrete ethos of each particular theological school derive from its relation to the history and traditions of higher education as symbolized by the University of Berlin, on the one side, and on the other side, from its relation to some tradition of organized Christianity, as symbolized by Ecumenical Councils (Orthodox) or by place names emblematic of various reforms (Trent, Augsburg, Geneva, Canterbury) or emblematic of various revivals (Northampton, Massachusetts; Azusa Street Mission in Los Angeles, California).[1] More exactly, theological schools differ from one another precisely because the ways in which they relate to the turnpike to Berlin vary, and because the ways in which they relate to the road to Azusa (or Northampton, Canterbury, Geneva, Augsburg, or Trent) vary, and because the ways in which they interrelate these two sets of relations themselves vary. If one's expectations and hopes regarding a theological school are going to be concretely appropriate to the school in *its* concrete reality, then it is important to attend to the way that school weaves these factors together. To that end it will be useful to sort them out and map some of the quite different ways in which they may be combined.

There is nothing odd about "theology" associating with "school." A school, we might say, is a particular community of persons whose central purpose is to understand some subject truly. The community includes some persons whose understanding of the subject matter is acknowledged to be somehow more advanced or deeper than the understanding of other members of the community; they are recognized to be skillful at helping the others develop and deepen their understanding. It is customary to describe the interaction between these two groups by saying that the former teach and the latter learn. However, teaching and learning are effectively accomplished only when both are done as subordinate moments in one common quest for truer understanding. Furthermore, since that quest always involves a struggle against various kinds of impediments, it requires appropriate methods and disciplines that serve as strategies in the struggle. It is not so much teaching and learning that make a school but the disciplined common, communal struggle to understand more truly.

What distinguishes a theological school is that the subject it seeks to understand truly is *theos*, God. However, God cannot be studied directly, as though God were immediately given like the page of a text. Nor can God be studied by controlled indirection the way, for example, subatomic particles, which also are not immediately given, can be studied indirectly under the conditions of controlled manipulation in the laboratory. Therefore it is more accurate to say that what distinguishes a theological school is that it is a community that studies those matters which are believed to *lead* to true understanding of God. Thus, for example, schools as communities of study of scripture have always been central to the life of both Judaism and Christianity precisely because scripture was believed to be a body of "sacred" texts whose study would lead to truer understanding of God. A synagogue is by definition a place to study Torah; "school" was an early image for the church, the "school of Christ."

However, while there is nothing odd about "theology" associating with "school," the association immediately pluralized "school." Far from naming the essence that makes theological schools basically all the same thing despite apparent differences, "theology" indicates one range of factors that accounts for the irreducible differences among theological schools. "Theology" does not name the unifying factor; it names one pluralizing factor. This can be seen in relation to three of the characteristic features of a school: the subject matter that focuses its common endeavor; the "understanding" it seeks through study of that subject matter; and the kind of community the school is.

DIVERSE SUBJECT MATTERS

Theological schools are academic hamlets located at crossroads, one of which is the road from (select at least one): Nicaea, Trent, Augsburg, Geneva, Canterbury, Northampton, Azusa Street Mission, and so forth. Each of those place names is the emblem of a different way of construing the *subject matter* on which a theological school focuses. Indeed, they are so different that it is difficult to find a relatively neutral generic term for this subject matter. To refer to the subject matter as "the word of God" easily appears to favor either the Lutheran "Augsburg" or the Calvinist "Geneva" road; and any effort to clarify that easily leads to complaint that the Augsburg Road is being privileged over the Geneva Road, or vice versa. To refer to it as the Christian "tradition" will raise the objection that that implicitly favors the Counter-Reformation Roman Catholic "Trent" Road. To refer to it as "Christian experience" sounds too easily like a privileging of the revivalist "Northampton" Road or the charismatic "Azusa" Road. And any effort to clarify "experience" is likely to arouse complaints that one of those two is being favored. If, in an irenic move, one suggests it is "scripture, tradition, and experience," one will be charged with covert preference for the Anglican "Canterbury" Road! Hence, for convenience' sake, I am going to borrow a phrase from G. K. Chesterton and refer to the subject matter on which theological schools focus as "the Christian thing." I will use the phrase "nominalistically," simply as a place-holder for all communities of practice and belief who call *themselves* "Christian."

The point is: the Christian thing is construed in a number of different ways. To be sure, they overlap at many points in many unsystematic and unsystematizable ways. Nonetheless, they are irreducibly different. The Christian thing may be construed as a piece of good news about something that has actually already happened to human history or, indeed, to the entire cosmos, and all the implications of that news for our attitudes and values and orientation in life: "God has already decisively overcome evil and is actively at work liberating the whole creation from its bondage; live accordingly." Or the Christian thing may be construed not as a report about what is already actual, but as the offer of a possibility: "Here is the possibility of forgiveness of your sin and release from your burden of guilt; or, the possibility of coming into truly authentic human life and leaving behind a deformed, inauthentic life; all you have to do is appropriate it for yourself in joy and trust." Or, the Christian thing may be construed as an entire ethos, a total way of life complete with the necessary institutional framework, traditional structures of relationships among persons, values, norms, and so forth. Or the Christian thing may be construed as a total interpretation of reality or of the whole of experience, something like a body of theory that gives, at least in principle, a single unified explanation of everything.[2]

There is no one "core" or "basic" or "essential" material theme or doctrine, nor any one pattern of them, that *is* the Christian thing. The generally accepted conclusion of historical studies is that there never has been. There is not even a past, perhaps originating, "essential" or "core" construal of the Christian thing from which Christians have departed in different ways and to which they might return.[3]

The important consequence is this. Since the "subject matter" on which theological schools focus (in the belief that its study will lead to truer understanding of God) is itself construed in irreducibly different ways, then that which makes all the schools nonetheless of the same kind (namely, theological schools) cannot be that they all finally study the same subject matter.

This is a radical simplification of the actual situation, of course. It wrongly suggests that each theological school exhibits allegiance to some one way of construing what Christianity is all about. In fact, theological schools vary in the way they relate to the construal of the Christian thing to which they are tied by history. Many quite intentionally and explicitly adhere to one construal. Others, equally intentionally, are internally pluralistic on this score. They distance themselves from any one construal by including within their communities persons with allegiances to a variety of construals of the Christian thing or persons proposing original syntheses of older construals. They may all study what they do study to the same *end*: understanding of God. But that is a different matter. Insofar as the concrete particularity of each school is shaped by its central subject of study, theological schools differ from one another precisely *because* they are theological and, among Christians, that involves different construals of the immediate subject matter of theology.

DIVERSE "UNDERSTANDINGS"

The diversity of ways in which the Christian thing is construed makes the world of theological schools irreducibly pluralistic for a second reason. Different construals bring with them significantly different notions of what it would be to "understand" God truly. Note: What is at issue here is not the conflict among different concepts of God. Rather, it is a matter of different concepts of *understanding* God.

What is it to understand God? The dominant answer, from the second century through at least the sixteenth century, on all sides—Orthodox, Roman Catholic, and Protestant "scholastic"—would have been, "To understand God is to have a kind of wisdom or *sapientia*."[4] However, left at that, "wisdom" obscures important differences. This wisdom concerning God embraces contemplation, discursive reasoning, the affections, and the actions that comprise a Christian's life. But the ways in which these four are interrelated vary enormously. Each way of interrelating contemplation, discursive reasoning, affections, and action amounts to a different way of leading the Christian life. They might be called different types of "spirituality" or "piety." However, in current usage both spirituality and piety tend to connote mainly inward states, and that is an inadequate characterization of some of these ways of understanding God. We shall simply refer to them as different types of Christian life.

They are not to be confused with the different ways in which the Christian thing has been construed, which I discussed in the previous section. The construals of the Christian thing are different ways of construing the immediate *subject matter* on which we focus in theological schools as the way to come to a better understanding of God. By contrast, what we are attending to now are different pictures of just what it is to *understand* God by way of focus on that subject matter. Obviously, the two intersect in a bewildering variety of ways. A particular theological school is helped to be made the concretely distinctive school it is through the way in which it combines (a) a tendency to construe the subject matter in one way rather than another with (b) a particular picture of what it is to understand God. That is why it is important to distinguish the two factors and discuss each separately.

Christian thinkers in the third and fourth centuries made contempla- *la* tion central.[5] They reasoned that Christianity has to do with the fulfillment of human life, and that our fulfillment comes in contemplation. In making this judgment they were shaped, as all Christians are, by the intellectual tradition centered on the question, "What is the best life for a human being? What life brings full realization and happiness?" The common assumption was that there were only two truly human ways to life: the life of political action and the life of contemplation. The dominant assumption in classical Athens had been that the citizen's life of political action was to be preferred because in it one fulfilled what is highest in human nature, the capacity for free and rational action. It was action in the public realm aiming at the common good. Involvement in the political life of the city of Athens was enormously expensive and time-consuming. It presupposed one was rich enough to be free of having to labor for a living. Political action itself largely involved rhetoric, trying to persuade others to adopt one policy rather than another. Such speech exercised and exhibited *logos,* which does not so much name one's rational capacities as it refers to the rationality inherent in effective rhetoric. Plato's project, successful in the long run, was to reverse these assumptions. He sought to persuade Athenians that the way of contemplation was higher than the way of political action. Contemplation was a way of understanding. The contrast to contemplation, or *theoria,* from which the English word "theory" is derived, was not (as it is in current English) action or *praxis* (cf. "practice"). Rather, the contrast term was some other way of understanding, having to do with guiding human action ("practical" understanding) and with making things ("productive" understanding).

Thus we get two definitive characteristics of contemplation. First, what distinguishes contemplation from these other ways of under-standing and makes it the highest form of life is the nature of its subject matter. Contemplation is the way to understand that which does not and inherently cannot change. Practical understanding, by contrast, is the way to understand wise political action, and that is notoriously changeable. In Plato's view that which cannot change is inherently the most rational and the "real" reality. Its contemplation involves the fullest realization and hence the happiness of creatures of a rational nature such as human beings. The second definitive mark of the way of contemplation is that it is inimical to the way of action. The way of contemplation involves all of one's energy and attention and a disengagement from the distractions of the everyday world, including political action.

A philosophical development contemporaneous with third-century Christians introduced a third definitive mark of contemplation. Until then contemplation was discussed as a way of understanding unchanging things that combined discursive reasoning, or coming to understanding by a process of thinking things through, and immediate intuition, coming to understanding by a kind of intellectual direct "seeing" of how things unchangingly are. In the third century the philosopher Plotinus, and the Neoplatonic philosophical tradition that followed him, sharply distinguished between these two and identified contemplation solely with an immediate intuition of unchanging reality.

To third-century Christian thinkers it was obvious that the Christian life centers on that understanding of God which brings to full realization our humanity and happiness. They identified this with the biblical "blessedness." It was equally obvious to them that such understanding is identical with the way of contemplation. God is the most real and utterly unchanging reality. The heart of Christian life is contemplative understanding of God.

However, this judgment created a serious problem. As Christians, these third-century thinkers also held that the best way to contemplate God is through meditation on sacred scripture. Now, if there is anything obvious about the biblical texts it is the high premium they place on action—precisely that with which contemplation was said to be inherently incompatible. Understanding God in and through some sorts of action had to be combined with understanding contemplatively. This was worked out first by redefining "action" and then by subordinating it to contemplation.

Scripture was interpreted as commanding either ascetical acts or acts of charity. In the third century stress fell on defining action as ascetical practice, as "acts" ultimately directed at oneself to purify one of all engagements with the everyday world that distract from pure contemplation.[6]

By the fifth century Augustine was acknowledging that "action" includes acts positively done in love for the neighbor's well-being, that is, acts of charity, in addition to acts done negatively to purify oneself. Together they are a walk of life defined by Christian perfection. That is, they are acts defined by the degree to which they are formed and guided *only* (i.e., perfectly) by God-given love for neighbor and for God. Augustine seems increasingly to have restricted these acts either to activities serving the neighbor's more basic needs or to those connected with religious service.[7] They may be performed by anyone in any position in society. It does not matter whether one is by God's providential decree placed in the role of politician, engaged in public action for the common good, or in the role of a lover of wisdom (philosopher), engaged as a private person in contemplation of eternal truths, or in some combination of the two: "A man can still lead a life of faith in any of these three lives and reach the eternal rewards. What counts is whether he lovingly holds to truth and does what charity demands."[8]

No longer is the "action" in which our humanity is realized primarily political action, as it was in classical Athens, action in the public realm for the public good. Rather, acts of charity are acts outside the public realm, that is, private action, aimed at the well-being of private persons, oneself, and one's neighbors. Such action constitutes the practice of a Christian life through which one can come to understand God.

This way to understanding God in and through action can be combined with the way of contemplation by being subordinated to it. As early as the mid-third century Origen of Alexandria[9] had urged that the actions enjoined by scripture constitute a "practice" that begins a spiritual journey and comprises the Christian life of most people in time; it flowers into pure contemplation in the afterlife as the ultimate and certain reward of faithful practice. This pattern of thought became normative in Western as well as Eastern Christianity. Actions of charity and asceticism, including the discipline of meditating on scripture, lead to a certain understanding of God in this life, but Augustine stresses, doing these actions does not itself constitute the full actualization of human life. Acts of love for the neighbor and of ascetical self-discipline are therefore a burden. Nonetheless, Augustine held, because they are burdens laid on us by God they must be accepted willingly in love for God. Doing them requires the "right use of worldly things," which involves discursive reasoning or *scientia*. Thus discursive thought is indirectly involved in understanding God through action infused by love. However, this entire way to understanding God, including *scientia*, is prior to, inferior to, preparatory to, and so subordinated to the way of understanding by contemplation, or *sapientia*.[10] The Christian life, in short, is construed as mainly a life spent actively preparing by disciplined loving for a future fulfillment of our humanity in a perfect contemplation of the unchanging God.

This picture of what it is to understand God has tended to have a high correlation with distinctive cultural situations. As Robert Schreiter has pointed out,[11] it is characteristic of contemplative understanding of God, or *sapientia*, that it has a strong interest in integrating all aspects of the world into a single meaningful whole. It goes with a sensibility that sees the world as an elaborate code of analogies, in which everything at the material level of reality refers to a higher level of spiritual realities, which in turn refer still higher to God. Hence it is characteristic of this picture that the dominant metaphor for coming to understand God is a "path" or "journey" up through the levels of meaning in the cosmos until one grasps God. Such a picture of how to understand God tends to predominate in cultures that see human life as a cycle replicating the cycles that make the world a unified whole. These cultures tend to be ones that, on the one hand, will sacrifice other things to maintain a unified view of the world, and that, on the other hand, maintain important rites of passage by which human life is tied in with the recurring cycles that make the world one. Such cultures tend to value conformity to the underlying patterns of the universe far more than they value personal growth as one's own personal achievement. Cultural situations in which contemplative understanding of

God thrives tend to be highly homogeneous and intolerant of pluralism.

This picture of Christian life shapes the nature of a theological school in distinctive ways. When it dominates, the understanding of God that is the aim of theological schooling is basically an understanding by way of contemplation as one is empowered for that by loving one's neighbor and God. It tends to be correlated with construals of the Christian thing as either good news about a divine act that has transformed the fallen cosmos so that it is again genuinely a harmonious whole, or as an ethos that embraces all of human life, or as a total interpretation of reality. In the first two cases the subject matter on which one focuses contemplatively tends to be treated intellectualistically as the mind's guide to the contemplation of the structure that makes reality a harmonious whole. In the last case the subject matter is treated more practically as a guide to how to order life so that contemplation is possible. In any case, theological schooling centers on disciplines of spirituality. This notion of what it is to understand God has been definitive in Eastern Orthodoxy and enormously influential in Western European theological schooling. Under various terminological guises it continues to shape deeply many North American theological schools historically rooted in Roman Catholic and certain Anglican movements.

A second notion of what it is to understand God gives much greater 𝟚 place to understanding by way of discursive reason. In the thirteenth century, it grew out of the earlier view centering on contemplation under the impact of newly recovered writings of Aristotle. Thomas Aquinas, for example, preserves a number of themes central to the earlier view. He continues to hold that human fulfillment is fully realized only in *sapientia* or contemplation of that which is most unchanging, God. He also affirms the traditional conviction that the best way to contemplate God is through meditation on scripture and the practice of its injunctions. Moreover, he maintains the traditional subordination of understanding through acts of charity to understanding by immediate intuition in contemplation.

Indeed, he radicalizes it. He holds that immediate intuition or vision of God comes *only* in the hereafter. *Sapientia* is reserved for the eschaton. Nevertheless, there is a way of truly understanding God in this life. His study of Aristotle helped Aquinas recover the role of discursive reasoning in *theoria* as it was understood before Plotinus. This is the way of understanding one has when, in a relatively disengaged fashion, one observes (in Latin, *speculari*) what is going on and thinks through what are the patterns or principles that explain what is happening. It is understanding by way of *scientia,* or speculative *theoria,* rather than by way of *sapientia,* or immediately intuitive *theoria.* Where Plotinus had limited contemplation to the latter, Aristotle had seemed to combine the two in contemplative understanding. Aquinas follows Aristotle's lead. For him, understanding by way of contemplation is rich enough to embrace *scientia* as well as *sapientia,* discursive reasoning as well as intellectual intuition.

Indeed, for Aquinas there are two kinds of *scientia* or speculative understandings of God.[12] They differ in what they "observe" and in what they led to. Discursive reasoning can lead to understanding of God either by meditation on the everyday world or by meditation on scripture. Either will lead to some kind of understanding of God because each in its own way is given by God. To attend to both of them in their God-relatedness is, as Augustine had taught, one important way in which to love God with one's mind. From Aristotle's writings Aquinas acquired a set of concepts and some theoretical principles that he could use as tools to reason discursively from what can be grasped in the books of scripture and in the book of the world to an understanding of God.

They result in two rather different kinds of *scientia.* Observing (*speculari*) what goes on in the world and reasoning discursively from that lead to what Thomas calls *scientia divina,* "divine knowledge." It is not so much understanding of God as it is understanding of God-related matters. It leads, more particularly, to understanding how all things are related to One Unknown (who, on other grounds, one understands is God). Meditatively observing in faith what goes on in scripture and reasoning discursively from that leads, by contrast, to what Thomas calls *scientia dei,* "knowledge of God." It is not so much understanding of what and how God is, as it is understanding true things to say about God, such as, "God is merciful." They are true to say because they derive from God's revelation communicated in scripture. But because they are said of a transcendent God, we have no grasp of how they apply in God's case, that is, of the "mode" of their application in God's case.

This picture of what it is to understand God tends to have a cultural location that is characteristically different from the one that correlates with understanding by way of *sapientia* or wisdom. Where understanding by way of *sapientia* tries to grasp the unity of the world, understanding by way of discursive reasoning or *scientia* tries to construct a system of propositions to explain the world. Furthermore, it is characterized by a drive to show that its understanding is sure, demonstrably preferable to competing explanations. That lays a high stress on specialized skill at analysis and sophistication about the methods and strategies for "demonstrating" something. As Schreiter has pointed out in his reflections on the sociology of theology,[13] such a picture of what it is to understand God tends to predominate in cultural situations marked by high specialization and differentiation, like urban societies and their economies, and marked by a plurality of competing worldviews. They are more complex and pluralistic societies than those that tend to correlate with understanding God contemplatively.

On this picture, the understanding of God that is the aim of theological schooling is basically understanding by way of discursive reasoning. It is done in faith and done as a way of loving God. It is a way of Christian life to which acts of neighbor love are integral but subordinate. Both the acts of love and the discursive reasoning are a preparation for future fulfillment of our humanity in contemplative vision of God. But in this life, understanding of God is by way of discursive reason.

This has had important consequences for theological schools. Because such understanding focuses on truths established by discursive reasoning, it tends to correlate with a construal of the Christian thing as a total interpretation of reality. Theological schooling consequently focuses on cultivating capacities for reasoning, capacities for formulating and testing the propositions by which those truths are expressed. This notion of what it is to know God has been enormously influential in both late Western medieval and modern theological schooling. It continues to shape many North American theological schools historically rooted in certain Roman Catholic communities, especially those in which neo-Thomist theology and philosophy were dominant, and schools rooted in the Reformed tradition,[14] especially those rooted in

British and Dutch scholastic Calvinism of the sixteenth and seventeenth centuries.

A third picture of what it is to understand God stresses understanding that comes by way of the affections. It too grew out of the earlier view centering on contemplation as *sapientia*. That earlier view had also held that contemplative understanding of God comes by way of love for God. But as articulated by Augustine, for example, that love was quite specifically a love of the mind, in obedience to the biblical injunction: You shall love the Lord your God with all your heart, soul, *mind*, and strength. Contemporaries of Aquinas who stood in the Franciscan tradition developed this thought a step further. They urged that loving was distinct from reasoning and went beyond it. The Franciscan Bonaventure, Aquinas's great theological debate partner, held that sapiential contemplation "starts with knowledge and reaches its completion in love,"[15] and may do so in *this* life.

What is distinctive about this tradition is that it associates love with will rather than with reason. According to Nikolaus Lobkowicz, Bonaventure is following Thomas Gallus's contention that "instead of applying the *intellectus theoreticus*" (i.e., our capacities for discursive and "speculative" reasoning, on which Thomas Aquinas focused), we "ought to reach God by the *summus affectionis apex,* the 'tip of the will': 'It is by this communion (*unitio*) that we have to know things divine, not in terms of the sobriety of our intellect.' "[16]

The picture that God is understood by way of the affections is shared by a number of later Christian movements that otherwise differ strongly from Bonaventure's Franciscan tradition and, indeed, in varying degrees differ from one another. They all agree that God is not to be understood chiefly either by way of contemplation (*sapientia*) or by way of discursive reasoning (*scientia*). They differ in how they understand the affections that replace *sapientia* and *scientia*. They have all deeply influenced theological schools in North America.

Beginning in the late seventeenth century, the pietist movement tends to distinguish the affections from both reason and will and associates them instead with feeling states. Love for God is more focused, perhaps, in one's "heart" than in one's "mind" or "strength." In the eighteenth century the picture that one understands God through love as a feeling state deeply shaped the early Methodist

42

movement through John Wesley's experience of a heart "strangely warmed." As his work on the *Religious Affections* shows, it was also central to Jonathan Edwards's understanding of the great revival that began in his parish in Northampton, Massachusetts.

Different versions of basically the same picture continue through the nineteenth century in both theologically liberal and theologically conservative circles. No longer are the relevant affections associated with love, however. Among liberals, "affections" tends to mean "religious experience." For some that designates a distinctive type of experience, perhaps the experience of the numinous, that combination of intense fascination and terror one experiences in encounter with the uncanny or the holy. For others the relevant affection or feeling state is more like a dimension of all human consciousness, and hence a dimension of every particular experience, than it is some one class of experiences among others. Perhaps, as it was for Friedrich Schleiermacher, human consciousness may be understood to have several levels. At very least, one is at once conscious and (most of the time) self-conscious. Underlying it all is a level of consciousness of which one is not often aware, of a "feeling of absolute dependence" on some reality that is not itself in any way dependent on us. Such understanding of God as we may have comes from attending to that feeling.

Conservative American theological circles were more deeply shaped throughout the nineteenth century by continuing waves of religious revivals on the American frontier. There, understanding God was often identified with a "personal knowledge" of God that came, not so much through any particular affection such as love, but rather through the very intensity of one's emotions, intensity so great that in the surge of emotion distinctions between love, fear, guilt, and joy blurred entirely.[17]

In one distinctive version of this, "affections" mean quite specifically the ecstatic experience of possession by the Holy Spirit as evidenced, for example, by speaking in tongues. From a revival meeting in 1906 in the Azusa Street Mission in Los Angeles, in which such a second Pentecost occurred, this particular stream has had powerful and broad impact on many Christian traditions in North America through the charismatic movement.[18]

This picture that God is understood by way of the affections tends to have much the same cultural location as does the view that God is understood by way of discursive reasoning or *scientia:* It is a culture marked by the high differentiation and specialization of social roles characteristic of urban societies and their economies, considerable pluralism of subcultures and worldviews, social fragmentation, personal anonymity, and rootlessness. Such a cultural setting tends to generate a deep hunger for certainty about one's worldview in its competition with other worldviews, about one's identity in the face of social rootlessness and anonymity, and about one's unsubstitutable significance as a person in the face of specialization that reduces one's personhood to a single socially useful role. Where understanding God by way of discursive reasoning addresses these problems by trying to explain the world and to establish the sure validity of its worldview, understanding God by way of the affections grounds certainty in the sureness of immediate experience and grounds a sense of personal significance in the intensity of the intimate face-to-face communities in which those experiences occur and flourish.

All of these variations on the picture that God is understood by way of the affections, it may well be said, are a far cry from anything Bonaventure had in mind when he stressed that understanding comes through a love which goes beyond reason. Their important differences from Bonaventure and from each other arise from differences about what is central to human nature. They are differences regarding precisely what it is about us that makes it possible for us to understand God. But for all their differences, they share in taking feeling states or experience or emotions to be at the heart of Christian life.

This picture of the Christian life tends to correlate with a construal of the Christian thing as an offer, as news about a possibility of new and fulfilled or blessed life that one may appropriate for oneself—and the appropriation is by way of the affections. Where this picture predominates, theological schooling is organized around the goal of preparing leadership for Christian communities that is knowledgeable about the conditions under which such experiences occur, may be nurtured, and will flourish. When such schools are located in a cultural context marked by the "triumph of the therapeutic,"[19] there is a strong tendency to construe those conditions in psychological and sociological categories and to equate the requisite knowledgeability with counseling skills and related psychoanalytical and social-psychological theory. Evidence of that tendency is widespread in Protestant theological schools, both conservative and liberal, that have roots in religious communities shaped by one or another of these movements of revival. Given the history of Protestant Christianity in North America, most schools do have such roots. Nor is this tendency entirely lacking in Roman Catholic theological schools.

A fourth picture of what it is to understand God roots understand- 4
ing in action. It first surfaces in the generation after Bonaventure in the thought of Duns Scotus as yet another development of the Franciscan version of the Augustinian heritage. Scotus shared the Augustinian conviction that ultimate human fulfillment lies in love for God, and he shared with Bonaventure the traditional Franciscan view that love for God is more an act of will than of reason. But he "replaced the innocuous notions of affection and 'affective knowledge' by the notion of 'practice' "[20] or *praxis,* which he had thoroughly reconceived. (Scotus seems to have been the first medieval thinker explicitly to ask the question, "What exactly is *praxis?*" Indeed he seems to have been the first Latin author to use the expression *praxis* in a philosophical or theological context.)[21] Broadly speaking, Scotus takes *praxis* to be any action that is conscious and deliberate, is something other than a purely "mental act," and is capable of being either right or wrong. Human life is defined, not simply by intellectual acts, but by *praxis,* by a complex mix of those acts that are different from purely intellectual acts and, while analogous to many activities of animals, are generically different from them.

Scotus has very nearly revived Aristotle's notion of *praxis,* with the glaring difference that because Scotus does not define *praxis* by reference to the public realm or the common good it lacks any political connotations. But then Scotus disagrees with Aristotle. In Scotus's view, Aristotle had rightly held that understanding of human behavior in politics and ethics has to be practical and not contemplative understanding because behavior is so changeable. However, Aristotle wrongly held that the unchanging God can be understood only contemplatively. Against this, Scotus insisted that God is the "doable knowable" *(cognoscibile operabile).* That is, God may be understood by way of any action which is true *praxis.*[22]

With this notion of *praxis* Scotus effectively subverts the other three pictures of what it is to understand God. He removes action from its subordinate role and makes it central. Recall that from the third century onward the actions enjoined by scripture had posed a problem to Christian thinkers because action was perceived to be inconsistent with contemplation. Of human action, that is, of politics and of ethics, as of all changeable things, one might acquire practical understanding and acquire it precisely by way of engaging in the action, but the unchanging God one can hope to understand only by way of contemplation undistracted by action. Hence action is given only a subordinate role in our coming to understand God. Action might be ascetical, playing the role of purifying us of distracting entanglements. Or action might be works of neighbor love, done in joy because God commanded them, but burdens because they do distract from contemplation. Or action might be the actions involved in worship by which we express our inadequate love for God and pray for the grace of an adequate love for God. Taken together, these actions make up the way of Christian perfection and are in the service of and subordinate to contemplation, in which alone is understanding of God to be found. Scotus's idea of action reverses this. Action's role in understanding God is not limited to our purification. It is not limited to acts of worship. It is not to be understood as a burden distracting us from the effort to understand God. Rather, since *praxis* comprises our entire life as human life, it can be so shaped that it is itself the way to an understanding of God which may then flower into that love for God in which we are one with God.

For third-century Christians *sapientia,* contemplative understanding, might here and now yield human fulfillment in vision's union with God. For Thomas Aquinas *scientia,* understanding by discursive reasoning, might help prepare us for a future intellectual vision of God. For Bonaventure understanding of God might start in reason's contemplating *(sapientia)* but then must go on beyond reason to the completion of understanding in will's affectionate union with God. But for Scotus, because understanding God culminates in precisely will's love of God, it must begin here and now neither solely in reason's *sapientia* nor solely in its *scientia,* but in will's deliberate and conscious action, that is, in *praxis.*

As Nikolaus Lobkowicz points out, "One only has to forget for a second that for Scotus the ultimate secret of will, and thus of practice, is love, in order to be reminded of statements such as: the only knowledge able to reach God is practical, not theoretical (Kant); the only source of meaning in the whole universe is *praxis* (Marx)." Of course Scotus says nothing of the sort. Nonetheless, his picture of what it is to understand God "anticipates, and in a sense paves the way for, the notion . . . that it is an atheoretical practice [i.e., practice without *theoria*] in which God is encountered or missed."[23]

There have been a number of variations on this picture of what it is to understand God, largely in late nineteenth- and twentieth-century Protestantism. Some of these versions take "action" in a highly individual and private way: To understand God is to understand God's will for me in this particular situation; understanding God's will consists of the rigorous effort to clarify what my unconditional moral duties oblige me to do. Or, in a less moralistic and more psychological mode: To understand God is to act in such ways in this given situation involving another person that I may discern how God's grace is at work in the trans-actions between us to correct what is amiss and, where life is broken, empower for new life. Alternatively, "action" may be taken in a more public and political way: One comes to understand God as one engages in action with others in the public realm struggling to redress some social or economic injustice by taking realistically prudent political action. Morally such situations are inescapably ambiguous, but in their midst one may—though one's companions in the struggle may not—discern the grace of God at work judging the evil resisted and forgiving the evil committed (cf. Reinhold Niebuhr). In this version, the *praxis* in which one comes to understand God is public in the classical Athenian sense, but the atheoretical understanding itself is entirely private.

Currently the most influential version, of course, is associated with movements shaped by liberation theologies: We come to understand God as we are a part of a community that is united by a common history of oppression and struggles for liberation by radically changing the arrangements of economic and social power that have made the oppression systemic in our society. In that action we encounter the God who is already at work in world history ahead of us and on behalf of the oppressed to establish God's kingdom of justice and peace. In this version, *praxis* is understood quite differently than it is in the others. Both *praxis* and an atheoretical understanding of God are communal, intersubjective, and hence, in that sense, public. There is a place for *theoria* in this practice. Out of *praxis* that aims at transforming oppressive social power arrangements arise fresh theoretical understandings of the structure and dynamics of oppressive relationships within society. These new theories may then guide further transformative *praxis*. Theory is a dialectical moment *within* practice.

This *theoria* is not so much theoretical understanding of God as a theoretical understanding of society and ourselves in it. However, it can be shaped by the atheoretical understanding of God we already have. To understand God as the One who liberates oppressed people into a realization of their true social humanity, for example, can put us in a position to recognize the falsity of the social relationships our society imposes on us.

The picture that God is understood in action tends to be correlated with cultural situations marked by deep social change or by newly widespread consciousness in parts of a society of the need for deep social changes. They need not be cultures marked by high degrees of differentiation and specialization of social roles. Nor need they be highly pluralistic societies. They need not be highly urbanized societies. But they do need to be marked by sharp constrasts between small elites who control massive economic, social, and political power, and large groups whose consciousness of their relative powerlessness is sharply rising. In such societies, this picture of what it is to understand God tends to be best sustained in relatively small Christian communities that can retain a degree of communal identity in the midst of these social changes without moving to the margins of social turmoil and withdrawing from active participation in the reformist or revolutionary movements that cause the changes.

Where variations on this picture of what it is to understand God prevail they deeply shape theological schools. The schools differ in the degree to which the action in and through which God may be understood is thought of as Christian communal action and, if it is, in how far it is precisely political action. They share, however, the view that Christian life and therewith Christian ministry are above all an active life. Accordingly, the common life of a theological school that educates those who lead and nurture communities of Christians in that life must in high moral seriousness focus above all on the nature and demands of that activity and on analysis of the society in which it must be lived.

It is precisely because theological schools are *theological* that they are irreducibly plural. The pluralism is a consequence of the irreducibly plural ways in which the idea of "understanding God" is itself theologically understood, combined with the irreducibly diverse ways in which the subject matter (the Christian thing), whose study is believed to bring us to a better understanding of God, is construed. Together these two points bring with them important pointers regarding how to go about better understanding any particular theological school. In the interest of following the recommendation that any such effort ought to be kept as concrete as possible, it would be important and fruitful to ask whether there is some one dominant assumption within the school as a community about (a) how the 1 Christian thing is best construed and (b) how one best goes about 2 "understanding" God. Since a society's ethos is rarely entirely coherent, it is likely to be even more fruitful to ask whether there is tension among two or more sets of assumptions on these matters widely held within the school as a community.

Rarely are these assumptions stated self-consciously and explicitly; even more rarely are they stated in official school publications. Rather they are assumptions almost wholly implicit as the structures, patterns of behavior, and common talk of such communities. One can hope to find symptoms of them in several ways. One is to explore how intensely 1 the school identifies with Geneva Road or Azusa Street, Augsburg or Trent Road, and so forth. The historic traditions within Christianity emblematized by these place names characteristically bring with them commitments to specific answers to our two questions. The more intensely a school identifies with such a tradition, the more deeply the tradition's commitments on these matters will shape the school's ethos. This is the rare case in which the school's assumptions may be explicitly, in a reliable way, in its official documents. Increasingly, however, a great many schools, especially Protestant ones, are not very intensely identified with any one Christian tradition.

A second place to look for symptoms of a theological school's 2 implicit ethos-shaping theological commitments is the structure of the curriculum it requires of its students and the relative richness of the courses it offers them. For example, a curriculum that seems to privilege courses having to do with religious experience, worship, spirituality, counseling, and the like over, say, systematic and philosophical theology may reveal a commitment to the assumption that God is understood affectively rather than discursively; while a curriculum relatively more rich in offerings in ethics, sociology of religion, liberation theology, and the like than in offerings in historical theology, patristics, liturgics, and mystical traditions may reveal a commitment to the view that God is better understood in action than in contemplation.

Yet another place to look for assumptions that shape a given theological school's distinctive ethos is its organization of activities not strictly academic, such as worship or social action. To what extent is such activity organized by the faculty as a matter of school policy and to what extent by students at their own initiative? To what extent does it engage faculty energy and to what extent student energy? Major differences between faculty and student responsibility for the very occurrence of such activities may suggest tensions between different sets of implicit commitments regarding what is central to the Christian thing and how best to go about understanding God. One has, in short, to be an amateur anthropologist studying the school's ethos as participant observer to discern those deep theological assumptions that help make a given theological school the distinctive social reality that it is.

DIVERSE COMMUNITIES

A third theological factor that pluralizes theological schools is their understanding of the kind of community they are or ought to strive to be. Earlier I characterized a school as "a particular community of persons whose central purpose is to understand some subject truly."[24] A theological school in particular is a community whose central purpose is to come to understand God more truly. The fact that what the community seeks to understand is God presumably has implications regarding the sort of community it is. The central issue here can be focused by asking the question as concretely as possible: How does a given theological school understand the relationship between itself as a community and a Christian congregation as a community? Granted that a theological school surely has *some* kind of relationship to the Christian church, just what is that relationship?

Not all theological schools have explicit, formal answers to this question. Nevertheless, some answer is always implicit in the way the school conducts its common life and the reasons conventionally given for doing some things in the way in which they are done. The answer is theological in the sense that, if challenged, theological reasons would be given in support of it. At least three broad types of answer to this question can be found among American theological schools. What is important for our purposes is that a school's answer to this question shapes its peculiar ethos.

The first type simply identifies a Christian theological school with a Christian congregation. The school community's common life is ordered to its being a congregation. Of itself that does not constitute the community as a theological school. Something more is needed for it to be a school; we shall take that up in the next chapter. However, on this view it is more determinative of the community's particularity and identity that it is a Christian congregation than that it is a school. To be school requires first that precisely this community *be* church. This shapes the school's ethos in deep and distinctive ways. On the Trent or Canterbury road it means that eucharistically centered worship is the basis of the school's community. It means that focus on everyone's spiritual formation is central and not peripheral to the community's common life. Furthermore it means that the spiritual health of members of the community is somehow the responsibility of the entire community. On this view, the fact that the school community is a worshiping community is not just terribly important; it is the foundation of its being a community at all.

When a theological school understands itself in this way it tends to develop an ethos in which high value is placed on its being a resident community set apart from the "world" so that there will be maximum time, energy, and attention focused on that which defines it as a community. Such schools tend to be placed physically in rural or small town settings. At its most extreme this ethos tends to foster a certain anti-intellectualism, seeing academic work itself as a possible distraction from the spiritual shaping that is the basis of the community.

This view and its ethos are evident in North American schools in Catholic traditions. There, theological schools are simply assumed to be religious communities living under orders. Such schools see themselves as modern embodiments of medieval Cathedral schools or monastic schools which were, unambiguously, ecclesiastically ordered communities. This picture may be exhibited quite unambiguously, of course, in many North American Roman Catholic theological schools operated by religious orders or by a diocese, even when the schools' communities in fact include persons not literally "in orders." This is reflected in the conventional structure of Roman Catholic theological education in which theologates are a subset of seminaries. "Seminary" covers schools at the high school and college levels as well as theologates. What makes them "seminaries" is that their common life is that of a community of worship aiming at the spiritual formation of its members as priests. "Theologates," academically the most advanced, the institutions that provide professional education for ministry, what this book calls "theological schools," are first of all "seminaries." This view becomes more ambiguous when increasingly large numbers of men and women students are admitted who are not "in orders" and require a different sort of spiritual formation.[25]

Basically the same view underlies the ethos of many Episcopal theological schools, although with a good bit of ambiguity generated, perhaps, by the way differences in church polity and theology of ordination alter the clarity of the idea of being "in orders." Nor is this view of the relation between theological school and congregation and the ethos that goes with it limited to Catholic traditions. In 1754 Thomas Clap, self-consciously a Calvinist theologian, the rector of Yale College, then still self-consciously a school in the Reformed tradition, forbade Yale students to worship anywhere except at the college church on the grounds that the school itself, ordered to educate ministers, was a religious society "of a superior nature."[26]

A second and more complicated view of the relation of theological school to church, however, was more characteristic of New England Congregationalism and mid-Atlantic Presbyterianism. There "school" was an amplification of the study of a congregation's senior minister.[27] Future clergy were apprentices schooled by the minister as he conducted his weekly ministerial rounds. The student or students and the minister did not constitute a church; they were related *to* a church in the way in which clergy and congregation are understood to be related to one another in the Reformed tradition. Looked at one way, clergy (and student clergy) and laity are all together one congregation. But with regard to the preaching of the Word they are differentiated, and the relation between them is hierarchical. Nonetheless, clergy and their students do not themselves comprise a Christian congregation. This view, and the ethos it tends to create, persists in this tradition long after theological education has passed from the studies of ministers to theological seminaries.

A particularly clear illustration of this is provided by the founders of Union Theological Seminary, New York, in their preamble to the school's constitution. The constitution was drafted in 1836, just before the school opened. After noting the need for well-trained ministers, and that in New York and Brooklyn there were promising persons who could not go away from home to get such training, and professing their allegiance to the Presbyterian church, they announced their intent

> that its students, living and acting under pastoral influence, and performing the important duties of church members, in the several churches to which they belong, or with which they worship, . . . shall have the opportunity of adding to solid learning and true piety, enlightened experience.[28]

The theological school provides "solid learning." It is a community constituted by the pursuit of learning. The students bring "true piety." To be sure, the school is not indifferent to the health of that piety. Worship is an important part of the common life of the school. But it is not foundational to its being a community as, precisely, a theological school. Nonetheless, the school community is *essentially* related to church communities. The churches nurture the "true piety" of students who live under their "pastoral influence."

The school is not *a* Christian congregation, but it is related to a number of Christian communities by virtue of the fact that its students (and faculty) are active members of them. And this is what will provide "enlightened experience." As Robert Handy points out in his comment on this preamble, Union's founders made a "distinctive contribution" to theological schools of this type when they included this theme in their vision for their school. "Enlightened experience" was to come through performing the duties of church membership while "acting under pastoral influence." In effect, its founders institutionalized "supervised field work" in the very structure of the school. "It was later widely copied, for their aim was to draw on the rich educational and religious resources of what by then was America's largest metropolitan area for preparing ministers.[29]

This way of understanding the relationship between theological school and church tends to create an ethos that has probably been the most influential one in Protestant theological schools in America. Union did not originate it. It had been pioneered by the founding of Andover in 1808, and by the time Union opened in 1836 more than twenty-five seminaries had been established. The prevailing ethos of schools with this heritage is profoundly shaped by the conviction that they are constituted as communities by academic purposes and not, as church communities are, by doxological purposes. Common worship tends to be highly valued and it is characteristic of schools with this ethos to include in the weekly schedule stated times for worship by the entire community. However, it is uncharacteristic for such a school to institutionalize in its common life a structure for nurturing and monitoring its students' "piety" (which would be the closest structural equivalent to "spirituality" in the first ethos I sketched). Furthermore, if situations arise in which academic interests compete with concerns for students' "piety" for added time or financial resources, the response characteristically shaped by this ethos would be to assign to the "churches" responsibility for "piety" and to assign priority within the school to the academic interests.

To be sure, it too is an ethos that places a high value on avoiding distractions. Until the early decades of the twentieth century, schools of this sort were strictly resident communities of unmarried male students. Schools tended to be located physically in rural settings or small towns. When they were in larger cities, they tended to be located in the suburbs. However, it was more important to avoid distractions from academic work than distractions from spiritual formation. As the founding document of Union shows, such a school would quite deliberately be set in the midst of a major metropolitan center on the grounds that this environment was necessary to, rather than a distraction from, its proper academic purposes.

Theological schools with this sort of ethos have tended to be especially comfortable associating with or being an organic part of other types of academic communities such as undergraduate colleges, graduate centers, and universities. This is a theological school ethos that values intellectual seriousness and disciplined rigor as the way in which to love God with one's mind. In the larger context of the Christian life it gives an especially highly valued place to the life of the mind. In its extreme form this ethos can tend to alienate the common life and familiar language of a theological school from the ordinary language and patterns of common life of the churches, giving rise to complaints that theological schooling is "irrelevant" to the "real life" of actual congregations.

A third pattern has had considerable influence in American Protestantism. Under the conditions of the frontier, where the population was widely scattered and revivalist movements became the dominant form of Christian religious experience, especially where the Methodist movement was influential, persons were appointed to circuit riding ministries before their "theological education" was completed. They might be thought of as a cadre of preachers. But since they tended to live a fairly isolated life of frequent travel they could not as a group be considered a community living together under orders. Nor could they be considered a part of a larger group of worshipers settled in one place. Their education took place by private reading and was monitored by examinations set by denominational officials.[30] As theological schools emerged, they were considered adjunctive to the actual practice of ministry. The activity of theological education often had the character of "extension" education. Theological students were certainly part of the church construed as a movement or a denomination. But they were not part of a settled local congregation by whose leadership they were schooled. And the theological school itself most certainly was not a congregation. Rather, the theological school was seen as basically a service agency to a denomination.

The ethos of theological schools sharing this view of their relationship to "church" is markedly different from the other two we have identified. The school is constituted a community, not by being a resident worshiping congregation nor by a common academic undertaking, but by the fact that it consists of a cadre of persons called by the

55

larger church to a mission in the world. Little value is placed on the school's being a resident community; much of the time its members must be away in mission, probably part-time, in the place to which the larger church, that is, the denomination, has appointed them. Many of them are married and have families who live, not at or near the theological school, but in the place where they are sent to minister. Shared worship when all are together as a school is valued. Indeed, given the roots of this tradition in pietist and revivalist movements, it is characteristic in this ethos to invest high energy not only in communal worship but also in Bible study and prayer in intimate small-group settings in which students' individual piety may be nurtured and formed. However, none of this constitutes the school as a community.

Rather, what constitutes the school community is its basic focus on equipping its students with professional ministerial skills and competencies. The students are already responsible for founding, maintaining, and expanding the programs and organizations of local congregations. Preparing them to fulfill these institutional responsibilities more effectively is the common activity that constitutes the theological school as a community. In extreme forms, this ethos tends to value training in what is demonstratively effective and successful in practice over academic learning, to value what sustains clerical careerism over what cultivates the capacity for critical reflection.

I have sketched three ideal types of community that a theological school might be or be committed to becoming. It might be a community under orders sharing a common religious discipline. It might be a community of quasi-clergy related to Christian congregations in the way in which clergy are supposed to be related to the congregations they lead, yet distinct because it is constituted by academic interests of special interest to clergy rather than constituted as a church. It might be the community of a cadre of persons sent individually in mission but concurrently sharing a program of training for that mission. There may well be other types of community to which some theological schools belong. If a theological school were a community of only one of these types it would probably be a relatively harmonious and calm community. In reality, most theological schools are strained communities because they implicitly mix two or more of these types in a single institution.

This suggests an additional set of questions to ask oneself about any particular theological school one is trying to understand. What type of community do the people who comprise it assume it ought to be? It is not sufficient to consult the school's bulletin or catalog for its official self-description in this regard. That may or may not accurately describe how the community's common life is actually lived out. Rather, one needs to attend to such matters as the systems of rewards that shape the community's common life.

Different systems may function in different aspects of that life. Official school policy, for example, might put pressure on students and faculty to invest significant amounts of time and energy in a common life of worship as though the school were a Christian congregation; while faculty put pressure on themselves and students to invest energy and time in scholarly study and writing; and students, concurrently, are under financial pressure that can be met only by taking positions with local congregations so time-consuming that their academic work is conducted on the pattern of extension education. Or the pattern among contrasting types of community that constitute the school might be very different. The point is that some such pattern characterizes every school and the tensions within it profoundly shape the distinctive ethos of that school.

If one is to have a realistic grasp of the school, one needs to be clear about this feature of its ethos also. This is especially important if, as we imagined in chapter 1, one harbors hopes of changing the school. Some kinds of change may be plausible if they involve a strengthening of a commitment to be a certain type of community which is already dominant in a school, but other kinds of change may be much less plausible precisely because they would involve a change in the type of community a school already is or a change in the current equilibrium among contrasting types of community.

IN A DISMAL FEBRUARY

Here we have three broad types of things to look for if, in a dismal February well after the fall, we want to get a firmer grip on the concrete reality of some particular theological school in which, perhaps, we have invested deeply felt expectations. If we may think of a school as a community of persons whose central purpose is to understand some subject truly, then a theological school is such a community that seeks to understand God. That is what makes it "theological," and that is also what helps make one school irreducibly different from another and in some ways peculiarly resistant to change. Precisely because it is a theological school, it will be helpful to ask three different sorts of questions about it, and then to ask how the answers to the three are themselves interrelated in the structures that pattern the school's common life: What construal or construals of the Christian thing are assumed in the way the subjects of study are addressed? What picture of what it is to understand God dominates the school's common life? How does the school seem to understand itself as a community in relation to churches?

What matters, of course, is how a school answers these questions in practice, not necessarily in its official public rhetoric about itself. The answer can be complex in regard to each of these questions. As we have noted, since God cannot be understood directly we must focus on other matters whose study we believe will lead to better understanding of God. But from the very beginning of Christianity there have been a number of different ways of construing this subject matter. All theological schools stand in some historical tradition in this regard. Some, because of mergers of schools, stand in more than one tradition. In some theological schools a traditional construal is simply assumed; in others one or more traditions of construal of the Christian thing are very self-consciously celebrated ("*This* is a school in the *Reformed* tradition, with the following consequences . . .!"). Still others self-consciously seek to be open to all construals of the Christian thing and attempt to distance the school as school from any one of them ("*We* are a truly *ecumenical* school!"). Sometimes one can see that one kind of construal is assumed in one area of the curriculum, say biblical studies, and quite another in some other area, say pastoral theology.

These differences will interconnect in complex ways with different assumptions about what it is to understand God: contemplatively, discursively, affectively, or actively. Here too schools inescapably stand in some historical tradition or traditions and differ from one another in the attitudes they adopt toward those traditions. Moreover, here too different assumptions about this matter may be made in different sections of the curriculum. This can be further complicated by the fact that different assumptions about what is involved in understanding God may be made in regard, say, to the school's common worship life than are made in its curriculum.

Finally, the answers made to these two types of questions will interconnect in complex ways with answers made to the question of how the school as community is related to church communities: Is the school itself an ordered Christian congregation; is it an expanded version of the academic aspect of the work of ministerial leadership in a settled congregation; is it an agency for the extension education of practicing clergy? Once again, every school stands in one or more historical traditions with regard to this question. And schools differ in the attitude they adopt to their own histories. Moreover, as we have noted, one answer to this question may be assumed by a school historically, another adopted by its faculty, and still another be mandated by financial constraints on students. Especially as one harbors hopes for significant changes in a theological school, it is important to understand a particular school *in* its concrete particularity. These are major theological factors that help make it the concretely particular school it is, and analyzing it in the light of these three questions will help give a realistic understanding of it.

Notes

1. In 1906 the Azusa Street Mission in Los Angeles, under the leadership of William J. Seymour, became, in Sydney Ahlstrom's phrase, "the radiating center of Pentecostalism" in the United States, from which Pentecostalism has grown into a worldwide movement. A brief account of the history of Pentecostalism may be found in Sydney E. Ahlstrom, *A Religious History of the American People* (New Haven, Conn.: Yale University Press, 1972), pp. 816–822.

2. For an elaboration of the notion of diverse construals of "the Christian thing," see David H. Kelsey, *The Uses of Scripture in Recent Theology* (Philadelphia: Fortress Press, 1975), ch. 8.

3. See, e.g., Robert L. Wilken, *The Myth of Christian Beginnings* (Garden City, N.Y.: Doubleday & Co., Anchor Books, 1972).

4. For a sketch of the history of the idea of "wisdom" as our understanding of God, see Farley, *Theologia,* pp. 33–39; p. 46, nn. 6 and 12.

5. For the following paragraph, see Nikolaus Lobkowicz, *Theory and Practice: History of a Concept from Aristotle to Marx* (Notre Dame, Ind.: University of Notre Dame Press, 1967), chs. 1–6.

6. Cf. Clement of Alexandria, *Stromata,* II, 10; VI, 9.

7. See Lobkowicz, p. 67.

8. Ibid., p. 64.

9. See Origen, *On the Gospel of John*, I, 16.

10. See Augustine, *City of God*, xix, 19; xv, 106.

11. Robert J. Schreiter, *Constructing Local Theologies* (Maryknoll, N.Y.: Orbis Books, 1985), pp. 85–87.

12. Cf. Victor Preller, *Divine Science and the Science of God* (Princeton: Princeton University Press, 1967), ch. 1; Ralph McInerny, *St. Thomas Aquinas* (Notre Dame, Ind.: University of Notre Dame Press, 1982), pp. 140–170.

13. See Schreiter, *Constructing Local Theologies,* pp. 87–91.

14. For similarities on this topic between Thomas Aquinas and the Reformed tradition, see Arvin Vos, *Aquinas, Calvin and Contemporary Protestant Thought* (Grand Rapids: Wm. B. Eerdmans Publishing Co., 1985), chs. 1 and 5; Farley, *Theologia,* p. 46, n. 12.

15. Lobkowicz, p. 74; see pp. 71–74 for the historical context.

16. Ibid., pp. 73–74.

17. See Ahlstrom, chs. 19, 20, 26, and 27, for a historical survey of successive waves of revival movements in American religious history.

18. See ibid., pp. 819–820; 1059–1060.

19. For the classic discussion of the "triumph of the therapeutic" as a movement in American culture, see Philip Rieff, *The Triumph of the Therapeutic* (New York: Harper & Row, Harper Torchbooks, 1966).

20. Lobkowicz, p. 74.

21. See ibid., p. 71.

22. See ibid., p. 74.

23. Ibid.

24. See above, p. 31.

25. For an account of a major study of Roman Catholic seminaries in regard to the above issues, see Katarina Schuth, O.S.F., "American Seminaries as Research Finds Them," in *U.S. Catholic Seminaries and Their Future* (Washington, D.C.: United States Catholic Conference, 1988), pp. 29–59.

26. Clark Gilpin, "The Seminary Ideal in American Protestant Ministerial Education, 1700–1808," *Theological Education* (Spring 1984), p. 95.

27. See Mary Latimer Gambrell, *Ministerial Training in Eighteenth-Century New England* (New York: Columbia University Press, 1937), esp. chs. 6 and 7.

28. Quoted in Robert Handy, *A History of Union Theological Seminary in New York* (New York: Columbia University Press, 1987), p. 8.

29. Ibid., p. 9.

30. See Douglas R. Chandler, *Pilgrimage of Faith: A Centennial History of Wesley Theological Seminary, 1882–1982* (Cabin John, Md.: Seven Locks Press, 1984), esp. chs. 1 and 2, for an illustration of how one theological school developed in this fashion.

3

Excellence as *Paideia*

There is a fourth, nontheological factor that pluralizes "theological schools." Ironically, often it brings with it a temptation to find an underlying unity that will overcome the pluralism of theological schools by showing that they all share the same essence. We have just seen that, far from unifying them, the fact that theological schools are *theological* makes them irreducibly different from one another because of different theological judgments about the nature of the Christian thing, what it is to understand God, and what sort of community a theological school is. But the next question must be: How shall that school go about schooling?

Concretely speaking, schooling requires accepted conventions by which it is organized and governed, however informal they may be. Schooling is inherently an institutionalized set of practices. What shall those institutionalized conventions be? How shall the distinction between "students" and "faculty" be specified? By what criteria, and why? Which disciplines should be exercised in the struggle to understand, and why? And how shall the network of interactions among students and faculty be structured and ordered? To what ends, and why?

Answers to these questions have always been borrowed from the larger host culture within which theological schools are placed. Cultures tend to adopt some model of schooling as the standard of excellence in schooling. Christian theological schools have always aspired to meet the going standards of excellence. That is to say, theological schools have characteristically acted in this regard as though they acknowledged a responsibility to be part of a larger public cultural life and to be accountable to its standards.

Late-twentieth-century theological schools in North America, however, exhibit the strain of trying to appropriate two quite different models of excellent schooling, both of which are by this time traditional in our cultural setting. One, *paideia,* which has its roots in the ancient Greco-Roman world, was unquestioned until the eighteenth century. It is an integral part of every tradition of Christian schooling, whether that tradition is on the road from Nicaea or Trent or Augsburg (or Geneva, or Northampton, etc.). The other model of excellence in schooling is the modern research university, for which we may let the founding of the University of Berlin in 1810 serve as the emblem. Each model brings with it different criteria by which "faculty" are distinguished from "students," different principles governing how faculty and students relate to each other, and different assumptions governing how a school's common life ought to be run. No accredited theological school in North America escapes the probably unresolvable tension created within its common life by trying to assimilate itself simultaneously to both models of excellence and their inconsistent demands. However, theological schools vary considerably in the ways in which they attempt to negotiate between the two. The way any one school does negotiate the two is a major factor making it the concrete particular school it is. Every theological school grows up at the intersection of the Berlin Turnpike with one or more of the roads: Trent Road, Augsburg Road, and so forth.

PAIDEIA

In current discussions of the nature and purpose of theological education Edward Farley has invoked the older of these two models of excellence in schooling when he describes his book *Theologia* as an essay "which purports to promote a Christian *paideia.*"[1] This model is rooted in an understanding of schooling already at least four centuries old by the time Christian churches appeared on the scene. It was the understanding of schooling dominant in the Hellenistic host culture of the earliest churches outside Palestine. The Greek word *paideia* meant at once "schooling," "culturing," and "character formation." Although, as we shall note, it underwent important changes between the fourth century B.C. and the fourth century A.D., the concept of paideia retained important continuities through this history. Its aim was to form in the souls of the young the virtue or *arete* they needed to function as responsible citizens. In its earliest form this schooling had focused on athletics and on the study of the poetry ascribed to Homer. The assumption was that by simultaneously subjecting the bodies of the young to physical discipline and their souls to the traditions and customs of ancient Greece as conveyed by literature, they would emerge deeply shaped by those dispositions or habits, that is, virtues, that make the good citizen. At the same time it meant that the ruling class were all genuinely "cultured" in the same way so that, whatever their differences of judgment on particular matters, they were unified by a shared picture of the good life and of what was to be most valued in it.

This was the manner in which educated, Greek-speaking Christians from the very beginning had been schooled, whether they were from pagan families or from Jewish families that had become assimilated into Greek culture. Fragments of quotations from Greek authors and adaptations of conventional Greek rhetorical devices and literary forms by the authors of some New Testament writings, notably the Acts of the Apostles, testify to this. Even more striking is the explicit use of the traditional concept of paideia in a letter written in A.D. 90 by the bishop of Rome, Clement, to the church in Corinth, which was badly divided by controversy. Werner Jaeger, who has written the classic history of the idea of paideia,[2] pointed out in a later book on *Early Christianity and Greek Paideia* that Clement not only uses literary forms and types of argument calculated to sway people formed by paideia but, beyond that, he explicitly praises paideia in such a way as to make it clear that his entire epistle is to be taken "as an act of Christian education."[3]

What early Christians inherited was both a practice of paideia and a body of literature about paideia. Central to the literature about paideia were Plato's writings, especially the *Republic* which, along with some of his shorter dialogues, can be read, so Jaeger urges, as a proposal for the reform of ancient Athens' paideia. Indeed, Jaeger points out, it was in Plato's time, in the fourth century B.C., that Athens developed humankind's first *"conscious* ideal of education and culture."[4] In Athens "a 'higher culture' grew up with its own representatives, the Sophists, whose profession was 'to teach virtue.' But . . . despite all their hard thinking about educational method and styles of teaching, and despite the bewildering multiplicity of subjects embraced in their higher culture, none of them really understood the assumptions on which his profession was based."[5] To solve these problems, Plato proposed in the *Republic* a reform of paideia that was inseparable from a reform of the social structure and governance of the *polis*. This generated a differentiated proposal of reformed paideia, with significantly different modes of education for persons filling different functions in the city. In particular, it led to a proposal that those responsible for the protection of the city, the "guardians," be "cultured" in a way that inculcated civic traditions and virtues particularly needed for their tasks, especially courage. By contrast, those responsible for ruling, the "philosopher kings," were to be "cultured" in a way that formed in them the "philosophical virtue" that was grounded in knowledge of the Good itself and not, as were the guardians' virtues, simply trained into them by custom and practice. Plato retained the traditional pattern of understanding paideia in terms of political goals.

Of course Plato's utopian proposals were never adopted by early Christian churches and were not part of the practice of paideia inherited by them. But at least four interrelated themes in Plato's proposals about the education of ideal rulers took on a life of their own and did shape ordinary paideia as the Christians knew it centuries later. First, Plato argues that, instead of focusing on disputes about which virtues are the needful ones and how they are to be distinguished one from another, it is more important and fruitful to attend to what they have in common and inquire into what Virtue is in itself—the *essence* of virtue. To know that is to know the Good. Hence, to be shaped by *arete* simply *is* to know the Good.

The next theme concerns the nature of the Good. In Plato's analysis, the Good is the highest principle of the universe. Greek philosophers before Plato were accustomed to calling the highest principle "God" or "the divine." Plato's followers assumed that he had been founding a new religion. The understanding of Plato that early Christians inherited assumed that the goal and deep foundation of paideia was knowledge of the divine.

The third theme has to do with the teacher of paideia. Taking his own teacher Socrates as the ideal teacher, Plato argues that, strictly speaking, virtue cannot be taught. The Sophist proposed to teach virtue by conveying information about what other thinkers had taught about virtue and by training in techniques of rhetoric and argument. But what is needed in order to be shaped by virtue is "to recognize one supreme standard, which was binding on all alike because it expressed the innermost nature"[6] of human beings. Knowing the Good involves not only knowing the divine but also a deep knowing of one's own humanity. Like Socrates, who always had claimed that he had nothing to teach anyone, the teacher of virtue can at most serve as a midwife for someone else coming to that knowledge of self which is at the same time knowledge of the divine, that is, knowledge of the Good. It comes through contemplation that yields intuitive insight or *gnosis* of the Good.

The final theme has to do with the student. Paideia requires conversion, "the wheeling around of the 'whole soul' toward the light of the Idea of Good, the divine origin of the universe."[7] Conversion has to happen in order for one to have intuitive insight into the Good. It comes as the culmination of a long educational process like "slow vegetable growth."[8] Like vegetable growth, it requires a climate and nutrients that, Plato believed, must be provided by the social atmosphere of the city. Unlike the Sophists' highly individualistic view of paideia, Plato stressed its inherently social nature.

It is important to note one feature of Plato's "self-conscious ideal" of paideia: It is the result of the hunt for the *essence* of the subject studied in paideia, "the Good." Plato thought that one could show the underlying unity of the apparent plurality of the virtues by discovering something that was identically the same in all of them, the Good, the essence of moral virtue. It is one and the same thing in all of the virtues, even though the virtues themselves differ from one another. It is the one subject that we seek to understand better through paideia. Hence, although particular, concrete occasions of paideia, the actual practices of paideia, we might say, appear to be both many and enormously diverse, they are "really" all identical with one another because they are practices through which people are shaped by one selfsame reality, the Good. This is not to say that the idea of paideia itself logically requires that one adopt the view that there is one essence underlying a plurality of occasions of paideia. That was Plato's contention. His was not the only "self-conscious ideal" or theory of paideia; the Sophists had their own. But Plato's was the way of understanding paideia that historically most deeply influenced Christian theological schooling. In consequence, the hunt for the essence of paideia's subject matter came to seem perfectly natural.

In the century and a half between Clement of Rome's letter to the Corinthians and Clement of Alexandria's Christian school of the Catechetes, Christian spokesmen went from perhaps unself-conscious reliance on traditional pagan paideia (in order to make their cases persuasive to both pagans and fellow Christians) to a self-conscious ideal of Christian paideia for its own sake. It was, we might say, in third-century Alexandria, in the time of Clement and his successor Origen, that there first developed the *conscious* ideal of Christian education and culture as something integral to the Christian thing itself. This is the crucial point: Paideia was built into the very way the Christian thing was construed.

Of course, the received practice of paideia had itself undergone major changes between the rise in fourth-century B.C. pagan Athens of the "first conscious ideal of education and culture" and the rise in third-century A.D. pagan Alexandria of the first conscious ideal of *Christian* education and culture. What remained unchanged was of utmost importance: The aim of paideia is to shape persons in such a way that they are literally "in-formed" by virtue. However, the governing interests guiding the practice of paideia had decisively shifted from political to religious interests.

Within two generations after Plato the political autonomy of the Greek city-states, which had been the original context of paideia, had been destroyed by the relentless spread of Alexander's empire from Macedonia to India. Alexander recognized the value of Greek culture as a unifying force in his cross-cultural empire and encouraged the spread of Greek paideia in non-Hellenic cultures, but not to the end of culturing virtuous *self*-ruling citizens! During the social and political turmoil of the centuries following Alexander's death—in which his empire was dismembered, the "members" seemed continuously to war with one another, and then were largely absorbed into Rome's growing empire—the practice of paideia continued to be the dominant force shaping the educated classes. But by the third century A.D. it was a practice focused not on shaping virtuous political agents, but rather on preparation for that conversion of soul which would bring religious knowledge of the divine. Plato's contentions that virtue is knowledge of the Good, that knowledge of the Good is at once knowledge of one's own humanity and knowledge of the divine, and that it comes only through a conversion of the soul had all been separated from his contention that the proper home for such knowledge is public life in the *polis*.

By the third century A.D. the practice of paideia treated all the classical philosophical traditions—Stoic, Epicurean, Aristotelian, but most of all Platonic—with religious interests. Using them, teachers "led their pupils the way to that spirituality which was the common link of all higher religion in late antiquity."[9] Furthermore, it was increasingly stressed that in undergoing paideia one needed divine assistance; one could not expect to accomplish conversion and come to knowledge of God on one's own unaided resources.[10] Paideia had to do with the interior and entirely private life. "Greek paideia," writes Jaeger, itself "became a religion and an article of faith."[11]

This was the frame of reference in which it was unavoidable that educated Greek-speaking Christians would understand the Christian thing from the late first century (cf. Clement of Rome) onward. It was not only an effective device in commending and defending the Christian faith to pagans—"See, Christianity is paideia too, aiming at the same goal, but superior in the way it does so"—no, more deeply, it was the Christians' own way of taking Christianity. In their view, the Christian thing is not "like" paideia; it does not merely make use of received paideia, as Clement of Rome had done. Rather, as claimed by Clement of Alexandria and, with much greater intellectual power, Origen, his pupil and successor as head of the Alexandrian Catechetical school, Christianity *is* paideia, divinely given in Jesus Christ and inspired Christian scriptures, focused in a profound conversion of soul, and divinely assisted by the Holy Spirit.

As paideia, the Christian thing is inherently a school. In the fourth century under Origen's leadership the Catechetical school in Alexandria was the most influential institutionalization of this school. It provided schooling, not principally for future clergy, but first of all for those who wished to be baptized, and even for those who wished merely to inquire into Christianity. We may let it serve as the symbol for the rise of paideia as the model of excellence in theological education.

Paideia requires texts as its subject matter. In ancient Athens the subject matter had been Homer. Here we touch on a second major change that slowly took place in the practice of paideia before Christian churches appeared on the scene. The subject matter had slowly expanded to include Greek poetry at large. Then paideia had come to mean Greek literature as a whole. "Only relatively late were the more rational branches of education added . . . and the system of 'liberal arts' invented . . . ; finally philosophy was added,"[12] above all, from the second century on, "divine Plato." Ironically, Plato's dialogues, intended as a challenge to the notion that paideia would be accomplished by ways of conveying information, were themselves included in the mass of information conveyed in the name of teaching knowledge of the Good. It needs to be stressed that the interest in which the "liberal arts," including literature and culminating in philosophy, were read was religious. These texts were studied in the conviction that doing so would lead to deeper knowledge of the divine. Now, the central subject matter of paideia in Christian schooling was the literature of the Bible. Origen applied the traditional forms of Greek scholarship to the biblical texts, producing critical editions, commentaries, and scientific treatises. However, this was done in the service of something else. The dominant interest in studying scripture was to come to know God through that conversion of the soul that yields *gnosis,* intellectual intuition of God. That was also the interest in which pagans read Greek literature. It required them to move from literal interpretations of the texts to allegorical interpretations in which the religious insight of the texts was uncovered. Origen followed suit, interpreting biblical texts allegorically with a power that made itself felt for centuries thereafter.

Alongside commentary on scripture, Origen formulated the subject matter of Christian paideia in a second way. He wrote more or less systematic reflections on the implications of the content of scripture regarding human nature, the predicament that requires conversion and how that predicament could have come about, the conditions under which one can be saved from one's predicament, and what all this implies about the nature of God. He produced the first great "Christian philosophy" which dealt, not with all the branches of traditional Greek philosophy (e.g., "logic," "physics," "politics"), but only with what was customarily called "theology," reflection on divine things (although Christians of the time avoided the term "theology" because in their setting it usually had to do with pagan gods). This too, secondarily to scripture, was part of the subject matter of Christian paideia, as the writings of pagan philosophers were in pagan paideia.

Furthermore, Origen insisted that Christian paideia had to be practiced in conversation with the pagan paideia dominant in the church's host culture. In his view pagan paideia was "the gradual fulfillment of the divine providence,"[13] culminating in the paideia which was Christianity. Accordingly Christian paideia had to include schooling in the best of pagan philosophy. That paideia became *the* model for excellence in theological schooling was simply inherent in the way the Christian thing was construed by Christians and pagans alike in a Hellenistic culture that understood itself to be paideia.

As a schooling, Christian paideia must be seen as a process of slow ("vegetable") growth requiring a climate and nutrients. Plato had taught that they must be provided by the social atmosphere of the *polis*. By the time Christian churches appeared on the scene, "polis" was no longer a living concept. Within two generations after Origen the intellectual leadership of the Christian churches in Cappadocia were calling for the churches themselves to develop that "atmosphere" by developing a distinctively Christian literature in the broad sense. Gregory Nazianzen and his younger contemporary Gregory of Nyssa, both bishops, worked very self-consciously to write and to encourage other Christians to write in the finest literary fashion of the age. Gregory of Nyssa's explicit rationale for this lay in his view that educational activity and the work of the creative artist, painter, and sculptor were essentially identical in the shaping of the human person.[14] In his view, excellent theological schooling is in conversation with its host culture not only by learning from it but also by contributing *to* the host culture's arts and letters. In this way Christian paideia, like paideia in Plato's day, bore on the public realm, but in a quite different sense of "public." For the tradition to which Plato had been heir, paideia was essential to the well-being of the public realm as the political realm, by forming virtuous citizens capable of filling political roles wisely; for fourth-century Greek-speaking Christians paideia, while it aimed to shape persons' private interiority rather than their public political activity, contributed to the well-being of the public realm as a cultural realm accessible to any literate, educated person, Christian or pagan.

Because the construal of the Christian thing of which it is an integral part is not only the earliest construal but has been historically much the most influential one, paideia has been the most influential model of excellence in theological schooling. Jaeger holds that this model

> can be pursued through the Middle Ages; and from the Renaissance the line leads straight back to the Christian humanism of the fathers of the fourth century A.D. and to their idea of man's dignity and of his reformation and rebirth through the Spirit.[15]

THEOLOGICAL SCHOOLING AS PAIDEIA

Theological schooling as paideia is ruled by a religious interest to know God by *gnosis,* an immediate intellectual intuition. That is compatible with at least three of the senses of "understanding God" we sorted out above (contemplative understanding; discursive understanding; affective understanding) and perhaps with some versions of the fourth (understanding in and through action). Even when, as with the Protestant Reformers, knowledge of God is reserved for the eschaton and theological schooling focuses on faith, schooling remains a practice of paideia—notably, in Calvin's academy in Geneva. Furthermore, it is compatible with the various construals of the subject matter of theological schooling (Word of God, Christian experience, Christian tradition—paideia as "Christian culture"—or various combinations of these). When the institution of the university developed in the Middle Ages and the writings of Aristotle were rediscovered, theological schooling stressed far more than it previously had discursive reasoning, technical logical skill, and academic specialization. Nonetheless, it continued to be a type of paideia, governed by paideia's characteristic religious interest. With the Renaissance, theological schooling among Protestants and Roman Catholics alike began to emphasize literary-critical studies of scripture and other texts, but still as a practice of paideia. Paideia proved compatible both with the more social understanding of human personhood that marked medieval life and with the more individualistic assumptions about personhood that marked much Renaissance culture.

In all these settings, theological schooling that meets paideia's standards of excellence exhibits four features in particular. First, it is ruled by a religious interest in coming to better understanding of God. This religious understanding comes in *gnosis,* immediate intuitive understanding. As we have seen, this means that at bottom all the senses of "understanding God" which we have sorted out can be and were understood as the fruit of paideia.

Second, theological schooling on the model of paideia requires divinely assisted conversion of the one who learns. This has implications for who can teach and what teaching is. It means that the identification of who is qualified to teach and the character of the relationship between "teacher" and "learner" are very complex matters. In principle, the relationship must be indirect. No one can directly give another person *gnosis* of God by teaching. In part this is because, as Plato held, knowledge of the Good cannot be taught. Additionally there is the theological reason that the condition of having *gnosis* is that one undergoes a conversion which finally only God can give. At most, the teacher "teaches" only indirectly by providing the context in which the student may be graced himself or herself to come to that combination of immediate self-knowledge and God-knowledge which is the aim of paideia. Among the factors that make that "context," of course, are those texts and practices whose study is believed to lead to understanding of God, that is, scripture and the practice of the way of the Christian life, including but not limited to worship of God.

Accordingly, there are two quite different sorts of capacities that qualify one to be a "teacher" in theological education as paideia. One is unusual learning in regard to the relevant texts and practices, that is, the subject matter. As we have seen, this holds true for all of the various construals of the Christian thing that we have sorted out. The other sort of qualification necessary for being a teacher is the possession of personal gifts for the indirect "teaching" that, as a midwife, helps another come to *gnosis*. It has always been difficult to hold the two together in balance. If the former is stressed, "teaching" becomes direct communication of information and ceases truly to be life-shaping paideia. If the latter is stressed, technique becomes dominant, the substance by which the student is to be "molded" is lost, and again schooling ceases truly to be paideia.

3   It follows, third, that theological schooling as paideia focuses on the student because it supposes that for the student to understand God some kind of shaping or forming of the student is required. Theological schooling thus tends to be individualistic.

4   Finally, theological schooling in this model is, in a qualified way, public schooling. Because understanding God cannot be achieved directly, it is sought by studying material whose study is thought to lead to understanding God. That subject matter, whether sacred texts only or inclusive of other "extra-Christian" or "secular" texts, is understood to be publicly available and publicly explicable. Furthermore, as paideia, theological schooling generates its own writings that are intended not only for use within Christian communities but also as contributions to the cultural life of the communities' host societies.

However, this is "public" schooling only in a qualified sense. It is open to and engaged in a "public" cultural life broader than the common life of the communities for whom the schooling is undertaken. But because its governing interest is "religious," theological schooling on the model of paideia has characteristically been disengaged from the public realm in the sense of the realm of political, social, and economic power, its arrangement and its management. This is not to say that the Christian churches have necessarily been disengaged in this way. To the contrary, whether they should be so engaged and, if so, how, has been a continuing point of disagreement among them. But theological schooling, even when undertaken by a Christian community itself committed to vigorous engagement in the public realm, has not itself been rooted in such engagement. Indeed, it has not on principle. Its model of excellence is an ancient paideia that once was so engaged because in ancient Athens it was ruled by political interests. But it came to be ruled by religious interests when the social conditions for the political interests were destroyed along with the social reality of the *polis*. The very idea of paideia became privatized and entailed economic, social, and political interests, that is, "public" interests, in one sense of the term, incommensurate with its religious interests.

It cannot be stressed too much that paideia as a model of excellence in theological schooling continues to be very powerfully influential in theological schooling today. There is a historical reason for that. From the second century on, the Christian thing has been understood as a kind of "forming" of persons' lives on the model of education as paideia. Every construal of the subject matter of theological inquiry and of what it is to "understand" God simply assumes the validity of this model. The idea that Christianity is some type of paideia has come to be so deeply built into all construals of the Christian thing that the two are inseparable. It would be sheer self-deception to suppose that one could reconceive theological schooling by abandoning paideia as a model of excellent schooling. Indeed, recent books about how best to understand theological education include proposals by both Edward Farley, in *Theologia,* and Charles Wood, in *Vision and Discernment,*[16] to take paideia as the central model quite deliberately and self-consciously. However, as we shall see in the next chapter, in the modern world it is not possible simply to settle for paideia as the model of excellent education. There is a second model that is as unavoidable as paideia. The two cannot be synthesized. There are different ways to negotiate between them, and that fact constitutes the fourth major factor that pluralizes theological schools.

Notes

1. Farley, *Theologia,* p. xi.

2. Werner Jaeger, *Paideia,* 3 vols., trans. Gilbert Highet (Oxford: Basil Blackwell, 1939–63), vol. II; idem, *Early Christianity and Greek Paideia* (Cambridge, Mass.: Harvard University Press, 1961).

3. Clement, furthermore, refers to the "paideia of God" and the "paideia of Christ" and closes with a prayer thanking God for sending us Christ "through whom thou hast educated and sanctified us and honored us." In this Clement echoes the frequent use of paideia by the Septuagint and by Ephesians. However, Jaeger argues, "it is clear that he applies it in a much wider sense in his letter and, while using Scriptural testimony, he himself conceives of paideia as precisely that which he offers the Corinthians in his whole letter. . . . There can be no doubt that what he takes over in his letter from a great philosophical tradition and from other pagan sources is included by him in this comprehensive concept of divine paideia, for if it were not so, he could not have used it for his purpose in order to convince the people of Corinth of the truth of his teachings." Jaeger, *Early Christianity and Greek Paideia,* p. 25.

4. *Paideia,* vol. II, p. 5 (emphasis added).

5. Ibid., p. 123.

6. Ibid., p. 125; for this entire paragraph, cf. ibid., chs. 4 and 5, passim.

7. Ibid., p. 295.

8. Ibid., p. 228.

9. Jaeger, *Early Christianity and Greek Paideia,* p. 46.

10. Ibid., p. 88.

11. Ibid., p. 72.

12. Ibid., p. 91.

13. Ibid., p. 67.

14. See ibid., p. 87.

15. Ibid., p. 100.

16. Charles Wood, *Vision and Discernment* (Atlanta: Scholars Press, 1985).

4

Excellence as *Wissenschaft*
and Professionalism

There have been two models of excellence to which theological schooling in North America has held itself accountable. The more ancient is paideia. We have examined it in the last chapter and noted its consequences for theological schooling. The second is only about a hundred and eighty years old. It is rooted in the modern research university, for which rigorous "scientific" research or *Wissenschaft* is the defining goal. It was at the founding of the University of Berlin that a decisive argument was won to include a theological school within the research university. Therefore we shall make Berlin the emblem of this model. The burden of that successful argument rested on the notion of a "profession" and a "professional school." Hence, when a theological school adopts the research university as the model of excellent schooling, it takes on not only a standard of appropriate schooling *(Wissenschaft)* but also a particular end for theological schooling (the production of "professionals"). We shall explore the origins of this model. Then we shall go on to review revisions of this model in modern thinking about theological education. We can then track the tensions that arise within theological schools as their paideia-shaped roads from Geneva, Trent, and others intersect with the Berlin Turnpike.

THE RESEARCH UNIVERSITY

The research university developed out of a century of university reform in Germany. This reform reflected a cultural spirit and value commitments that are usually associated with the Enlightenment, understood as a very broad cultural movement. From the Reformation on, universities in each German state had been dominated by the church established in that state. Within the universities the faculties of theology were dominant. During the eighteenth century there was a steady movement of reform to encourage free inquiry within the universities. These reforms involved greater independence from the established churches, a shift from Latin to German as the language of instruction, and greater prestige accorded to faculties of law and philosophy than to theology. The spirit permeating the entire movement focused on two intellectual values: critical historical methods of inquiry applied to every appropriate topic, sacred as well as secular; and reason as the final arbiter of all questions about truth. "Reason" and "rationality" were understood in a distinctively modern way that was shaped by the new learning symbolized by empirically tested Newtonian physics, the invention of calculus, and critical historical research. Usually the University of Halle is named as the first reformed university in Germany institutionalizing this modern spirit, soon followed by Göttingen and Erlangen.[1]

The University of Berlin, founded against the background of this century of reform, was the occasion for a historically decisive debate about whether theological schooling rightly belongs within a modern university. The university was created as part of a reorganization of the Prussian educational system in the wake of Prussia's devastating defeat by Napoleon. The reorganization was part of the larger movement in Europe to reform education in ways shaped by Enlightenment principles; Napoleon, for example, was reforming the French educational system at the same time. The founder of the University of Berlin is usually said to be the scholar Wilhelm von Humboldt, who proposed the founding of the university as part of a general restructuring of the educational system that he designed and initiated during a short sixteen-month tenure in government service as head of the section on cultural and educational affairs. In June 1810, to help him draft the provisional statutes for the new university, he appointed a three-person committee, including the theologian Friedrich Schleiermacher. Schleiermacher actually wrote the founding document. The university opened in October of 1810.[2]

As Daniel Fallon points out, von Humboldt and Schleiermacher
designed a university based on three principles.[3] The first principle was
the unity of research and teaching. In his reorganization of the entire
educational system von Humboldt envisioned both a major contrast
and a symbiotic relationship between secondary schools and the
university. The secondary school, or *Gymnasium,* deals only with
well-established and derived principles, conveying them to the student.
Universities, by contrast, "always treat knowledge as an as yet unsolved
problem, and thus always stay at research."[4] Conducting original
research, therefore, is central to what distinguishes a university from
secondary schools. The only degree to be given was the doctorate, the
research degree. Only persons who had published significant research
beyond the doctorate could even be considered for faculty positions.
Only full professors were to be considered members of the faculties
of the university. This was a radical educational innovation. However,
von Humboldt and Schleiermacher were educational conserva-
tives in insisting that the older picture of universities as teaching
institutions be retained. Rather than adopting the more radical
view that research should always be confined to non-teaching research
institutes they insisted that research needed to be accompanied by
teaching.

This changed the teacher-student relationship. Teacher and student
now have the same function: to cooperate in the promotion of
knowledge. The teacher does not exist *for* the student, as was the case in
paideia. Rather the teacher needs the student to achieve the goal of
research by, as von Humboldt put it, "combining a practiced mind,
which is on that very account apt to be more one-sided and less active
[the teacher's], with one which, though weaker and still neutral,
bravely attempts every possibility [the student's]."[5]

A second principle on which the university was based was the central
importance of the arts and sciences. This was viewed at the time as a
recovery of what was central to paideia. Study of the liberal arts had
come to be considered preliminary to more specialized study of one of
the professions, theology, law, or medicine. Accordingly, the faculty of
arts and sciences was considered the "lower" faculty and the faculties in
the professions considered the "higher" faculties. Moreover, the

faculties in the professions had often come to be ranked by law in a hierarchical order, with dominance given to the faculty of theology. The University of Berlin marked the emancipation of the faculty of arts and sciences from institutional domination by the higher faculties, especially theology.

Von Humboldt was explicit that, as had been the case in ancient paideia, such liberal arts schooling "transforms the character." However, he did not note the significance of one major difference. In his classic history of German universities Friedrich Paulsen points out that recovery of the centrality of the liberal arts at Berlin would have this character-transforming result "not on the basis of medieval church unity," nor, we might add, on the basis of the coherence of a Hellenistic view of what constitutes the good life, "but rather upon the basis of the unity of human civilization and scientific work, the unity based on the modern ideal of humanity."[6]

The "modern ideal of humanity" is the Enlightenment view. At its heart is a particular view of rationality, one defined by the idea of scholarly research that yields net increases in knowledge. To have one's character "transformed" is to have one's rational capacities brought out and honed through learning how to be an expert researcher.

The third principle exemplified by the University of Berlin was the protection of academic freedom. Its two mottoes were *Lernfreiheit:* the freedom to learn; and *Lehrfreiheit:* the freedom to teach. The former gave students the right to follow any curriculum; the latter gave scholars the right of free inquiry and was institutionalized in a provision for faculty tenure. Academic freedom was the direct application to higher education of the central value of the Enlightenment: reason's independence from all authority and its innate responsibility critically to scrutinize any claim to authority.

It is very important to notice the context of assumptions in which academic freedom was institutionalized. It was simply assumed that the university exists for the well-being of the state. In a way this is a return to the public context in which paideia was understood in classical Athens up through Plato: the context and goal of excellent schooling is the well-being of the public realm understood as a political realm.

Because the university existed for the state's well-being, the state, not the university, selected and appointed faculty members. The state funded each faculty member and the member's research through bilateral negotiations with each scholar separately. It may be that at the time there was no clear distinction made between concepts of state and society. In any case, von Humboldt and Schleiermacher offered no challenge to the understanding of the state they had inherited. They simply assumed that if the state provided the university with space for independent inquiry, the students educated that way would provide the state with enlightened servants through whom the state itself would become progressively enlightened.

This created, of course, an extremely ambiguous legacy. From the perspective of Enlightenment ideals it seemed exemplary. Writing before both world wars, Paulsen saw the University of Berlin as far more successful at institutionalizing Enlightenment values than were its French counterparts. Whereas the French model relied on centralization and standardization so that universities were transformed into "professional state-schools with hard and fast instruction and without scientific spirit" centralized in Paris at the expense of the provinces, the University of Berlin was the model for "an abundance of flourishing universities distributed throughout the country whose competition created greater efficiency." Moreover, their "free, non-political universities became important" even for "the political life of the German people."[7]

From a post–World War II perspective, the confidence that state self-interest would guarantee academic freedom and, conversely, that duly enlightened graduates functioning as civil servants would progressively enlighten the state strikes Fallon as "romantic heroism."[8] Direct state control of faculty appointments and finances made possible politically inspired direct state influence, especially in regard to opinion and policy. Inevitably, "by the end of the nineteenth century the German university had become a very conservative institution—in fact, as the historian David Schoenbaum remarked, 'conservative enough to survive Bismarck, William II, and Hitler, attenuated but largely intact.' "[9] It is not self-evident, although it is arguable, that Enlightenment ideals themselves bear part of the responsibility for the ambiguity of the legacy of the University of Berlin. What is clear is that the way in which the university institutionalized the public ends and roles of schooling did directly contribute to that ambiguity.

The research university, exemplified by the University of Berlin, became the normative model of excellence in higher education in the United States during the last third of the nineteenth century, though there had been movement in that direction for the better part of the century. For example, the University of Michigan, which had been chartered in 1817 with a rationale inspired by Napoleonic ideals, was shaped for a generation after 1835 by leadership explicitly emulating Prussian higher education. The model became decisive for American higher education, however, in 1876, when Johns Hopkins University opened as the first graduate school in the United States. Virtually all of its faculty by 1884 had studied in Germany and thirteen had been awarded German doctorates. Indeed, the Ph.D. degree was itself assumed directly from the German Dr. phil., the highest degree awarded by the German faculty of arts and sciences. "Throughout this period of birth and development of the American university the dominant influence, the overriding ideal, was the model of Humboldt's enlightenment university."[10]

What are the consequences of Berlin's influence? The Enlightenment involved major changes in what counted as "inquiring," "knowing," and "understanding," and research universities institutionalized those changes. When the research university became the normative model of the excellent "school" a new and quite different set of methods and aims came to dominate schooling, including theological schooling.

The overarching aim of a research university is inquiry leading to the mastery of the truth about whatever is studied. The German word for such inquiry is *Wissenschaft*. It is usually translated into English as "science." That is misleading, because in ordinary English "science," unless qualified as "life" or "psychological" or "social" science, usually designates the physical sciences, the "hard sciences." Better simply to characterize such inquiry as "critical research that is orderly and disciplined."[11] This becomes a powerfully influential model for inquiry in theological schools.

Such inquiry is characteristically "critical" inquiry in that it rationally tests *all* alleged bases of truth. Schooling on the paideia model in pagan or Christian academy, monastery, cathedral school, or medieval university had always been critical in the sense of testing arguments for clarity, logical validity, and coherence. But it acknowledged certain sources of information as authorities in secular as well as sacred studies. In particular, the sheer antiquity of a source was characteristically taken to establish it as an authority. For the research university, however, critical inquiry requires that no alleged authoritative source of truth, either sacred or secular, be exempt from rigorous testing of its veracity. It follows that inquiry turns quite literally into "re-search." One does not inquire into the truth by searching to discover what previous authorities said, the more ancient the better. Rather one conducts re-search, a second and independent search for the truth about the subject under consideration—a search, furthermore, that can in principle be *re*peated and so *re*confirmed by any other qualified inquirer.

Critical research is "orderly" when it attempts to locate its subject in the largest possible context of relations to other things. Inquiry in the research university shows an extraordinarily intense passion for building theories that are all-encompassing. The ideal goal is to develop and validate one unified theory that can outline the interconnections among all things. This is not simply a matter of exhibiting relationships among concepts. Ancient and medieval schooling engaged in inquiry that was orderly in that sense. Rather, two other kinds of relations are crucial here: natural or physical relations and historical relations. Consequently, "understanding" a subject consists in mastering how it is related to other matters, that is, how it may be located in the web of physical and historical relationships that make it what it is.

Note that "theory" means something quite different in the research university than it did in the context of paideia. In paideia, as we have seen, *theoria* is the understanding one may have of such reality as is unchanging and eternal. It is obtained by contemplation. It has no bearing on managing the changing worlds of physical nature or human politics. For coping with changing political situations one needs instead practical wisdom. For coping with the changeable physical world one needs the artisan's or craftsperson's skilled know-how. By contrast, in the research university "theory" is about nothing other than endlessly changeable physical and social worlds, and it is significant only to the extent that it is applicable to them. The very idea of "theory" now entails the movement from "pure science" to "applied science," from research to engineering, from theory to application.

Orderly inquiry, finally, is "disciplined" when it devises methods for exploring the relations among things, methods for critically testing all alleged authorities. They must be methods that rely on types of evidence appropriate to the subject, minimize the biases of the inquirer, and can be followed by another researcher to establish the same conclusions over and over again.

Only the results of critical, orderly, disciplined research can count as yielding "knowledge." Knowledge in this sense is by definition "public," that is, in principle accessible to anyone capable of understanding it and open to being re-searched by anyone who is skeptical of it.

In actual practice, inquiry in the research university has divided all possible subjects of inquiry into two broad classes, natural and cultural, the "sciences" and the "humanities," according to the types of discipline each requires. The disciplines and types of theorizing that constitute the "sciences" have created subject matters that simply did not exist within schooling on the model of paideia. However, the type of subject matter into which the humanities inquire simply *was* the subject matter with which paideia dealt.

That makes possible a continuing tension between the two models of schooling in the humanities. In a third-century A.D. pagan or Christian academy one might study ancient texts so as to become more deeply shaped by the virtues. On the model of paideia that is what excellent schooling aims at. By contrast, the disciplines that make inquiry in the humanities in a research university genuinely critical research yielding truly public knowledge are the disciplines of the historian. In a research university one studies ancient texts to re-search the truth about them, their origins, their meanings in their original settings, the history of their uses, the history of teachings about them or readings of them, perhaps the social or psychological dynamics that explain why such texts come to be written. Because theological schooling focuses so heavily on ancient texts, it clearly is going to experience deep tensions if it accepts the research university as its model of excellent schooling without giving up values central to paideia as the model of excellence.

RESEARCH UNIVERSITY AND THEOLOGICAL SCHOOL

That is precisely what began to happen with the founding of the University of Berlin. Prussia was a Protestant state. A Protestant faculty of theology was included in the university. It was by no means obvious that it should be. Given an Enlightenment view of what it was to "inquire" and to "know," no "inquiry" belonged within the university if it ended up appealing to some authority that could not itself be subjected to critical inquiry. For a decade there had been a public debate about whether theology failed this test. Schleiermacher argued that it did not or, at least, need not. Since he prevailed and a theology faculty was included in the paradigmatic research university, the structure of his argument continues to affect us for whom the research university remains the culturally dominant model of excellence in schooling.

Schleiermacher was solving a problem. Protestant theological faculties of Schleiermacher's generation had inherited a fourfold theological curriculum. In his historical sketch of its development, Edward Farley[12] argues that it was an uneasy and unself-conscious compromise between a pre-critical and a post-critical view of scripture. On the pre-critical side two subtle but decisive changes had taken place in Protestant theological schooling.

First, "theology" had been made objective. In theological schooling on the model of paideia, "theology" named one's understanding of God and, by derivation, the act of meditative reflection on scripture that was believed to lead to that understanding. However, during sixteenth- and seventeenth-century polemical controversies (Catholics vs. Protestants; Lutherans vs. Calvinists; everybody vs. "anabaptists"), "theology" came to name church teachings, truths that could be stated propositionally. Scripture was treated as the divinely inspired repository of these truths. The theological curriculum was a set of things one did with the truths scripture provided: exegesis drew the truths out of scripture; dogmatics arranged them in coherent systematic structures and defended them polemically; church history traced changes in practices and teachings that either exhibit faithfulness to those truths or decline; practical theology reflected on how the truths apply to daily life. Theological schooling involved a movement *from source of truth (scripture) to application.* To get there involved four areas of study, a fourfold curriculum.

The second subtle pre-critical change was introduced by the pietist movement. It arose as a reaction to this objectification of theology and the intellectualization of faith. Faith was more a matter of a heart warmed by love for God. Theology was reflection on scripture that yielded the truths that guide one into doing God's will. Theology was still objectified. Only now its truths were seen as a body of theory to be applied to practical cases. Furthermore, as Farley points out, for the pietists the "practice" that was the goal of theological education was not the individual person's practice of the Christian life. Rather, it was ministerial practice. Theological schooling was shaped by the distinctive roles played by clergy. It still involved four areas: exegesis uncovered the content of scripture; but now dogmatics was not so much a matter of systematic arrangement of that content as it was a matter of deriving a body of theory about the practice of the Christian life; church history was a narrative describing different forms that the church had taken at different times, so as better to understand the present time; practical theology was now the training of clergy in the skills they would need to help others practice the Christian life. Theological schooling involved a movement, not so much from source to application as *from theory to practice.*

On the critical side, this fourfold structure of theological schooling underwent a third, less subtle change. The rise of critical methods of historical investigation began to be applied, first to scripture and then to the institutional and intellectual history of the church. "Exegesis" and "church history" became, in the Enlightenment sense, "sciences." They were areas of orderly, critical inquiry. Thus the curriculum of theological schooling began to be fragmented. It divided into two major parts, one "practical" and the other "scientific"; and the three traditional parts of the "scientific" (exegesis, church history, dogmatics) tended to be divided among various disciplines in the faculty of arts and sciences.

This created a serious problem. The result was an ad hoc and uneasy compromise: The fourfold nature of the curriculum presupposed some sort of grounding in scripture as authority, whether as source of truths to be applied or as more indirect basis of theory to be applied; whereas the critical methods, as they gained hegemony, simply ignored the privileged position traditionally claimed for scripture. The rationale and structure of the theological school curriculum suffered a deep self-contradiction.

Schleiermacher developed an argument that at once offered a rationale for the inclusion of a theological faculty in the research university and offered a way to unify the fragmented curriculum for that faculty. His argument for the inclusion of theology rests on an implicit theory of human society: As the research university itself exists for the well-being of the state, so the theological faculty is necessary, in Farley's words, to "give cognitive and theoretical foundations to an *indispensable practice.*"[13] More particularly, the theological faculty's presence in the university is justified by its goal or purpose: to train leadership for this practice. The same is true of law and medicine. Every human society has had sets of practices tied up with basic human needs like bodily health or social order or salvation. Those practices require "professional" leadership educated in "professional" schools.

To be sure, this means that theology is not a pure science; it cannot be part of the faculty of arts and sciences (i.e., the "philosophical faculty"). Rather, it is a "positive" science. That is, it is rooted in something specifically historical and cultural (the Christian church) in contrast to something universal. But theology need not assign any privileged status to anything historical and cultural (say, the Bible) on the grounds that it is revelatory and so beyond the scope of critical inquiry. What justifies the inclusion of a school of theology in the university simultaneously unifies the theological curriculum. The theological faculty's curriculum is unified by virtue of its goal to train professional church leadership for their indispensable social roles.

This has had major implications for the structure of the theological curriculum. It must be at once "scientific" and "professional." There is a single, proper, normative structure to a theological school curriculum, argued Schleiermacher, because it is rooted in the inherent structure of the focal subject matter of the curriculum, the faith of the Christian church as something "positive" or concretely given in history and culture. Note: The essence hunt functions as prominently in this model of excellent schooling as it did in many versions of paideia. The purpose of a theological school and the structure of its curriculum are rooted in the historical and cross-cultural universal essence of the Christian faith.

In effect Schleiermacher proposed collapsing the traditional four areas into three. One area would be the study of the positively given historical community of faith itself. This includes study of scripture, dogmatics, and the history of church institutions and practices. Schleiermacher calls it "historical theology." It is one field because all its subject matters are studied by one discipline, critical history. On the one hand this helps legitimate the theological curriculum in a research university since critical history is a recognized type of *Wissenschaft*. On the other hand, it establishes the hegemony of critical, orderly, disciplined historical research in theological schools as the model of rationality and excellence in schooling.

But how does historical research decide which historical phenomena are indeed "Christian"? This calls for a second area. What is needed from this area is some grasp of Christianity as such, and here is where the search for an "essence" comes in. What is needed is a formulation of the "essence of Christianity." Essence here does not mean simply a commonality among all the details, a lowest common denominator abstracted from all periods and modalities of Christianity. Rather, for Schleiermacher the search for the essence of something is to address the question of its truth and value. In relation to Christianity, Schleiermacher calls this second discipline "philosophical theology." Its task is to show that there is a correlation between Christianity as a particular type of piety or religiousness, on the one side, and the structure and dynamics of human consciousness, on the other. This also helps legitimate the theological curriculum in a research university since critical, orderly, disciplined philosophical reflection and analysis is a recognized type of *Wissenschaft*.

The third area in Schleiermacher's proposed curriculum is aptly characterized by Farley as a "normative field which critically appre-hends the *rules* for carrying out the tasks of ministry."[14] This honors the "professional" character of the school. It is defined by the goal of the curriculum to educate professional religious leaders. Schleiermacher calls it "practical theology," but it is not a cluster of skills courses. It is a normative discipline, a body of theory related to the practice of the clergy. It derives its information about what is normative from historical theology. The historical-critical study of Christian community as a concrete cultural and historical reality provides the foundation for practical theology.

The movement of this theological schooling is still from theory to practice as it was in pre-Schleiermacher pietist theological schooling. But because the theory is based, not on historically and culturally conditioned biblical writings held to be beyond critical inquiry, but on the realities of Christian piety as manifested precisely *in* their historical and cultural facticity and relativity, it is an inquiry admissible in a research university. Moreover, because it is theory aimed at preparing leadership for a socially indispensable practice, it is of public importance and hence a research university ought to include it.

Theological schooling on the model of the research university brings with it, as we saw, a new understanding of "rationality" in inquiry. It is clearly compatible with three of the senses of "understanding God" we sorted out above. It certainly could be a way to discursive understanding of God. It definitely could be a way to affective understanding of God; that seems to be the genre in which Schleiermacher himself construed "understanding God." Given a revision in the way Schleiermacher understood the relation between theory and practice, it could also be compatible with understanding God in and through action. The model is not, however, compatible with contemplative understanding of God, since on the research university model scripture can be taken as a subject of study only if it is a subject of critical inquiry.

Furthermore, theological schooling on this model is compatible with some, but probably not all, of the various construals of the subject matter of theological schooling that we distinguished earlier. It surely is compatible with the picture that the Christian thing is Christian experience (that was Schleiermacher's own claim) and with the picture that it is "Christian tradition." It is very much more difficult to see how it would be compatible with the construal of the subject matter of theological schooling as "Word of God" (i.e., something historically given that is unconditionally and unqualifiedly revelatory).

In summary, theological schooling on the model of a research university is marked by four characteristics. First, it is ruled by "professional" interests. Because its justification as "excellent" schooling lies in its social function to train leadership for an indispensable practice in society, its central preoccupations focus on the characteristics of "excellence" in leadership in a particular institutional structure, namely the church, *as that bears on society in general*. Farley terms this focus on training church leadership the "clerical paradigm" for theological schooling. However, it is not the focus on clergy education as such that is decisive. Rather, it is the construal of church leadership as a role necessary to the well-being of the *society* (not to mention the "state") *as such*. That rightly introduces sociological criteria of what counts as "excellence." And the appropriate language to employ in discussing leadership with regard to its importance for society at large is the rhetoric of "professionalism."

Second, that which is focused upon with these professional interests 2 in view is a set of topics to be researched. Neither biblical texts nor any others are attended to in the belief that doing so may lead to an understanding of God. Rather, they are researched to learn what they can contribute to a better understanding of the essence of the Christian community and, more particularly, a better understanding of what makes for effective leadership of that community. No conversion is needed as a condition.

This has important implications regarding faculty. The principal criteria for selecting faculty have to do with their demonstrated capacity to engage in such research, to continue to contribute to knowledge through continuing research, and their ability to cultivate the same disciplined skills in critical inquiry in others.

This, thirdly, has implications for students and student-teacher relationships. The individual student is only incidentally a focus of attention in this type of schooling. The subject matter being researched 3 is the center of attention and students and teachers together engage in the research as a team. To be sure, they are unequal partners. The teacher has a greater fund of knowledge and more highly developed research skills. The student acquires both indirectly through the process of apprenticeship in research. And the aim of the apprenticeship is the acquisition of those research competencies; but the subject currently being researched is the immediate focus of attention. From the founding of the University of Berlin onward, the disciplines and methods of the historian have had hegemony in theological schooling. This student-teacher team of unequals requires a distinctive context. It most maximizes the freedom of their inquiries, protecting them from constraint by political, religious or academic authorities.

Finally, theological schooling on the model of the research university is a public enterprise in two senses of the word which are in some practical tension with one another. On the one side, it is "public" in the sense that it is accessible to any interested person who is competent in the requisite ways. Indeed, as schooling in critical research, it is accessible independently of the social and political opinions and location of either the researcher or the reader. On the other side, it is "public" in the sense of contributing to *res publica,* to the general well-being. Indeed, as schooling of leadership for a practice indispensable to the well-being of society in general, it cannot help but be importantly engaged in social and political issues confronting the society as a whole. The unresolved tension between these two ways of being "public" accounts for much of the conflict about theological schools' under- or over-engagement in the controversies of the day.

WISSENSCHAFT AND PROFESSIONALISM REDUX

Neither Schleiermacher's threefold theological curriculum nor his argument that it grows out of the essence of the Christian faith had much impact on theological schooling; but his rationale for including theology *as a professional school* in the research university has deeply shaped theological schooling in twentieth-century North America, especially in the United States. This has been true not only of the relatively few schools that are organic parts of research universities but also of the vast majority of Protestant freestanding theological schools. Schleiermacher's picture of the nature and purpose of theological schooling in a research university has provided a model of excellence for theological schools seen as a distinctive combination of "professional" schools and centers for critical inquiry. That is, it has generated a rhetoric in which theological schools describe themselves as precisely "professional" schools and not simply "theological academies" or "theological colleges" or "Bible schools"; and it has generated expectations that theological schools will be "graduate schools" whose faculties include persons skilled in a variety of ways of critical, orderly, and disciplined inquiry, who possess earned research doctorates, are backed to some degree by library resources, are productive of scholarly research that is published and discussed by peer researchers, and use pedagogical methods associated with the research university such as the research seminar, the research paper, and field-based research.

By the second quarter of the twentieth century, however, central elements of Schleiermacher's picture of a theological school had begun to undergo significant modification, so that it is a substantially revised version of Schleiermacher's vision that now serves as a model of excellence for theological schools. These modifications were first called for by W. R. Harper's 1899 manifesto, "Shall the Theological Curriculum Be Modified and How?"[15] When the University of Chicago was founded, a Divinity School was located at its geographical center. Harper proposed a revision of research university–related professional theological education that would take further advantage of psychological and sociological scientific research regarding how persons change and how institutions grow. Very influential major, comprehensive studies of theological education by Robert Kelly in 1924[16] and by William Adams Brown and Mark A. May in 1934[17] monitored the development of these changes in theological education in North America, worried when they did not develop sufficiently, and celebrated them when they did. They urged increased cooperation among theological schools to raise commonly accepted levels of standards of excellence in theological schooling. One measure of the influence of these studies is that an organization for such cooperation was founded and served to legitimate revisions in the Berlin model of excellence. As the organization developed into theological schooling's instrument for self-evaluation and academic accreditation, now called the Association of Theological Schools, those revisions tended to become institutionalized in standards for theological schools' academic accreditation. In 1957 H. Richard Niebuhr, Daniel Day Williams, and James M. Gustafson published a third comprehensive study of theological education[18] under the auspices of the American Association of Theological Schools (as it was then called), which in some ways urged restraint in these modifications. However, widely acclaimed as this third study was, it does not seem to have resulted in widespread abandoning of the modifications of the Berlin model that have become commonplace. The modifications have come at three points. What "professional" means has changed; the sorts of critical inquiry or *Wissenschaft* deemed relevant have changed; and the ways in which the two are related have all changed.

I "Professional" has increasingly come to be understood in a largely functionalist and individualistic way. A "professional" is someone who has the specialized skills needed to fill the function of meeting specific needs of his or her clients one by one. Everyone from the neurosurgeon to the hairdresser is a "professional."

Schleiermacher had proposed that a theological school educate persons able to lead church communities in their distinctive practices which, as it happens, are important for the health of society as a whole. He proposed that the school give future clergy the ability to do this by teaching them relevant information about the church and its faith, by cultivating their capacities for discriminating judgment about what is authentically Christian, and by helping them grasp the rules for carrying out the tasks of ministry. As the idea of "professional" changed, however, a theological school that sought to approximate the model of excellence provided by the Berlin model instead focused on equipping future clergy with skills they needed to fill certain functions in the lives of persons who were viewed more as "clients" ministered to mainly one by one than as fellow members of a congregation whose common life was built up out of cooperative practices that needed to be led as whole systems.

2 Correlatively, the sorts of critical inquiry deemed relevant to professional ministry have changed. In one way the change is a matter of a broadened range. If professional education must focus on equipping potential clergy with a variety of skills, then the sorts of critical inquiry that provide the theoretical background appropriate to different sorts of skills are what is needed. Accordingly a variety of human sciences, both social and psychological, have been added to historical and philosophical inquiry to provide bodies of theory to guide both the way one talks about the Christian faith and the way clergy are to fill their roles.

At the same time, the way these various sorts of *Wissenschaft* are related to professional clergy practice has changed from the relation Schleiermacher envisioned. This is the most decisive change. The changes regarding relevant sorts of inquiry involve more than a broadening of the range of what is relevant. Governed by the clerical paradigm, the aim of a theological school is to educate professional ministers.

At issue is what should inform the practice of ministry. We saw in chapter 3 that theological schooling on the model of paideia involves a movement from source, usually taken to be scripture, to appropriation, in which one is "formed" in specifiable ways—the source forms me, and I, thus in-formed, engage in ministry.

We saw earlier in this chapter that in post-Reformation theological controversies theology was increasingly objectified in "truths" that could be "applied" to "problems" in thought or action. Accordingly, theological schooling became a movement from source (scripture alone or scripture-and-tradition, depending on whether one was Protestant or Roman Catholic) to application. Indeed, we saw that among seventeenth-century pietists theological schooling became a movement from source to application in quite specifically clergy tasks. Thus, made knowledgeable about the contents of the source, I apply them in my practice of ministry.

Schleiermacher had proposed that a moment of theorizing be placed between the source and the application in practice. The "source" is simply a collection of historical facts and has no normative force to it that could "form" practice. It is philosophical theology, critical reflection on the nature, meaning, and truth of the Christian faith, that ought to inform practice. To be sure, "theology" had intervened between scripture and practice for Christians all along. But "theology" had been a process of organizing, clarifying, and generalizing what was already normatively present in the source. For Schleiermacher "theology" is not just a matter of generalizing what is already normative; it is a matter of theorizing from the given historical facts to uncover what their normative essence must be. Theology generates the normative, it does not simply generalize and systematize it. So theological schooling ought, he proposed, to be something like a movement from theory (not "source") to application (not "appropriation"). That would mean that theological schooling would cultivate persons' capacities to do this theorizing, to do "philosophical theology" *for themselves*. Furthermore, "practical theology" would cultivate their capacities to do theology in relation to the actual practice of ministry to identify the rules or norms governing that practice when it is authentically Christian ministry. Thereby they would also be capacitated to be discriminating about things done in the name of Christian ministry that ought to be reformed or abandoned.

In the twentieth century, however, theological schooling seeking to match this model of excellence relies less and less on theology as the body of theory that is to inform the practice of clergy tasks. Instead it is a variety of bodies of theory in the human sciences that are relied on to inform practice. There are, however, far too many of them for students to be schooled in how to do them for themselves as exercises in critical inquiry.

This is where the decisive change comes in this model of excellence in theological schooling. Schleiermacher had argued that, precisely in order to be the sort of "professional" school that society needs for its own well-being, a theological school must school future clergy in certain sorts of *Wissenschaft,* namely historical and philosophical, so that they can do the relevant theorizing, "do theology," for themselves. The movement of the schooling was to be from theory to application in ministry. But now students are informed *about* the prevailing theories in the field and then informed *about* the ways others have applied those theories to particular ministerial tasks. That information then serves as background to their training in the skills that the application suggests would be useful when undertaking those tasks.

To be sure, biblical, historical, and theological studies continue to take up a great deal of a theological school's time and space. However, they have tended more and more either to give background information that provides a "context" within which clergy need to be aware they are fulfilling their roles, or to give intellectually challenging and interesting alternative "options" or "perspectives" from which to view what they are already doing anyway in filling their roles. The irony is that much the same fate awaits the bodies of theory that have increasingly come to inform the practice of ministry. Students are not inducted into the relevant *Wissenschaft,* as Schleiermacher had proposed they should be. They are not schooled in critical inquiry or pure research that generates theory. Nor are they really schooled in doing the applied research that generates the array of skills they are taught. The movement of theological schooling has tended to become this:

from information about pure theory, "academic systematic theology," to information about applied theory, "academic practical theology" (chiefly counseling theory and church growth theory), to skills training; from science to technology to practitioner.

BETWEEN ATHENS AND BERLIN

The world of theological schools is highly pluralistic. I argued in chapter 2 that individual concrete theological schools differ from one another partly because they are *theological.* They have different understandings of the Christian thing, different construals of the central subject matter of theological schooling and different views of what it is to understand God. The burden of the last two chapters is that particular schools also differ from one another because they are *schools.* They seek to be adequate to some model of excellent schooling. However, in point of fact, they are faced with trying to be accountable to two quite different models of excellent schooling, for one of which ancient Athens is emblematic and for the other of which modern Berlin is emblematic. For historical reasons they cannot evade either model. Yet the models are in tension with each other and cannot be synthesized. They bring with them different ways of understanding the overarching purpose of theological schooling, different pictures of what makes for excellent teachers and students, different pictures of how students and teachers are to be related to one another in schooling, different pictures of the sense in which a school can be a community. Between Athens and Berlin, theological schools are caught between a rock and a hard place. The most that any school can do is negotiate some sort of truce, strike some sort of balance between them. There are many different ways in which to do that. The sheer variety of ways of negotiating between paideia, on the one side, and *Wissenschaft*-and-professionalism on the other is another major factor pluralizing theological schools.

Clearly, this suggests further questions to ask of any one theological school you are trying to understand in its concrete particularity. Does it tend to make one model central and honor the other only in subordinate ways? Look, for example, at the way the school's ethos patterns relations between students and faculty, the way it organizes the curriculum, and the apparently dominant purposes of individual courses; do these all suggest that the Berlin model is dominant, with its stress on *Wissenschaft*, while attention to paideia-like "formation" is subordinated or marginalized to the status of voluntary activities? Or is it perhaps like this: Expectations of faculty make the Berlin model central for them, but the structure of the school's common life tends to organize student life around the demands of paideia and its expectations. That is, does the school divide its common life between the two models, so that one dominates the school's intellectual style and the other its extracurricular common life, or so that faculty are held accountable to one model and students to the other? Are there structural features of the curriculum, of the ways in which individual courses are usually designed, of prevalent teaching styles that suggest an effort by the school to integrate the two models? Is one model in fact dominant and the other chiefly honored in the rhetoric of the school's self-description?

The first four chapters have suggested questions it would be useful to ask of some particular theological school you are trying to understand more deeply. In Part Two I shall sketch my own utopian proposal about how best to understand the nature and purpose of a theological school. I hope it will persuade you by its cogency. Even if it does not, however, I hope it will help make more concrete just what the force of those questions has been, just how they can be illuminating. Perhaps it may even prompt you to formulate an even better proposal of your own.

Notes

1. Cf. Friedrich Paulsen, *The German Universities and University Study,* trans. E. T. F. Thilly and W. W. Elang (New York: Charles Scribner's Sons, 1906), pp. 44–50; Daniel Fallon, *The German University,* (Boulder, Colo.: Colorado Associated University Press, 1980), ch. 2.

2. For this paragraph, cf. Paulsen, pp. 50–55; Fallon, pp. 10–20, 32–35.

3. See Fallon, pp. 28–30.

4. Quoted in Fallon, p. 17.

5. Quoted in Paulsen, p. 53.

6. Paulsen, p. 54.

7. Ibid.

8. Fallon, p. 36.

9. Ibid., p. 53.

10. Fallon, p. 52. For the entire paragraph, see Fallon, pp. 51–52.

11. See Edward Farley, *The Fragility of Knowledge* (Philadelphia: Fortress Press, 1988), ch. 5.

12. See Farley, *Theologia,* chs. 4 and 5.

13. Ibid., p. 86.

14. Ibid., p. 91.

15. W. R. Harper, "Shall the Theological Curriculum Be Modified and How?" *American Journal of Theology,* vol. 3, no. 1 (January 1899), pp. 45–66.

16. Robert Kelly, *Theological Education in America* (New York: George H. Doran Co., 1924).

17. William Adams Brown and Mark A. May, et al., *The Education of American Ministers,* 4 vols. (New York: Institute of Social and Religious Research, 1934).

18. H. Richard Niebuhr et al., *The Advancement of Theological Education* (New York: Harper & Row, 1957).

Part Two

A Proposal

5

Utopia

Now a thought experiment and an invitation: The experiment is one more utopian exercise in sketching what makes a theological school *theological* and what makes a theological school a *school*. Along the way the experiment will urge that there are a few issues that are truly basic. They are more fundamental than are any of the issues in which theological educators have tended to invest a great deal of attention and energy. They are more basic, it will be urged, because the ways in which they are decided pretty much determine how other issues in theological schooling are worked out. Further, the experiment will propose a language in which it may be more fruitful to state both issues and proposals than is the language often employed.

The invitation is to conduct your own thought experiment about what some theological school known to you is and ought to be. It may very well be that you see good reasons to disagree with the proposals sketched here. All the same, it may be that the issues identified here as basic strike you as the right issues to think about. In that case, this proposal is an invitation to discuss a shared agenda, even though the discussion leads us to differing proposals about how to deal with the issues. Or it may be clear to you that the wrong issues have been identified, that there are other issues more fundamental than the ones singled out here. Nevertheless, it may be that the modest conceptual scheme proposed here will prove useful in formulating those issues, showing why they are more "basic," and showing why your proposals about them are illuminating and fruitful. In that case, this proposal is an invitation to use a shared language to discuss what the issues really are as well as to discuss alternative resolutions of them. Or, of course, you may have reasons to believe that even the slightly technical language advocated here leads me to state the issues misleadingly. In that case, this proposal is an invitation to make a counterproposal about how best to *say* what the basic issues are in theological schooling and how best to resolve them. Naturally, I hope to persuade you of the wisdom of my own thought experiment; far more importantly, the experiment will have served its purpose if it stimulates and focuses fresh and continuing discussion of theological schooling by all of those who are involved in it, students and trustees, administrators and faculty.

THE THREE CENTRAL ISSUES

The next five chapters are devoted to developing a proposal about the purpose and nature of a theological school. That is, they elaborate a proposal about how to explain what makes a theological school *theological* and what makes it a *school*. As I noted in the first chapter, the proposal is a contribution to a larger, ongoing conversation about what is more frequently called "theological education" than it is called "theological schooling." That conversation raises three major interconnected issues which my proposal aims to resolve.

Since the relative success of this proposal depends on the degree to which it does show how to resolve these three issues, and since the proposal is organized by the way the issues depend on one another, it is important to identify them clearly here at the outset:

a) How shall the theological course of study be unified?

b) How shall the theological course of study be made adequate to the pluralism of ways in which the Christian thing is actually construed, that is, interpreted and lived in concrete reality?

c) How can "theological education" itself be understood concretely, that is, how can it be described so that what makes it "theological" is made clear *without* denying or ignoring its concreteness and the ways in which that concreteness makes it deeply pluralistic in actual practice?

A word about each of the three is in order.

The first two issues arise within the conversation about "theological education" itself; the third arises when one stands back from the conversation and reflects on the way in which it has been conducted. As the new literature about "theological education" began to grow during the past decade it quickly became clear[1] that for some participants the central issue facing "theological education" is the fragmentation of its course of study and the need to reconceive it so as to recover its unity, whereas for others the central issue is "theological education's" inadequacy to the pluralism of social and cultural locations in which the Christian thing is understood and lived.

Edward Farley's path-breaking *Theologia: The Fragmentation and Unity of Theological Education*,[2] which may fairly be said to have launched the conversation, urged that the major issue for theological education today is the fragmentation of the theological course of study and proposed a way to recover its unity. In quite different ways, so have such other widely read books as Charles Wood's *Vision and Discernment: An Orientation in Theological Study*[3] and Max L. Stackhouse's *Apologia: Contextualization, Globalization, and Mission in Theological Education*.[4] It has been a common student complaint for a long time, of course, that the theological course of study lacked "integration." The fact that a great many theological schools' curricula long ago fragmented, in H. Richard Niebuhr's phrase, into "a series of studious jumps in various directions"[5] is beyond dispute. It is important to underscore that the writers who focus on this issue stress that fragmentation of the course of study is unacceptable in a theological school not simply because it makes for bad schooling, but because it makes for bad *theology*. Generally they hold that a fragmented theological curriculum is unacceptable because it is inadequate to a unity that "the faith" or the "life of faith" is supposed to have. Because it fragments the integrity of the faith, it is inadequate to its theological subject. Writers in this group (Charles Wood is perhaps an exception) tend to assume that the Christian thing has some time- and culture-invariant essence or structure that makes it one selfsame thing in all times and places. Accordingly, a course of theological study would be theologically adequate if its organizing structure were derived from the inherent structure of the Christian thing. Hence they propose that unity can be restored to theological education by recovering for its course of study the structure and internal movement that is dictated by the very essence of Christian faith.

The centrality of the second issue is most passionately urged in *God's*

Fierce Whimsy,[6] written by Katie Cannon and the Mud Flower Collective. It is also pressed in various ways by several contributors to *Beyond Clericalism: The Congregation as a Focus for Theological Education,* a collection of essays edited by Joseph C. Hough, Jr., and Barbara G. Wheeler.[7] Many theological students, especially women, African Americans, and Hispanics, regularly and vigorously object that their "theological education" is in important respects inappropriate to the faith communities to which they belong and to the social and cultural worlds in which they expect to live and work in the future. Theological educators in this second group stress that the conventional course of theological study is inadequate to the pluralism of ways in which the Christian faith is understood and lived. They are impressed by the ways in which gender, race, and class differences shape both different understandings of Christian faith and different social worlds in which it is lived out. They contend that the conventional course of study in "theological education" unjustifiably privileges a very narrow spectrum of that diversity as though it were somehow "normative" and definitive of the Christian thing.

To be sure, justification for privileging certain construals of Christian faith is sometimes offered through the claim that these construals best represent the essence of the Christian thing. However, as writers in this group tend to suggest, that type of argument overlooks the fact that characterizations of the "essence" of Christian faith are themselves deeply shaped by the social and cultural locations of the people who make them. Theological education thus ends up being inadequate to a great many construals of the Christian thing that have not been privileged, and is also inadequate to a great many "worlds" in which the faith is actually lived. Here too it must be underscored that this group's contention is not only that this is educationally inadequate, but, more than that, it is *theologically* inadequate. It is theologically inadequate because its unwarranted privileging of a narrow spectrum of construals of the Christian thing amounts to a kind of idolatry, an absolutizing of a historically and culturally relative human construct.

Do we have to choose between these two issues? This is where the third issue comes in. It seems clear on the face of it that both of these first two issues do genuinely confront North American theological schooling today. Yet as stated they seem interconnected in a *negative* way. If we focus on coping with the loss of unity, are we not driven to postulate an inherent structure or essence to Christian faith that is the basis of the curriculum's restored unity and is more basic than and more important than all pluralism? Focusing on restoration of the unity of "theological education" seems to require us to treat pluralism as something relatively superficial or merely apparent. It seems to lead to minimizing the importance of the issues raised for theological schooling by pluralism.

On the other hand, if we focus on coping with a theological course of study's inadequacy to pluralism, are we not driven to deny that the Christian thing has any one underlying structure or that it is any one thing in and through all of its diversity? Focusing on the challenge to make theological schooling adequate to pluralism seems to require us to deny the usual basis for unifying the course of study. It seems to lead to minimizing the importance of the issues raised for theological schooling by the fragmentation of the course of study. Indeed, it seems to threaten us with an increase in that fragmentation as more adequate attention is given in the theological course of study to more and more of the diverse ways in which the Christian thing is concretely actual. Is it not the case that to stress the issue of fragmentation is to deny that there is any serious issue raised by pluralism, while to stress the issue raised by pluralism is to deny that there is any serious issue about fragmentation?

The answer to that last question is, "No, not necessarily." It only looks that way because of the terms in which the issues have been posed, especially the "unity and fragmentation" issue. A central theme of my proposal is that these first two issues appear to be mutually exclusive because of the unnecessarily *abstract* manner in which they have been formulated. They are both posed as issues about something called "theological education," which is conceived as a kind of process that is one self-identical reality even though it admittedly "takes place" in or is "contexted by" a great variety of institutions in a great variety of social and cultural locations. But the "process" cannot be disengaged so neatly from its institutional "housing" and social "husk." Part One of this book has been devoted to sketching some of the ways in which "theological education" is in actual practice something particular and concrete, and in its concreteness deeply and irreducibly pluralistic.

Thus the very way in which the conversation about "theological education" has been conducted gives rise to the third of the three issues to which this proposal is addressed: How can "theological education" be described so that what makes it "theological" is made clear *without* denying or ignoring its concreteness and the ways in which that concreteness makes it deeply pluralistic?

WHERE WE ARE GOING, AND WHY

As will be quickly evident, the proposal developed in this part of the book first addresses the third of the three issues sketched above as the way to get at the other two in their interconnectedness. Before launching into the development of my proposal, it will be helpful to have an overview of where the discussion is going and why. First I will summarize the proposal itself, and then I will outline the steps through which we will move in order to develop the proposal.

What is *theological* about a theological school? What makes a school "theological," as I argued in Part One, is that it is a community of persons engaged together in the enterprise of trying to understand *God* more truly. However, we immediately noted that God cannot be "studied" directly; "understanding God" always proceeds indirectly. So we modified our characterization of a theological school: It is, I suggested, a community of persons trying to understand God more truly by way of studying some other thing or things whose study is supposed to enhance our understanding of God.

What are these "other things," and under just what circumstances might their study lead to "understanding God"? We have noted that historically there have been a variety of subjects whose study has been taken to be the best indirect way to come to understand God more truly: scripture, tradition, "salvation history," liturgy and the dynamics of worship, religious experience, the historical Jesus, and so forth. These are the various *subject matters* that are the immediate or direct objects of study in theological schooling. However, they are not what make theological schooling "theological." They may perfectly well be the immediate subject matters of inquiries that lead to truer historical or psychological or sociological understanding with no necessary bearing on understanding God. If it were a distinctive subject matter (say, the Bible) that made theological schooling "theological," then every time scholars examined 1 and 2 Kings to help reconstruct the economic history of the ancient Near East, they would be engaged in "theological schooling"! We must look beyond its immediate subject matter to identify what makes theological schooling theological.

Each of the subject matters that may serve as an immediate object of inquiry in theological schooling may be studied in ways made rigorous and critical by any of several methods and "disciplines" of inquiry. Predominant among them in modern theological schooling have been the historians' disciplines, but the methods and disciplines of psychologists, sociologists, philosophers, and literary critics have also been widely used. However, none of these methods and disciplines is what defines the inquiry as theological or makes the schooling that engages in them theological schooling. There is no distinctive "theological method" that must be used to make all inquiries into all subject matters studied in a theological school genuinely theological. All of the disciplines actually employed in the study of various subject matters in a theological school are also used in a variety of types of schooling that do not claim to be and are far from being theological. We must look beyond the scholarly methods and disciplines it uses to identify what makes theological schooling theological.

What makes a theological school theological is neither its various subject matters nor the scholarly disciplines it employs but rather its overarching *goal:* to understand God more truly. But insofar as God can be understood, it is only indirectly and not directly. The way of indirection goes through some tradition, that is, through a complex of beliefs, truth claims, practices of worship, stories, symbols, images, metaphors, moral principles, self-examination, meditation, critical reflection, and the like. For Christians it is what I have chosen to refer to as the Christian thing. In actual concrete practice, it is diversely construed. It is, perhaps, more an extended family of traditions than *the* "Christian tradition." Nonetheless, the various subject matters that are the immediate subjects of study in theological schooling are studied insofar as they are constituents of the Christian thing. They are not studied because study of them one by one in independence of one another and free-standing, as it were, is going to lead to truer understanding of God. Rather, they are studied in their highly complex and variable interrelations *as* the Christian thing. In Christian theological schools, I suggest, they are studied insofar as their study leads to that understanding of God which can come in and through the Christian thing, that is, insofar as their study can lead to understanding God "Christianly."

The interconnections among a theological school's immediate subject matters are elusive. If the goal that makes a school "theological" is to understand God more truly, and if such understanding comes only indirectly through disciplined study of other "subject matters," and if study of those subject matters leads to truer understanding of God *only* insofar as they comprise the Christian thing in their interconnectedness and not in isolation from one another, then clearly it is critically important to study them *as* elements of the Christian thing construed in some particular, concrete way. But where does one find that?

That brings us to the heart of my proposal. I will argue that the Christian thing is present in concrete reality *in and as various Christian congregations or worshiping communities in all their radical pluralism*. This is *not* to claim that the Christian thing is only present concretely in the mode of actual congregations. It is to claim that for the purposes of addressing our three central issues about theological schooling it is the decisively important mode in which the Christian thing is present. My proposal will be that those three issues can be resolved if theological schooling is reconceived this way: A Christian theological school is a community of persons trying to understand God truly by focusing study of various subject matters through the lens of questions about the place and role of those subject matters in diverse Christian worshiping communities or congregations.

Some things this proposal is not: It is not a proposal that a theological school be defined by the overarching goal of being "for" congregations. The proposal might be misread as a suggestion that a theological school be seen as chiefly a research center and training school dedicated to promoting "church growth," celebrating (perhaps uncritically) the importance of churches to American history and culture, and devising "pro-church" ideological positions on major social policy issues. To the contrary, as I hope to show, this proposal entails that a theological school be as vigorously *against* Christian congregations and churches as it ought, in other ways, to be genuinely "for" them.

Nor is this a proposal that a theological school be "about" Christian congregations in the sense that they become the central subject matter studied in a theological school. The proposal does imply that congregations ought to be one of the subject matters that are the direct objects of study. However, the proposal does not imply any major changes in the traditional array of subject matters studied in theological schools. The proposal does not even imply that study of congregations should be given pride of place (and of curricular time and faculty energy!) over, say, biblical studies. The subject matters are not what define a school as "theological" and rearranging them or changing them will not of itself make a school any more genuinely "theological."

Furthermore, this is not a pedagogical proposal. It does not imply any particular recommendations to the effect that theological schooling ought (or ought mostly) to take place within particular congregations, or that classes ought to include selected parishioners along with theological school students, or that only persons who also lead congregations (or have recently done so) ought to do the teaching, and the like. Such suggestions may well have merit for certain schools under certain circumstances. It is, I shall argue, a contingent matter. Individual schools must decide such questions in the light of their unique histories, particular traditions, and concrete locations. It is doubtful whether such pedagogical questions can be helpfully discussed or answered in the abstract. In any case, this proposal carries no necessary pedagogical consequences and tends to imply that the effort to devise generally applicable pedagogical proposals of this sort is a dubious project.

What the proposal *does* argue is this: Study of various subject matters in a theological school will be the indirect way to truer understanding of God only insofar as the subject matters are taken precisely *as* interconnected elements of the Christian thing, and that can be done concretely by studying them in light of questions about their place and role in the actual communal life of actual and deeply diverse Christian congregations. The proposal will be that doing this would provide a way to make a theological school's course of study genuinely unified without denial of the pluralism of ways in which the Christian thing is construed, and it could make the course of study more adequate to the pluralism without undercutting its unity. A way to make this point is to

111

exploit two metaphors: We could think of questions about the communal identities and common life of diverse Christian congregations as the *lens* through which inquiry about all the various subject matters studied in a theological school could be focused and unified. We could think of questions about the place and role of the various subject matters within the common life and identity-formation of pluralistically diverse Christian congregations as the *horizon* within which all inquiry, teaching, and learning regarding any subject matter takes place.

The chapters making up Part Two develop this proposal. The initial move will be sideways. In chapter 6, I will address the third central issue noted above. I will suggest some ways in which to describe very concretely both congregations and schools, what pluralizes them, what goes on in them, and how that is somehow "unified" without denial of their deep diversity. In chapter 7, I will then follow my own suggestion and offer a sketch of what a congregation is. In chapter 8, I will apply the same method of description to sketch what a theological school is. Then building on these two chapters side by side, in the next two chapters I will draw out what happens when theological schooling is focused through the lens or within the horizon of questions about congregations. Chapter 9 will develop the proposal's implications regarding a theological school's course of study, the basis of its unity and of its adequacy to the pluralism of actual concrete construals of the Christian thing. Chapter 10 will develop the proposal's implications regarding education of church leadership, including clergy, and its implications regarding education in the several academic "disciplines."

It will be obvious that one background assumption has been important throughout this book: the best way to the universal is through the concrete particular. This maxim has shaped the book in several ways. So far as the task of this book is concerned, it means that if one wants to understand truly and Christianly the universal God, the "God of all," it is best to do it by going through the concrete particularities of communities of persons who describe themselves as engaged by and responding to the universal God.

Furthermore, so far as the "voice" of this book is concerned, this background assumption means that I can hope to address "universally" all who are involved in theological schooling only by writing openly and explicitly out of my own concretely particular situation in theological schooling. This book grows out of my experience teaching theology in a university divinity school that has no organic relation to any Christian denomination, was historically associated with the Reformed, in contrast to Lutheran or Anabaptist, branch of the Protestant movement, and has now become thoroughly interconfessional in both student body and faculty. Furthermore, I reflect on these matters as a Protestant Christian whose theological views have been most deeply shaped by the Reformed theological current within the Protestant river, as that was channeled by nineteenth-century theological liberalism and then intersected first by that peculiar eddy in liberalism called "neo-orthodoxy" and then by various other theological eddies still swirling in the last half of the twentieth century. This is hardly a unique location for a North American white male theologian. But it is mine and is certain to shape my reflections in specific and concrete ways, to many of which I may be largely oblivious.

The background assumption of this book means, finally, that so far as its content is concerned the best hope of saying things of general relevance to persons involved in all types of theological schooling today lies in making some particular and fairly concrete proposals that may turn out to be directly pertinent only to a few types of theological schools but may provoke and help other persons in other types of schools to think through these issues for themselves.

Notes

1. See, e.g., David H. Kelsey and Barbara G. Wheeler, "Mind Reading: Notes on the Basic Issues Program," *Theological Education,* vol. 20, no. 2 (Spring 1984), pp. 8–14.

2. Edward Farley, *Theologia.*

3. Charles Wood, *Vision and Discernment.*

4. Max Stackhouse, *Apologia: Contextualization, Globalization, and Mission in Theological Education* (Grand Rapids: Wm. B. Eerdmans Publishing Co., 1988).

5. H. Richard Niebuhr et al., *The Purpose of the Church and Its Ministry,* p. viii.

6. Katie G. Cannon et al., *God's Fierce Whimsy* (New York: Pilgrim Press, 1985). Cf. I. Carter Heyward et al., "Christian Feminists Speak," *Theological Education,* vol. 20, no. 1 (Autumn 1983), pp. 93–103.

7. Joseph C. Hough, Jr., and Barbara G. Wheeler, eds., *Beyond Clericalism* (Atlanta: Scholars Press, 1988).

6

Borrowed Language

The third of the three central issues that have surfaced in the discussions of the nature and purpose of theological schooling is how to understand theological schooling concretely. This is, of course, a highly relative matter. There is no absolute standard of "concrete" description against which to measure the degree of abstractness of other descriptions. No thinking or language somehow devoid of abstraction is possible or desirable. Concreteness in expression is a matter of degree. Nonetheless, we have reason to believe that in dealing with our subject, it is best to speak as concretely as is possible under the circumstances. My contention is that decisions about the terminology we use in describing theological schooling are decisively important in this regard. In particular, we need to pay attention to a few terms that will be of crucial importance for this thought experiment. The rest of this chapter will be devoted to a closer look at the concepts "pluralism," "understand," "action," and "practice."

Consequently this will be the most technical chapter in the book. Much of what I have to say is borrowed from others who have, to my mind, clarified these notions admirably. It will be an exercise in borrowing language and explaining why it is borrowed. It is quite possible to make sense of the following chapters without working through this one. However, much of the defense of posing the issues as I do is given here. Without this somewhat more abstract and careful discussion, what is argued later on may be reasonably clear but why it is argued may be more obscure.

PLURALISMS AND VARIATIONS

It is already clear that I have made a decision to describe certain features of the heritage and situation that shape a theological school as "pluralistic." That is not an innocent conceptual decision. Why not instead use "various" and speak of "variations"? It is relatively uncontroversial to say descriptively, for example, that theological school students and faculty come from a variety of social and economic backgrounds, or that they may exhibit a variety of ways of concretely practicing the Christian faith. It is a fair question to ask whether we have committed ourselves to more than this descriptive remark if we decide instead to write of socioeconomic "pluralism" and of a "pluralism" of ways of being Christian.

Perhaps we have. Much current discussion of cultural, religious, moral, and intellectual pluralism uses the concept "pluralism" in a way that seems to shift from a descriptive use ("such diversity does in fact exist") to an evaluative and even celebratory use ("such diversity is a good thing and should exist"). Indeed, some high-flying, abstract, and vague talk of pluralism seems to assume the validity of a thorough relativism about these diversities ("each variation—culturally, religiously, morally, or intellectually—is as good and true as any of the others"). Does the very use of the concept "pluralism" smuggle an evaluative judgment into what presents itself as a descriptive account of factors that make a theological school concrete? Moreover, does the use of "pluralism" involve the unargued assumption that any construal of the Christian thing, and concrete practice of the faith, and so forth, is as good as any other? If so, that is a serious danger that needs to be guarded against when we use "pluralism" in relation to a theological school. Such judgments might be valid, but they need to be argued and not simply assumed. They ought not to be settled before they are argued simply by the choice we make of the terms we will use.

On the other hand, it seems that use of "variety" has even greater drawbacks. To speak of a variety of construals of Christianity or of social and economic locations is to suggest a set of variations on a theme. To speak in that way of factors that make a given theological school concrete is to speak very misleadingly. It suggests that in regard to each "diversity" we can identify some one thing, the "theme," that all

116

the variants share and which is normative for all of them. It suggests that the respects in which they differ, that is, whatever makes them "variations," are relatively less important than the one thing they share (the "theme")—unless they so distort the theme as to make it unrecognizable, in which case the diversity is a decline and deformation. It suggests that the one thing they all share may be entirely abstract. No actual variant may ever be identical with the theme; the theme may be a wholly ideal entity abstracted from the array of variants.

But nothing is more concrete than the differences among the racial, gender, and socioeconomic locations of persons involved in theological schooling, nor more concrete than the differences among the practices through which persons have sought to understand God, nor more concrete than the differences between the ways in which models of excellent schooling have been institutionalized. These are the sorts of differences that help make theological schools concrete. It cannot be assumed at the outset that any one construal (of the Christian thing, social location, way of understanding God, model of excellent schooling, etc.) is the one Christianly correct version. Nor is it self-evident that any of these sets of differences amounts to a set of variations on a single abstract theme. The relations among them may be far more complex and unsystematic, more like overlapping resemblances among members of an extended family than like minor modifications of one common and underlying genetic structure in identical twins. Even less is it to be assumed that we are capable of identifying such a theme that could be used normatively to identify which "variants" are closer and which further from what is Christianly acceptable in a theological school. The very possibility of identifying such a theme would need to be demonstrated.

For these reasons I have chosen to speak of the "pluralism of pluralisms" rather than the "variations" with which every theological school must deal. To speak of issues raised for theological schools by this or that type of "variety" risks diverting analysis and critique away from the concreteness of theological schooling into a hunt for abstract thematic essences and ideal structures. To speak instead of this or that "pluralism" raising issues for theological schooling at least has the advantage of tending in current usage to keep the focus of analysis and critique on what is concretely actual.

PRACTICES AND ACTIONS

We shall be speaking of a focus in a theological school on questions about "particular Christian congregations" as a means to understanding God Christianly. The common life of Christian congregations consists of a multitude of kinds of common activities: worship, preaching and listening to sermons, education, mutual pastoral caring, counseling, action for the well-being of the larger society, and the like. Craig Dykstra has shown that it is illuminating to analyze the educational activities in a congregation by using a technical sense of the concept "practice."[1] More broadly, in *Art in Action* Nicholas Wolterstorff has relied on the concept "practice" for an illuminating analysis of art and its place in Christians' common life.[2] I propose to generalize the point. I shall suggest that we think of congregations and of theological schools as comprised of complex networks of interrelated practices.

Here "practice" will be used in a somewhat narrower way than it usually is in ordinary English. Following, albeit at considerable distance, philosopher Alasdair MacIntyre's analysis of "practice" in *After Virtue,*[3] I will mean this by "practice":

A practice is any form of socially established cooperative human activity that is complex and internally coherent, is subject to standards of excellence that partly define it, and is done to some end but does not necessarily have a product.

Note several features of this description of "practice."

Practices are human *activities:* "activities" is used in a limited, technical way here and one needs to be careful about what one reads into it and infers from it. Activities are comprised of human acts or actions. Act and action are not simply identical with "behavior"; some behavior is not action.

Roughly, the distinguishing mark of action is that it is "intentional," it is "done on purpose," it has an end or motive.[4] Some behavior is intentional action. But some behavior is nonintentional. A standard illustration is the case of a man who repeatedly moves an arm in a sweeping gesture. We ask, "Why are you doing that?" If it is possible to give an intention as answer (call it a purpose, or a reason, or a motive), as in "I want to hail a cab," he is performing an act. But if all there is to be given is a causal explanation, for example, "I suffer a rare but medically understood muscular spasm," it is still clearly a piece of human behavior but it is not, properly speaking, an "act."

Actions are not as such "practices"; practices are *cooperative* human activities. That brings out two interrelated features of practices. They are *social;* they are done by two or more persons acting together in an interactive, social way. Secondly, they are governed by *rule-like regularities.* One learns how to engage in a practice by learning its implicit rules. One's enactment of a practice can be (and usually will be) subject to evaluation and, if necessary, correction by reference to its implicit "rules." Mostly the rules that seem to govern practices are implicit in them and have never been codified. Often people who are most adept at a practice are quite incapable of formulating even its most basic rules, although some of them may be skilled at coaching less adept people on how to "do it better" in an ad hoc way.

Note further that central to the concept of action is stress on its *bodiliness.* For that reason the possibility of answering the question, "Why are you doing that?" by identifying an intention is not inconsistent with also answering the question by identifying a cause. Indeed, it may well be that this question asked of genuine actions always requires both sorts of answers. Intentions, in any case, are not causes and it is a profound conceptual confusion to treat them as though they were. Sometimes, to be sure, the question "Why are you doing that?" cannot be answered by identifying an intention because there is none; all that can be provided is a cause. In that case, what is in question is a piece of behavior, but it is not an act.

Of course, sometimes (much of the time?) we do not know what to say when we are asked why we have done something. That may be because we do not understand the relevant causal "mechanisms." Or it may be because we are in varying degrees unclear about our intentions. In order to have a purpose or an intention, and engage in intentional action, it is not necessary always to be self-awarely clear about all of them. Indeed, we may be quite unconscious of some of our intentions. We may have unconscious purposes and motives. Furthermore, there may be *causes* (and not simply further motives) for these intentions having become unconscious, and psychoanalytic theory may have identified some of those causes. Clarity in self-awareness is a matter of degree, however, and in principle the degree of clarity is capable of being increased. We can hope to come to greater clarity and greater ability to say what the intention or (more unusually) complex of intentions are in our acts. One of the functions of psychotherapy is to assist that growth in clarity.

Not all pieces of bodily behavior are acts; nor are all acts pieces of *overt* bodily behavior. We engage in "mental acts." They are private in that they are unobservable. We read silently, think unspeakingly, imagine unexpressively, daydream impassively. It is not simply that a body somehow houses these mental happenings. Nor does the body merely provide them necessary physiological conditions. Beyond that, it is probably the case that our bodies are as deeply engaged in our mental happenings, including mental acts, as they are in our overt behavior. In the one case as in the other "acting" involves bodily changes. We probably imagine, think, and read silently with our bodies quite as much as we walk, speak, and make things with our bodies. None of this is done without the body. It is organic, bodily persons who read, think, imagine, dream, and hallucinate. Some of such behaviors we do intentionally and we may call them "mental *acts*." Some of them, however, like night and day dreams and hallucinations, happen *to* us. Like muscular spasms, they are caused but not intended.

Now, most if not all mental acts are capable of being overtly performed bodily. Using our bodies, we can say aloud what we are reading, thinking, imagining, and daydreaming silently. Sometimes we can also enact them bodily. We may, in the broadest sense, "act out." When we do, we are *performing* these intentional acts bodily. Private mental acts and public bodily acts are the same type of thing: intentional acts. It is the same concept "act" we employ in both cases. Consequently it is profoundly misleading to say of the overt public act that it is an "outer manifestation" or "expression" of an inner mental act. That wrongly suggests that the two are quite different sorts of realities, that the inner mental act is logically independent of, prior to, and—most important of all—the cause of the "meaning" of the outer act. Rather, in these cases the overt bodily intentional action is an observable performance of an unobservable embodied mental act. They are two modes of enactment of the same type of intentional action.

These are some features of the concept "act" or "action" that are used in our description of practices. If we choose to discuss both theological schools and Christian congregations in terms of practices, this concept of act will have important consequences. It will focus attention on the concrete bodily character of those who engage in the practices in question, subverting all tendencies to draw a systematic distinction between "physical" or "natural" or "material" practices, on one side, and "spiritual" or "intellectual" practices on the other. Furthermore, by holding "inner" intention and "outer" behavior together in a single dialectical whole, and by denying any difference in kind between mental and overt acts as *acts,* indeed, as bodily acts, it will subvert all tendencies to draw any *systematic* distinction between "interior spiritual life" and "engagement in the public realm."

A second notable feature of our description of practices: Because they are socially established, practices have a history. Indeed, they can be seen as traditions of human action, in distinction, although not separation, from traditions of thought. Practices are not spontaneously invented in the moment as improvisations to deal with passing and novel problems. They are instead already established, relatively settled and accepted over a period of time as social conventions. By the same token, however, they are deeply rooted in larger cultural settings that shape them. As those cultures undergo historical change, so do practices. To stress that practices have a history is to stress that they are historically and culturally relative.

Because, third, they are cooperative and complex, practices are necessarily institutionalized to some degree. By "social institution" I mean an established and relatively fixed arrangement of social status, roles, and various sorts of power among a group of people engaged in some sort of common activity. The complexity, formality, rationality, and rigidity of these arrangements are a matter of degree and vary enormously from practice to practice. However, among persons engaged in complex cooperative activities some degree of institutionalization is inherent in their practice. These persons will have different roles to play in their cooperative activity, different responsibilities, different authority, different power, and different status.

Thus "practices" and "institutions" ought not to be contrasted to each other; they entail each other. This contributes to the complexity of the practice. Some of a set of practices will be those of maintaining, monitoring, and, if needed, modifying the institutional arrangements of the rest of the practices.

This need for practices to maintain the institutionalization of other practices creates one of the possibilities for practices becoming deformed. A practice, we said, is done to an end. But the more formal and complex its institutional patterns are, the stronger will be the tendency for their maintenance to become an end in its own right. That end may then compete with and tend to supplant the practices' proper end. Nowhere is this clearer than in the case of that highly formal, highly rigid, allegedly highly rationalized form of institutionalization known as "bureaucracy," which so notoriously deforms many of the practices it organizes.

Because, fourth, practices are forms of cooperative human activity and are institutionalized, they inescapably have a "material" base. As forms of human action, practices are forms of bodily action. Whatever else they are, the human beings who act are living bodies whose continued action requires the care and feeding of those bodies. Furthermore, as institutionalized cooperative activity, practices involve various kinds of tools and instruments and all manner of material media of communication among the cooperators. It would be a mistake to look at this material base of practices as merely a "precondition" for practices but not really "part" of any practice. The two are not logically distinct. One can see this by noting the impossibility of defining any given practice without including in the definition either reference to bodily action or reference to physical media of communication among practitioners and the physical tools they employ in the practice. This is an important point to stress because it underscores that practices have concrete social and cultural locations in their larger host societies. Access to the sorts of material base that different practices require is determined by the ways those host societies arrange social, economic, and political power. Consequently, practices will tend to have some interest in preserving social arrangements that give them access to the resources they need and some interest in resisting changes in those societal arrangements that might limit their access to the resources they need. This obviously creates another possibility for practices becoming deformed: inherent within them is the possibility of their coming to fill an ideological role.

Because, fifth, they are ordered to ends and are partly defined by certain standards of excellence, practices inherently require self-critical reflection. Self-critical reflection is not a separate practice in its own right; it is an integral part of a practice. Like the whole of the practice, self-critical reflection itself must be a cooperative activity.

As *critical* reflection, it finds its criteria partly in the end to which the practice is ordered (As currently practiced, does this practice realize its end? If not, what is amiss?) and partly in the standards of excellence that partially define the practice (How excellently do these particular cooperators engage in this practice, and if not very excellently, are they really engaged in the practice they say they're engaged in, or are they doing something else? How excellently did the Somoza government govern Nicaragua; and if not very excellently, was it perhaps not really engaged in the practice of "government" at all, but rather in the practice of commerce and trade, treating the nation as a single privately owned corporation for the personal profit of the Somoza family and its associates?). Beyond that, however, critical reflection must raise questions about the practice itself: Why become involved in it at all? Insofar as engagement in this practice brings with it commitment to certain claims about reality, are they true?

As *reflection*, critical reflection is not logically prior to practice. It presupposes that the practice is already going on, a practice that already is and has been critically self-reflective. So reflection doesn't simply follow practice either. It asks, "What is this practice? In what ways does it shape the actions and the personhood of the people engaged in it? How has it changed through history?" or even, "What would the characteristics be of a practice in some ways analogous to this one but radically different from it in other regards?"—reflections that imagine utopias, lead to radical reformations and to revolutions. Thus critical reflection does not involve a movement from detached theory to practical application. Rather, it involves a circular movement from practice to critical reflection and back to corrected practice, or to radically transformed practice.

To summarize: As socially established cooperative activities, practices are historically and culturally relative, to some degree institution-alized, materially based, and inherently critically self-reflective.

Clearly, in order to engage with others in a practice requires that one have a certain range of abilities and capacities that the practice may call for. What is in question here are not skills and techniques but "conceptual" capacities. These conceptual capacities are deepened by disciplined participation in the relevant practice. Some involve far more shaping of one's personal identity than do others. This will vary a great deal from practice to practice. Consider the differences between the abilities and capacities called for respectively by the game of football and by farming, by creating and maintaining human communities and by painting, by physics and by the worship of God.

TO UNDERSTAND

We will be speaking of "understanding God," indeed, of trying to understand God indirectly *by way* of "understanding other matters within the horizon of questions about particular Christian congregations." We noted in chapter 2 that in Christian history there have been several different notions of how to go about understanding God: through contemplation, discursive reasoning, the affections, or action. But we did not reflect on what it is "to understand" in any of these ways. What is it to "understand"? This is the final somewhat technical concept we must examine with care.

"To understand" is no one thing. That is obvious in a broad and vague way when we consider some of the various ways in which we speak of trying (and often failing) to understand: We speak of hoping to understand the instruction manual that accompanies a new word processor and of trying to understand a novel like James Joyce's *Ulysses;* though both are printed texts, what it is to understand one is quite different from what it is to understand the other. Neither is quite what we are after when we try to understand some particular human person. That, in turn, is still different from what we mean when we say we have failed to understand one of Beethoven's last string quartets. And then there are those who say they would like to understand the meaning of life.

Furthermore, what it is to understand any one of these may vary depending on who is trying to understand and what the context is. It is one kind of thing to understand a person when she is my wife in the context of our life together, another to understand her when she is a potential buyer and I an advertiser in the context of contemporary American consumerist culture, still another when she is a client and I a psychiatrist in a psychotherapeutic context, even though these various senses of "to understand" overlap in various ways.

Surely these various senses of "to understand" have something in common? If not, then we are using the expression in wildly equivocating ways. There is one thing all these uses of "to understand" do have in common. It can be generalized like this: "To understand" something in some context is to have some abilities in relation to that "something." Charles Wood puts the point well:

> To understand a map is ordinarily to be able to find one's way around by it. To understand an order is to be able to obey it if conditions permit, or to know what obeying it would involve. To understand algebra is to be able to perform and apply various mathematical operations in appropriate circumstances, and to know when and why a particular operation is right or wrong. . . . One who understands a text will be able to make use of the text in ways that demonstrate—and in some sense even constitute—understanding.[5]

A more complete account of each of these "understandings" could be given in terms of specific abilities and capacities. The abilities differ from one another a great deal. Note that while it is important to relate "understand" to "be able to use," to relate "understand x" to "have certain abilities in relation to x," it is just as important to stress that "to understand" is not *identical* with "to agree" (e.g., with a text) or "to obey" (e.g., a command) or "to follow" (e.g., a map). Among the abilities that in some sense constitute understanding are abilities to assess critically, to entertain what is understood in an "as if" or imaginative mode, and mindfully and deliberately to disregard that which is understood. There is no one core of which all these abilities are merely variations. To understand is no one thing.

There are three further points to be made about "understanding" as sets of abilities. The first is that, within limits, we may grow in understanding. There are degrees of understanding because abilities admit of degree. To grow in understanding something is to grow in a set of abilities in relation to what is being understood. The growth comes through our engagement over a period of time in certain relevant practices. It was implicit in our discussion in the previous section that practices are patterns of activity that are governed by rule-like regularities: thus the judiciary, the making of western music on the piano, and batting a baseball are all rule-governed activities and hence are *practices*. Practices usually involve criticism, that is, rules according to which our activity has to be corrected in certain respects from time to time.

The traditional name for what grows through these practices is *habitus*. A *habitus* is a settled disposition to act in a characteristic way. Sometimes it is a disposition to engage in a certain practice. *Habitus* is thus rather like what in English is called a habit, but with major qualifications. Where many habits dispose us to act automatically in mechanical and rigid ways, *habitus* dispose us to act in a certain characteristic way (say, prudently) but to do so intentionally (as opposed to automatically), thoughtfully (as opposed to instinctively), self-critically (as opposed to mechanically), and inventively (as opposed to rigidly) in light of the actual circumstances of the action. Here we are considering specifically cognitive *habitus,* dispositions to act in regard to something in ways that comprise understanding it. In short, growth in understanding comes through some kind of discipline that leads to acquiring capacities to act according to relevant rules.

One distinction among these various sorts of growth is important for our purposes. Growth in some sorts of abilities shape who we are far more deeply than does growth in other sorts of abilities. Growth in our abilities to trust, for example, or to take risks, abilities that are integral to understanding "faithfulness," shapes us very deeply, whereas growth in our ability to manipulate checker pieces according to the rules of the game of checkers and to design strategies as we play, abilities integral to understanding checkers, scarcely shapes us at all. Coming to understand certain things is existentially significant in ways in which coming to understand other things simply isn't.

Understanding, secondly, is guided by our interests. We can bring this out by reflecting on the question, "Just which abilities constitute 'understanding,' say, this map, and why?" As Charles Wood points out, "The cab driver and the cartographer may have somewhat different understandings of the same map."[6] That is, they may have somewhat different sets of abilities in relation to the map. The differences between their sets of abilities are dictated by the different objectives they have. The cab driver wants to find a particular address; the cartographer wants to assess the reliability and complexity of the map. And their differing objectives are rooted in different interests: The cab driver is interested in getting around the city; the cartographer is interested in the art and science of mapping urban areas. The differences in their "understandings" of the map are rooted in different interests.

We recognize this point informally all the time in everyday life. To understand other persons will require different sets of abilities depending on whether our objective is to be their friends, sell them something they don't really need, or command them in the heat of battle. To be sure, these sets of abilities may well overlap in various unsystematic ways. Nonetheless, they will be different. What it is "to understand" other persons will vary depending on our objectives and interests. Similarly, a person whose objective is to acquire a sense for a particular historical period and a person whose objective is to savor a skilled writer's use of the mother tongue will have to bring somewhat different sets of abilities to a historical novel; they will have different understandings of the same novel.

These interests, or, to speak more concretely, the people who have these interests, are always "located" culturally, socially, economically, and politically. This is the third point to be made about "understanding" as sets of abilities relative to what is to be understood. Because these abilities are guided by interests and the interests are located in some society and its cultures, understanding is always "situated."

That has two important distinguishable but interrelated consequences. One is that the abilities that comprise "understanding" are in varying degrees culturally formed. To understand is always to understand in some cultural context, in terms provided by the culture's conventional practices and traditions. The other is that to be located in a society is, concretely, to be situated at some point in the distribution of power and status *within* that society. To the extent that social, economic, and political power is inequitably distributed and to the extent that this inequality generates tension or conflict within the culture, the interests that guide understanding may be shaped by one's location *in* these tensions—shaped either as an interest to right the inequality (perhaps because one is oppressed by it) or as an interest to preserve it (perhaps because one benefits from it).

Now, both consequences of the fact that interests are "situated" can lead to distortion and bias in understanding. The term "ideology" is sometimes loosely used to refer to distortion and bias rooted in both of these consequences of the situatedness of our interests. However, "ideology" properly connotes unself-conscious bias that functions to deny or obscure inequalities from which some people benefit and by which others are oppressed. Hence "ideology" is probably best reserved for that distortion and bias in understanding whose guiding interests are located, not simply in some culture, nor simply on one side or the other of an intrasocietal conflict, but quite particularly on the privileged side of such a conflict. However that may be, it follows that the abilities that comprise what it is "to understand" must include critical and self-critical abilities to detect and correct ideological and other distortions.

There are, to be sure, other ways to explicate what it is to understand something. It is possible, indeed common, in contemporary theology to assume that the concept "to understand" must be explained in terms of a philosophical analysis of the structure and dynamics of human consciousness or subjectivity which the philosophical analysis shows to be identical among all human persons. Explained that way, understanding is taken to be some one phenomenon which is the presence to consciousness of something called *the* meaning of that which is understood. On this explanation, understanding is, as Wood puts it, a phenomenon "experienced, as it were, in the privacy of one's mind, apart from any practical entanglements or consequences."[7] When this sort of analysis of the concept "to understand" is used in relation to theological schooling it does tend to yield an "essentialist" picture: It suggests that to understand God or anything else is some one phenomenon and that what is understood is some one meaning. It tends to yield an individualistic picture of theological schooling; it suggests that to understand God is a phenomenon experienced "in the privacy" of students' and teachers' individual minds. And it tends to yield a picture of theological schooling in which the life of faith is disengaged from the public realm. It suggests that to understand God or anything else is a phenomenon in consciousness "apart from any practical entanglements or consequences."

By contrast, "to understand" (God or anything else) has been analyzed here in a way that excludes "essentialist" implications by insisting that to understand is itself not some one thing, but rather an indefinitely large number of capacities and abilities. Furthermore, the analysis does not push toward an essentialist picture of the subject matter that is understood, because it does not require us even to mention anything called "the [essential] meaning" that must be grasped in any successful effort to understand a subject matter. So too, by tying understanding to capacities and abilities for engaging in practices that are inherently social, our analysis of "to understand" avoids individualistic implications. And precisely by tying understanding to dispositions to act, our analysis avoids disengaging the effort to understand from the public realm.

We have been sharpening a few tools. With this preparatory clarification of the concepts "pluralism," "practice," "action," and "understanding" in hand, we may now proceed to refine our proposal. These concepts are central to the proposal. In ordinary usage they are remarkably vague notions and quickly create confusion. If we take care to use them only in ways guided by the analysis we have given them here, we may be able to make our proposal both more clear and more persuasive.

Notes

1. Craig Dykstra, "Reconceiving Practice," in *Shifting Boundaries: Contextual Approaches to the Structure of Theological Education,* ed. Barbara G. Wheeler and Edward Farley (Louisville, Ky.: Westminster/John Knox Press, 1991), pp. 35–66.

2. Nicholas Wolterstorff, *Art in Action* (Grand Rapids: Wm. B. Eerdmans Publishing Co., 1980). See esp. pp. 1–19, 65–91.

3. Alasdair MacIntyre, *After Virtue* (Notre Dame, Ind.: University of Notre Dame Press, 1981), pp. 175–283.

4. Of the extensive literature in philosophical psychology dealing with the concepts "action" and "act," cf. esp. G. E. M. Anscombe, *Intention* (Oxford: Blackwells, 1957); Anthony Kenny, *Action, Emotion, and Will* (London: Routledge & Kegan Paul, 1963); A. I. Melden, *Free Action* (London: Routledge & Kegan Paul, 1961); R. S. Peters, *The Concept of Motivation,* 2nd ed. (London: Routledge & Kegan Paul, 1963).

5. Charles Wood, *The Formation of Christian Understanding* (Philadelphia: Westminster Press, 1981), pp. 16–17.

6. Ibid., p. 19.

7. Ibid., p. 17.

7

Congregations

A theological school is a community of persons trying to understand God more truly by focusing its study of various subject matters within the horizon of questions about Christian congregations. That is the thesis we need now to refine.

Understanding God must proceed indirectly. If a community of persons sets out to understand God more truly, it is going to have to go about it by focusing on something else whose study is believed to lead to truer understanding of God. What should that be? This is a point at which the diversity of construals of the Christian thing that we noted in chapter 2 becomes decisive. In some construals of the Christian thing the answer would be, "Study of Christian scriptures (or, scriptures in tradition) is the indirect route to truer understanding of God." In other construals the advice would be, "Study religious experience," or "Reflect on liberating *praxis*," or "Study Christian tradition (or at least the first five centuries of it)." Each of these is an important element of the Christian thing, but only as it stands interconnected in various ways with the others. The Christian thing itself, I suggest, can be encountered concretely *in and as Christian congregations;* its major and most demonic distortions can also be encountered in the same place. Consequently, I propose that the answer to our questions ought to be: "Focus study of all of the above through the lens of questions about Christian congregations in all their diversity and often appalling ambiguity."

OBJECTIONS AND OFFENSE

In making this proposal I am building on a suggestion first advanced by James F. Hopewell. Growing out of years of involvement in a group exploring different ways to study congregations[1] and his own ground-breaking *Congregation: Stories and Structures*,[2] Hopewell wrote an essay, "A Congregational Paradigm for Theological Education." Theological educators from a variety of types of theological schools were gathered in a seminar to discuss not so much Hopewell's paper itself but the issues it raised for theological schooling. The papers for that seminar, including my own, have been published as *Beyond Clericalism*.[3] The papers raise a number of major objections to the general proposal I now want to explore further. The objections are serious and I agree with them. However, in thinking them through I have come to believe that they provide guidance for shaping my proposal more rigorously than it would have been otherwise and, ironically, provide strong arguments in favor of the proposal! It is enough to outline the objections here and explore their force; detailed response to them will come later.

There are three broad sorts of objections to the proposal that theological schooling focus on study of Christian congregations. The first is that it is an inherently sectarian proposal. *A* Christian congregation is not, for most Christians at any rate, identical with "Christian Church." To the contrary, the practices, beliefs, and history of any one congregation, as well as the proper concepts to use in describing and analyzing it, have their home in a much larger Christian tradition.[4] If a theological school wants more truly to understand God, surely it would be better—to make a counterproposal—to focus its study on that greater tradition than on individual congregations within it.

Moreover, for a second objection, the proposal is far too parochial. There are far greater reaches of reality than what may be found within the common life of particular congregations.[5] If a theological school wants to understand God more truly, if *truth* is really the issue, surely it would be better to focus study on the foundations that justify our getting involved in a congregation in the first place. Perhaps—to make another counterproposal—it would be wiser to focus on common human experience, or at least on distinctively religious experience of which the experience of a congregation is one variation.

The third objection is that the proposal is too complacent about Christian congregations. It is too uncritical in its assumption that by studying Christian congregations one could come more truly to understand God. That assumption is uncritical of congregations' faithlessness. They are faithless to God, faithless to what they themselves say is their mission in the world, faithless in their idolatrous captivity to society's values. Moreover, in their faithlessness, congregations become blind to social injustice and tend to reinforce and sanction the injustice. They become ideologically captive.[6] If a theological school wants to understand God more truly, surely it would be better—to make yet another counterproposal—to focus study on the Word of God that not only calls congregations into being and nurtures them but also judges and corrects them.

Behind these reasoned objections and giving them their power lies a deep offense. Christian congregations are occasions for offense. One need hardly be a theological educator in a seminar about theological schools to feel that. The morally earnest, the spiritually perceptive, the intellectually sophisticated, not to mention the aesthetically sensitive, are often scandalized by the actualities of Christian congregational life. And justifiably so. The phrase "the scandal of particularity" has usually been associated with Christian claims about Jesus of Nazareth. The claim that God is uniquely present among us, sharing our common human lot as this one particular first-century Jew, is offensive the way apparently arbitrary, exclusivist, and arrogant claims often are. But the phrase applies with even more cause to traditional Christian claims that congregations are, or are somehow part of, the "people of God," the "body of Christ," the "bride of Christ," that they are communities on which the Holy Spirit is particularly poured out. It is natural and appropriate to be scandalized that such claims should be made of just these all-too-well-known groups, faithless to their self-descriptions, thoroughly assimilated to the value system of the larger culture in which they live, complacent and at ease, often trivial and banal, subtly using the rhetoric of the faith to sanction their privileges and to obscure society's injustices.

So, of all unlikely candidates, why pick Christian congregations as the lens through which to focus study of scripture, experience, and tradition? The general answer lies in our maxim: The way to the generally relevant and universally true passes through the particular and concrete.

Scripture, for instance, may very well be that which both nurtures and judges congregations. But it does these things in concrete actuality only as it is used in certain ways in the common life of actual congregations. Or it may well be that it is elements, perhaps "religious" elements, of our "common human experience" that ultimately justify our becoming part of some congregation's common life. But that experience is never conceptually unformed. In order to see how it is actually formed in such a way that it warrants our taking this step, we need to see how experience is shaped by the common life of congregations in their cultural settings. So too, it may well be that congregations are largely constituted of traditional practices that are part of a much larger church tradition. But that tradition is nowhere concretely actual except as practiced in particular congregations. What one may study independently of congregations are relative abstractions from the concrete actuality of particular congregations of Christians like "the history of dogma" or "the history of liturgy" or "the history of canon law." The abstraction from concrete social reality in each case tends to create the illusion that theological ideas or practices of worship or church legal systems have ghostly lives of their own that transcend the concrete particulars of the communities that more or less believe the dogmas, practice the liturgies, and follow the rules.

It is in the common life of congregations that all these factors of the Christian thing come together to transform and empower persons' lives. The Christian thing can be *concretely* encountered *in and as Christian congregations*. Indeed, it is *by comparative study of congregations* that one can see how different construals of the Christian thing make real differences in the ways persons' lives are shaped and empowered. If it is believed that study of some or all of these construals of "the content of the Christian thing" yields truer understanding of God, then, the proposal goes, it is best to study them as concretely as possible. One place in North American societies where they are most concretely available is the common life of Christian congregations. The Christian thing may, to be sure, be encountered elsewhere, say in the lives of exemplary persons, but no other place so insistently claims for itself that it instantiates and enacts the Christian thing as does the Christian congregation.

The way to the generally relevant and universally true passes through the particular and concrete. That is the reason for urging that study of all the subject matters to which theological schools attend, in the hope of understanding God more truly, be focused through the lens of questions about particular Christian congregations. However, it does not by itself answer any of the major objections to giving congregations this kind of systematic importance. I believe those objections can be answered. However, the answers must lie in the details of the way this proposal is worked out. Consequently, responses to the objections will need to be scattered through the rest of this chapter as the proposal is elaborated and developed.

A WORKING DESCRIPTION

Then how do we identify a congregation when we see one? What is going to count as a "Christian congregation"? We need to identify criteria by which to judge which groups belong within the circle of Christian congregations so that we can tell concretely just what it is that we recommend theological schools select to focus their studies. We need to identify the criteria to which congregations hold themselves accountable. We need to identify ways in which, for all their differences from one another, Christian congregations are nonetheless somehow "one" with one another in a more embracing "whole." We need to specify how congregations are not only located within but are somehow integral to larger social and cultural systems. We need to identify the methods of inquiry that should be used in the study of congregations. Only when we can identify these matters will we be in a position to respond to objections to the very suggestion that a theological school focus on the study of congregations.

To do all this we need an appropriate language. I propose to use the language of "actions" and "practices" sketched in the last chapter. I propose we think of Christian congregations as comprised of complex networks of interrelated practices. The *public worship of God* is, I suggest, the central practice of the set of practices that comprise a Christian congregation. There are, of course, an indefinitely large number of other practices that are part of the common life of Christian congregations: pastoral care of the ill, the troubled, and the grieving; nurture and education of children and adults; management of property; raising of funds; maintenance of institutions; and so forth. They are all ordered, however, to the practice whose end is to worship God.

It must be stressed that the practice of worship is a *response* to the odd presence of God. Historically, for Christians and Jews, the ways in which God is present have been understood to be unpredictable, unmanageable, and thoroughly peculiar: in dreams and a burning bush; in an Egyptian slave insurrection; in a crucified Jew. More exactly, it has been God's presence in memories of these occasions, remembered as promises of God's presence on equally unpredictable and peculiar occasions in the future. The response of worship has mostly been a response in the meantime, between memory and fulfilled promise. For Christians, almost by definition, the normative and decisive presence of God is in the life story of Jesus' ministry, crucifixion, and resurrection appearances. Christian worship is a response in joy, awe, and gratitude for the memory and promise of the sheer fact of God's presence in Jesus of Nazareth.

Consequently, this practice's end is internal to itself. That is, worship of God is not done to any further end. Rather, this practice is a celebration of God's presence for its own sake. Accordingly, it is misleading to characterize a congregation as "a redemptive community." It may be that on occasion the community is redemptive. However, to characterize the community that way suggests that the community's *central* practice is to "redeem" people. Rather, at very best, its practices are ordered only to being *a context* in which redemption may take place. If anything is redemptive it is God's own peculiar ways of being present in history, and congregations are constituted by the practices in which they respond to that redemptive presence.

When Christians' worship is understood in this fashion as a "practice" (in the somewhat technical sense of "practice" we have adopted), then James Hopewell's description of a congregation turns out to be unusually fruitful: "A congregation is a group that possesses a special name and recognized members who assemble regularly to celebrate a more universally practiced worship but who communicate with each other sufficiently to develop intrinsic patterns of conduct, outlook, and story."[7] To bring out its fruitfulness I shall first suggest an expansion of our working description of "Christian congregation" and then elaborate it piecemeal, drawing attention to its implications for theological study and the responses it implies to objections to focusing theological schooling on study on congregations.

What is a Christian congregation? As a working description I will adopt the following expansion of Hopewell's description:

A Christian congregation is a group of persons that gathers together to enact publicly a much more broadly practiced worship of God in Jesus' name, regularly enough over an indefinite period of time to have a common life in which develop intrinsic patterns of conduct, outlook, and story, and that holds its conduct, outlook, and story accountable as to its faithfulness to biblical stories of Jesus' mission and God's mission in Jesus.[8]

IDENTIFYING CONGREGATIONS

Our working definition provides an answer to the question, "How do we tell which groups belong within the circle 'Christian congregations'?" After all, the proposal that a theological school focus study by attention to Christian congregations is useless unless we can identify which groups should and which should not be considered candidates for study. The working description provides a very permissive answer: The phrase "in Jesus' name" is definitive. Let groups describe themselves into or out of the circle. Any group of persons who gather to worship God regularly enough for an indefinite period of time to have developed a common life in which arise intrinsic patterns of conduct, outlook, and story *and* explicitly do so "in Jesus' name" as a deliberate act of self-identification should be considered a Christian congregation for our purposes.

"In Jesus' name" functions at once descriptively and normatively. It requires us to draw two distinctions where only one grew before: Christian vs. non-Christian, and faithful vs. sinful.

The original question concerned description: Descriptively speaking, which groups count as "Christian congregations"? The answer given here is: Let each group's self-description stand. If a group characterizes *itself* as one that meets in Jesus' name, let it be counted a Christian congregation. We will let "in Jesus' name" be a necessary condition of a congregation's "Christianness."

This has implications concerning the subject matter of theological schooling. It is a matter of theological controversy, of course, whether "in Jesus' name" is a *sufficient* condition of a congregation's "Christianness." More controversy turns on what further conditions a congregation would have to meet if the self-description "in Jesus' name" is not sufficient. Those controversies ought to be left open by a theological school so that the structure and merits of arguments on both sides can be rigorously tested. Indeed, it is precisely by raising these controversies in the process of studying actual congregations that the meaning and importance of contested theological views are best understood.

Adopting "in Jesus' name" as the necessary minimal condition for a counting as a "Christian congregation" for the purpose of a theological school's study does not, of course, require any particular answer to the quite different question whether God is truly known and worshiped by groups who do *not* worship in Jesus' name or whether God is redemptively present to them. That is a further question open for exploration in theological study.

Adopting this necessary minimal condition does mean, however, that any congregation that takes on this self-description thereby also affirms that there is a difference between Christian and non-Christian congregations and that the difference matters. What matters is the way the community's identity is shaped and the ways in which its members' personal identities are shaped. The difference it makes is a difference in *who* they are.

"In Jesus' name" also functions normatively. Any group that describes itself as gathering to worship God in Jesus' name thereby adopts a criterion to which it commits to hold itself accountable. Its worship is intended to be faithful to Jesus. No matter how a group may understand Jesus, he has been identified as a necessary criterion by which its conduct, outlook, and story must be assessed. This means that in addition to the distinction Christian/non-Christian congregation, there is the distinction faithful Christian/unfaithful Christian congregation. Conceptually speaking, any particular congregation might be truly "Christian," that is, deliberately assume the communal identity that goes with worshiping God in Jesus' name, and at the same time in some ways be faithless to Jesus. It can at once be "Christian" and "sinful."

This too has implications regarding the subject matter of theological schooling. These distinctions between "Christian" and "faithful" are purely formal. Whether they are accepted as distinctions in reality depends on different views of the church. It depends on controversial theological views about whether "faithfulness" should be *added* to "in Jesus' name" as a necessary condition of genuinely being a Christian congregation. Here too, the controversy ought to be left open for reasoned debate in a theological school. It is precisely by raising these controversies in the context of the comparative study of congregations that the full meaning and importance of contested theological views are best grasped.

One qualification of this way of identifying what counts as "Christian congregations" needs to be made. What if there were a congregation that adopted the self-description "in Jesus' name" but never, as a part of its practice of worship in that name, engaged in critical reflection on its own faithfulness to that norm? For reasons we shall discuss below, such a group should probably be excluded from the class "Christian congregations" on the grounds that it evidently did not understand what it means to describe itself that way.

SELF-CRITICAL CONGREGATIONS

According to our working description, a congregation is a group that gathers to worship God in Jesus' name and holds its conduct, outlook, and story accountable as to its faithfulness to biblical stories of Jesus' mission and God's mission in Jesus. Consider what is entailed in this. Worship, we have said, may be understood as a social practice. As we went to some length to show in chapter 6, critical self-reflection is inherent in any practice. Insofar as a congregation is constituted by a complex set of interconnected practices, critical self-reflection is inherent to the common worship life of a congregation. In our working description of congregations we have, in capsule form, the norm against which a congregation's conduct, outlook, and story are reflectively to be guided and critically to be assessed: the stories of Jesus' mission and God's mission in Jesus. Hence, a group that never engaged in critical self-reflection on its faithfulness to its own self-description "in Jesus' name" would seem not to have understood what is involved in describing itself "in Jesus' name" and should not be considered as a Christian congregation.

But how are Jesus' missions and God's mission in Jesus to be characterized? How are the norms to be stated? Once again, the differences we noted in chapter 2 among construals of the Christian thing are decisive—and divisive. Different pictures of the significance of Jesus and of his relationship to God will yield significantly different but frequently overlapping formulations of the norms against which a congregation's life is to be assessed. One generalization may be ventured, however. In their diverse ways, all construals of the norms to which a congregation holds itself accountable tie worship of God to a commitment to truthfulness. Faithfulness to "Jesus' name" entails faithfulness to the truth. In one way or another critical self-reflection by a congregation involves not only attention to whether various features of its practices are faithful to the One to whom they are responses, but also involves attention to whether engaging in some particular practice or, indeed, to this entire set of practices is itself truthful.

There are several different sorts of untruth that constantly require critique and correction. As we have noted, practices are always historically and culturally situated and relative. One consequence of this is that practices shaped by one cultural and historical setting may become increasingly esoteric, private, and disengaged from the public realm as its host society goes through historical and cultural changes. In that case, the practices' growing unintelligibility and inappropriateness to the public realm require critique and imaginative reflection on how they should be revised.

A second consequence of a congregation's practices' social location is that they are threatened with ideological distortion. Precisely because a congregation has "material" bases and is necessarily located at some point in conflicts within a society which may tend to privilege its access to the material resources it needs, a congregation's practices are always in danger of serving to preserve the social arrangements from which they profit and of obscuring the inequalities inherent in those arrangements. When that happens the practices are filling an ideological function. They have also become idolatrous. The material interest being protected has displaced God as that to which response is being made. In that case, a congregation's practice requires a different sort of critique, and calls for creative reflection about how to avoid ideological captivity and idolatry.

Even more radically, the fact that the practice of worship of God inherently requires critical self-reflection means that it inherently requires critical examination of whether and why we should engage ourselves in the Christian thing at all, and hence in the common life of this or any congregation. Inherent in faithfulness to the One to whom worship in Jesus' name is a response is the call rigorously and critically to examine the truth of the Christian thing itself. Exactly how that is to be done is, of course, a highly controversial matter. The point is that by their own self-descriptions Christian congregations require that it be done and, therefore, doing it will be part of the work of a theological school whose study is focused through the lens of questions about congregations. This implies a response to one major objection to the entire proposal that theological schooling focus its efforts to understand God more truly through questions about congregations. The objection was that congregations are by and large far too ideologically captive to their host cultures to be suitable as the lens through which theological schooling is focused. However, the point is that given our working description of Christian congregations, theological schooling focused by study of congregations would welcome and endorse the most vigorous and detailed exposé of the cultural captivity and ideological functioning of congregations and their practices. By their very self-description as groups gathered to worship God in Jesus' name, congregations commit themselves to continuing self-critique in the light of norms that expose and judge exactly such idolatry, even though they may not do it very rigorously! Far from ignoring this idolatry, theological schooling focused by study of congregations would highlight it. In this regard theological schooling would be *against* a congregation.

By the same token, our working description's stress on the self-critical moment in Christian congregations' practice of worship has

141

implications concerning the subject matter of theological schooling. A theological school's focus on the congregation in order better to understand God must involve several kinds of critical and constructive theological work. It requires what might best be called "theology of culture," theological reflection on critical implications of cultural change for congregations' practices, and it calls for envisioning possible constructive reshaping of a congregation's practices insofar as they are ways in which the congregation tells its story in and to its host culture. For example, it requires examination of the ways in which the roles and status assigned to women in a congregation reflect the ways in which they are assigned in society at large, to test whether they are in accord with what the congregation itself claims are the implications of worshiping God "in Jesus' name" in a manner "ruled" by New Testament stories about Jesus. It requires moral theology, critical normative assessment of the congregation's practices insofar as they are morally accountable conduct. It requires doctrinal theology for critical assessment of the ideological distortion and faithlessness of its practices insofar as they are statements of its outlook, and it calls for constructive proposals of preferable formulations of its outlook.

PUBLIC AND ECUMENICAL CONGREGATIONS

Our working description stresses that a Christian congregation is a group that gathers to enact publicly a much more broadly practiced worship of God in Jesus' name. The connection between "broadly practiced" and "public" is crucial if "worship" is not to be misunderstood or understood far too narrowly.

It is immensely important that "worship" not be understood narrowly. At this point we must face up to a methodological problem. Here, as in this entire discussion of the notion of "Christian congregation," no sharp line is possible between descriptive and normative remarks. Once again we encounter the consequences of the variety of ways in which the Christian thing can be and has been construed. Different comprehensive or synoptic judgments about what "the faith is all about" or what "the basic message of the Word is" or what "the point of the Christian life is" bring with them different theological norms by which to judge what is, is less, or is not at all adequate and appropriate as worship of God in Jesus' name. One has always to make choices about the terms to use in description, and both the choices and the terms will inescapably be theologically laden, and therefore shaped by some normative commitments.

It is my hope to elaborate the concept "worship" in a way that will be compatible with the wide range of ways of understanding what is the Christian thing that we identified in chapter 2. However if, in light of your construal of what Christianity is all about, this sketch of what worship is requires alteration, alter it! What is important is the proposal that theological schooling's effort more truly to understand God be focused through questions about Christian congregations whose defining practice is worship, however "worship" is understood. It will be impossible to assess the fruitfulness of that larger proposal to a particular theological school if the understanding of "worship" and of "congregation" it takes for granted is inapplicable in a particular tradition. If those descriptions need to be modified to make the larger proposal more applicable, let them be modified! If the concrete content of the proposal sketched here is irrelevant to you, test whether at any rate it might be illuminating to rethink theological schooling along analogous lines, that is, as focused through questions about the Christian community described in some other way.

Elaboration of what worship is may usefully begin with two relatively noncontroversial negative remarks and then move on to positive characterization. To begin with, as James Hopewell pointed out,[9] worship "in Jesus' name" must not be understood as cultic worship in the strict sense. "Cultic worship" is a practice performed by a person empowered by the deity to serve as intermediary between human beings and divine powers by presiding over an esoteric ritual (usually a sacrifice) which evokes an appearance of divine power for the benefit of the worshiper.

The benefit for the worshiper might be anything from the success of an undertaking, to recovery from illness, to becoming immortal. Worship of God in Jesus' name is not cultic in this sense precisely because, as response to God's presence, definitively in the life, death, and resurrection appearances of Jesus, it does not seek to evoke God's presence but to celebrate it as an already given gift. Hence it permits no religious specialist to be intermediary between divine power and us and no esoteric ritual with the capacity to evoke divine presence.[10]

For much the same reason, worship of God in Jesus' name cannot be a practice whose defining end is to receive something from God. The fact that it is worship in Jesus' name means that the benefit which it is appropriate to seek of God is somehow predefined by "Jesus' name." It is defined as *already* given to us in the peculiar ways in which God has been and promises to be present, notably "in Jesus." Hence this worship of God is a practice whose defining purpose or end is nothing other than expression of joy, awe, and thanksgiving for the sheer fact of the gift of God's presence. However, in that context, petitions are made to God as part of a response in gratitude and joy. The response involves the community's total life. That means that acknowledgment of one's dependence upon God and of one's deepest yearnings (which, after all, are also part of the totality of life) is an appropriate part of the practice of worship. However, in this context petitions to God no longer define the practice of worship in a self-referencing way ("The point of worshiping God is to receive what we need"); rather petitions are themselves transformed into acts of thanksgiving as part of the practice of referring all our lives to God as a response to God's peculiar and disconcerting mode of presence.

More positively, the practice of worship of God in Jesus' name embraces everything involved in responding to God's presence. It is the practice of referring to God the entire life of the community *and* the world in which it lives. Perhaps the best comprehensive term for the practice of this worship as a whole is simply "discipleship." In its fullest sense, the practice of the worship of God in Jesus' name involves the shaping of the totality of persons' lives as an appropriate response to God's strange way of being present in the life of Jesus of Nazareth.

The tendency to understand "worship" more narrowly as limited to the "proclamation of the Word" and "the celebration of the sacraments" is understandable. It has legitimate roots in tradition. If, as discipleship, the practice of worship involves the shaping of the totality of our life as a response to God's way of being present, then discipleship needs constantly to be reminded of what it is responding *to*. Moreover, in order to be an appropriate response, it needs constantly to be tested and reformed *by* what it is responding to. That reminding, testing, and reforming is a major part of what goes on in conventionally and narrowly understood worship: the proclamation of the Word and the celebration of the sacraments. Clearly the two are at the core of the practice of worship. However, even as the core they are only part of a larger, more complex cooperative social practice, the public worship of God. It is for this reason that Bishop J. A. T. Robinson, noting that the end toward which the service of Holy Communion is ordered is its last line, "Go out into the world" (Latin: *Ite missa est* = Go, it is sent, or, more colloquially, Get out! Get to work!), claimed that celebrating the Eucharist is a profoundly political act.[11]

Thus our working description of Christian congregations underscores two central features of the practice that constitutes them: the practice of worship is a public practice and it is a broadly shared practice. These two points imply responses to two important objections to the proposal that theological schooling be focused through questions about congregations, namely, that it is parochial and that it is sectarian. They too have implications regarding the subject matter of theological study.

The practice of worship in Jesus' name is a public practice in at least two senses. It is a practice, we said, in which persons' lives are being shaped in their totality as appropriate responses to God's strange way of being present in the life of Jesus of Nazareth. In the quasi-technical language we sketched in chapter 6, what is being shaped are the emotions, passions, beliefs, and intentions that enable someone to act in distinctive ways. They are acts in which persons are capacitated to engage self-critically in a distinctive social practice. What is being shaped is the life of a community of bodied persons who are agents in a public realm shared with many others, most of whom do not engage in this practice of worship. This more broadly shared public realm is an arena in which social, economic, and political power is arranged and rearranged. Discipleship in that realm inescapably involves *some* sort of engagement of those arrangements of power, ranging from compliance with them to direct attack on them. Public worship of God inherently involves politically significant social action.

There is a second way in which the practice of worship in Jesus' name is a public practice. Every enactment of this worship of God is located in some cultural setting. It must be done in such a way that it is understandable to any interested person in that culture. It cannot be an esoteric practice intelligible only to initiates. It must be conducted in language and expressive gestures at least some of which are already familiar to nonparticipants. Thus the cultural setting shapes the ways in which this practice is in fact celebrated in that place. The practice of worship is thus always localiz*able* in temporally extended actions requiring particular, concrete physical and spatial location; and that constitutes a congregation.

Clearly, the inherently public character of the practice of worship implies a response to the objection that our central proposal is too parochial. The objection assumes that attention to the common life of congregations would tend to disengage theological schooling from serious attention to the broader world of the congregation's host culture and its global setting. However, if a congregation is understood to be constituted by a set of practices, and if the central practice is understood to be the worship of God in Jesus' name, and if that worship is understood to be inherently public in these two ways, then the objection seems to lose force. Attention to congregations whose practice of worship is the practice of shaping persons' identities for discipleship in the shared public arena could not be parochially limited to what de facto goes on within congregations.

They would necessarily have to attend to what is known about how persons' identities are shaped in general, and to what is known about the ways in which social, economic, and political power is arranged and could be rearranged in the public realm. So too, attention to congregations whose practice of worship is necessarily shaped by its cultural setting would not be parochially limited to what goes on "within" congregations but rather have to question the value of any sharp contrast between "inside" and "outside" and attend to what is known about the cultural settings that inescapably shape its enactments of worship.

Equally clearly, the inherently public character of the practice of worship has implications concerning the subject matter of theological study. A theological school's focus on congregations in order more truly to understand God must, if congregations' constituting practice is truly *public* worship, involve two things. It must involve study of the "languages" in which its practice of worship will be intelligible in a *1* truly public way. That is, it must involve study of the dominant images, symbols, and stories by which the congregation's host society tells itself who and what *it* is, what its vision of the "good" or "fulfilled" human life is, what its central values are. As participant in that culture, a congregation will be as deeply shaped by those "languages" as is any other group in the culture. It could not avoid using those languages if it wished. Moreover, as we have seen, if it is to be true to itself, it could not wish to avoid use of those "languages." Its constituting practice of worship must necessarily be "public" in the sense of being to some degree generally comprehensible rather than esoteric. That can only be accomplished by employing the "languages" common to its host society.

At the same time, a theological school's study of these languages must be a critical study. The vision of the "good" life, the central values, even the corporate identity expressed by a congregation's host culture in its dominant languages will in various ways stand in tension with the *2* congregation's own understanding of its own communal identity, its own picture of the good life, its own central values as they all are defined "in Jesus' name." Theological schooling will need to focus on those tensions and conflicts and the various strategies congregations employ in negotiating them when they use the host culture's languages to practice their own discipleship.

A theological school's attention to congregations will involve a second kind of study if congregations' constitutive practice is genuinely *public* worship of God. Worship in the full sense—worship as discipleship—involves shaping persons as agents and thus involves action in the public realm which consists in arrangements and rearrangements of social, political, and economic power. How are persons' identities formed and changed? How are social arrangements of power rearranged? There is a good deal of well-founded knowledge about these matters, and theological study focused through questions about congregations and their constitutive practices must attend to it too. More importantly, theological study must attend to those disciplines by which to *assess* the truth of old and new claims about how persons' identities and societies' power arrangements are shaped and changed. It is not that theological schooling has an inherent responsibility to discover these truths. It is rather that theological schooling, if focused by attention to congregations, does have an inherent responsibility to keep in review congregations' wisdom or foolishness about how to go about enacting their central practice in such a way that persons' lives are in fact shaped appropriately as responses to God's presence in Jesus of Nazareth and review the wisdom or foolishness of the concrete ways in which congregations enact their discipleship publicly.

A congregation, according to our working definition, is constituted by the practice of the worship of God; and "worship," we warned, will be understood too narrowly if its public and its universal features are not held together. Thus far we have been exploring the content and implications of the public character of worship; now we must turn to the characterization of it as "much more broadly" practiced.

A local congregation gathers to enact "much more broadly practiced worship." It is precisely that practice whose public character we analyzed above, that *is* the worship of God, that is "broadly" practiced. It is the same worship that is practiced by Christian congregations globally in every type of social and cultural location. Empirically, of course, it does not look that way. It is not simply that cross-culturally the worship of Christian congregations uses vastly different "languages" shaped by different cultures. Beyond that, in a crazy-quilt pattern, enactments of the practice of worship differ profoundly cross-culturally and within the same cultures because of deeply differing construals of what the Christian thing is all about and, consequently, what the features of an appropriate response to it should be. Nonetheless, it can be argued[12] that despite all the variations, it all is a response to the *same* thing: the stories of Jesus' mission and of God's mission in Jesus. Those stories provide all celebrations of Christian worship with a common lexicon of images, metaphors, and parables. Moreover, the pattern of movement, the plot, as it were, of the stories about Jesus provides the basic structure of the movement of all Christian celebrations or enactments of the practice of worship.

That pattern or movement in the stories about Jesus, that structure, functions something like a "depth grammar" in all enactments of the practice of the public worship of God in Jesus' name, by virtue of which all its culturally and theologically diverse instances bear family resemblances to one another. The varieties can be seen as dialects of a single language-family. They are quite different dialects often, but nonetheless recognizable as dialects of one family because they overlap enough so that some of the "grammar" that governs each of them is the same in all of them. That grammar is rooted in the basic patterns, the plot movements of the stories of Jesus' life, his ministry, crucifixion, and resurrection appearances read as stories of the peculiar way God makes Godself present to us. This is not only true of what we called the core of the practice of worship, that is, in the proclamation of the Word and the celebration of the sacraments. It is also true of the whole of worship in Jesus' name in what we called discipleship. It is all enacted as a response to God's presence and all seeks to be appropriate to the odd structure and movement of that presence (crucifixion and resurrection!). This is not to say that the practice of worship is always, or very often, in fact appropriate to that structure and movement. To the contrary, it is constantly faithless and in need of reform. This is only to claim that the practice constitutive of Christian congregations is a practice inherent in which are norms for its own assessment, something like a grammar common to Christian congregations.

This implies a response to the objection that the proposal to focus theological schooling through questions about congregations favors a sectarian or radically "congregationalist" view. Most Christian congregations would reject the suggestion that they are somehow identical with the church as such. No, they would say, there is "more" to the church than just our congregation. At issue is how to understand the relation between church and congregation.

Some pictures of the relation are to be rejected. Consider some possibilities: See "the church" as an abstract (theologians') ideal of which individual congregations are concrete and relatively enduring particular instances? No, because the church universal is as concretely actual as is any local congregation. See the church as an invisible reality marked by permanence, of which congregations are relatively impermanent manifestations in ecclesial "events" or "acts"? No, because congregations too are enduring realities with concrete location in physical and social space. See the church universal and local congregations related to each other as are a great commercial enterprise and its local outlets (as the Coca-Cola Company is related to local Coca-Cola bottlers and distributors worldwide)? No, because it suggests that just as no local Coca-Cola distributor is more than a small part of a greater whole, so no local congregation is more than a fragment of the universal church's reality. To the contrary, there is no reason why, were it truly faithful to its own identity, each congregation could not have and be the fullness of whatever "church" is.

Our working description of congregations provides a more fruitful way to understand the relation between particular congregations and the church. Precisely because particular congregations are constituted by their enactment of a more broadly practiced worship, theological schooling focused by questions about congregations could not be content with a sectarian attention to individual congregations. It would need to attend to the more broadly shared features of a congregation's practice of worship by *comparative* study of congregations in the same culture and cross-culturally (synchronically) and through history (diachronically). Attention to particular congregations, when they are understood in terms of the practice of the public and universally shared worship of God, could only be carried on by reference to the "greater church." As we have seen, the public character of congregations' practice of worship means that the practice of worship is always localiz*able*. It always has some concrete location in space, culture, and history. Hence congregations constituted by that practice are always concretely located socially, economically, and politically. The greater church is always actual in history only insofar as it is thus located. However, the broadly shared character of congregations' practice of worship means that the practice of worship can never be localiz*ed*. That is, it can never be simply and finally identified with any one local enactment of the practice. The enactments are all culturally and historically conditioned and relative; the practice cannot be flatly identified with any of them. The greater church, with which particular congregations are in some way "one," that is, the church "catholic" or "ecumenical," while always necessarily localizable, always present as particular congregations—though not necessarily *only* present as local congregations (whether or not it is present in other ways can remain an open question)—is never localiz*ed*, never exhaustively present as nor simply identical with a local congregation. When the public and the broadly shared characters of the practice that constitutes congregations are held together, it is clear that the proposal to focus theological schooling through questions about congregations need not imply a sectarian view of the church.

The more broadly shared character of the practice of worship also has implications regarding the subject matter of theological study. Two are evident. If congregations are constituted by the enactment of a more broadly practiced worship, then study focused by questions about congregations must locate the congregations it studies in history. It must study them diachronically or through time. Study of any particular congregation thus inescapably is study of it *in* its own tradition, in its likeness to other congregations in previous historical periods who share its basic construal of what the Christian thing is all about, what it is to understand God, and so forth (see chapter 2). At the same time study of that same congregation also involves comparing it with congregations in earlier periods whose enactments of the universally practiced worship of God are markedly different.

It is evident, secondly, that if congregations are constituted by sharing in more broadly practiced worship of God, study focused by questions about them must compare and contrast congregations that are contemporaneous. It must study them synchronically, or at the same time, in a cross-cultural way to probe the ways in which the broadly practiced worship may be enacted in quite different dialects. In short, focusing theological study by attending to congregations necessarily entails a globalization of the frame of reference of theological study.

CONGREGATIONS AS SOCIAL SPACES
AND SOCIAL FORMS

A congregation is a group that gathers to worship God "regularly enough for an indefinite period of time to have a common life in which develop intrinsic patterns of conduct, outlook and story." The congregation is a distinctive social form that the worship of God has assumed in the history of the Christian movement. As James Hopewell points out, the distinctiveness of this social form can be seen by contrasting it with other "sorts of collectivities by which humans corporately express their religion."[13] In human history, worship has often been focused by family loyalties, honoring ancestors, and ritually celebrating major moments in a family's life cycle. But "a congregation differs from a family at prayer. The local church bears a distinctive name to indicate . . . that the congregation is not synonymous with a particular bond of flesh."[14] In another social form, worship can be the celebration of the common piety of political units—a city or an empire. But, as Hopewell points out, worship in Jesus' name draws a sharp line between the congregation enacting that worship and "all bonds of compatriotism." In yet another social form, Hopewell notes, persons can gather occasionally and informally at a religious shrine, each to perform her or his own individual meritorious rituals of devotion. They may do this in support of a resident community of religious specialists, say, a congregation of monks. Or they may do it as observers of rituals actually performed by the shrine's priests and other functionaries, who guarantee ceremonial proficiency and continuity. In neither case do these worshipers communicate with each other enough to develop common patterns of outlook and story.[15] In each case, the collective is a set of simultaneous individual acts of worship. But worship in Jesus' name is the practice of a community with a common, communal identity, not an aggregate of individuals, because it is a response to the way God's presence in Jesus has made them a new extra-familial family of God's adopted "children," a new extra-national "people," a single "body."

It is abundantly clear from the history of the Christian movement that actual enactments of the practice of the worship of God in Jesus' name are constantly assimilated to one or more of these alternative social forms of worship. However, it is equally clear from the history of the reform of Christian worship that critical reflection reveals these assimilations to be inconsistent with the enactment of a much more broadly practiced worship of God "in Jesus' name." Unusually large gatherings in North American churches at Christmas and Easter tend to suggest that they are at least as much celebrations of loyalty to family and its tradition as they are response to God's peculiar ways of being present in Jesus of Nazareth. For most of European history from the emperor Constantine's embrace of Christianity onwards there has been a strong tendency to identify worship of God with loyalty to and reverence for the tradition and authorities that constitute the Holy Roman Empire, or its competing fragments in the Middle Ages, or their successor nation states, or one's home town and its familiar "way of life." From the time of martyrs during Roman imperial persecution, Christian worship has often taken the form of pilgrims' ritual devotions at shrines dedicated to persons deemed to be unusually holy in the hope that the saint would intercede with God to meet the pilgrim's individual needs, whereupon the pilgrim returns home. However, one theme the recurring reforms of Christian worship have in common is that none of these alternative social forms for the worship of God can be normative social forms. In one way or another as social forms they are inadequate to, or sometimes inconsistent with, the practice of worship of God "in Jesus' name."

We may generalize the point: A Christian congregation is a social form defined by its social space. What makes this social space distinctive is largely the medium by which members communicate with one another in the practice of worship and in the practices that are the effects of that communication. The communication takes place in various activities: preaching, praying, singing, action for the well-being of neighbors and society, educating, self-governing, and so forth. The medium in which these kinds of communication take place relies heavily on biblical texts and their metaphors and images. This is not to deny that both the social form and the social space of Christian congregations are also deeply shaped by social forms and cultural symbols prominent in the congregations' host cultures. To the contrary, one of the themes of this chapter is that theological schooling focused within the horizon of questions about congregations is inadequate *theologically* if it fails to attend as much to sociological and cultural analyses of congregations as it does to theological analyses. The point here, however, is to draw out implications of the narrower truth that a Christian congregation's social form is also shaped by its social space, which in turn is importantly and distinctively, if not exhaustively, shaped by the way biblical writings are used in the congregation's common life.

The use of these biblical materials has two types of effect. The biblical narratives and related writings are used in the activities comprising the community's common life to help shape and even transform the personal identities of the group's members. The shaping is as much a forming of their identities as agents, as embodied centers of power, albeit usually quite limited power, in a shared public realm, as it is a forming of them as patients, centers of a private inwardness or subjectivity.

At the same time, use of these biblical writings in the activities comprising the common life of the community has the effect of shaping a communal self-identity. Use of these materials helps shape relatively stable patterns of communal outlook, conduct, and narrative self-description. Among these will be relatively long-term patterns in which roles, responsibilities, authority, power, and relative status are arranged within the community's common life.

Together, these two effects mean that the social space created by the practice of the worship of God in Jesus' name is moral and even political in character. Thus a congregation is a space in which individuals' personal identities are shaped in such a fashion that they are disposed to act in characteristic ways in the public realm. And a congregation is itself a social space defined and structured by certain arrangements of responsibility, power, and status. The history of Christianity exhibits quite a variety of these arrangements of responsibility, power, and status that structure congregations' social space.[16] Some arrange responsibility, power, and status in rigorous ways so that persons' roles within the congregation are fixed for life hierarchically in a pattern that assigns different levels and degrees of status and authority to different people. Others arrange them so loosely and fluidly that there is near parity of status and power within the congregation and different people take on different responsibilities at different times. Between these two extremes still other congregations assign different responsibilities to different persons through a democratic process in which there is parity of status, but assign different sorts and amounts of power to different responsibilities. The point is that each of these is a different way in which congregations' social space may be structured as a concrete, if relatively small, political and moral reality. It has a particular social form.

An important consequence follows from this. It is inadequate to characterize a congregation simply by stressing its "intersubjectivity."

True, it *is* an intersubjective community. That is, a congregation is a community of subjects in which the consciousness of each is shaped by its relations to all the others through awareness of the others' presence. This happens by way of shared experiences of love and fear and sorrow, mediated through a shared system of symbols by which to express those experiences. But it is all of that only insofar as it is constituted by a complex network of practices in which a group of human bodily agents cooperate. As we have taken pains to point out in chapter 5, practices inherently have material bases. A Christian congregation as a distinctive social space inherently is an arrangement of very material powers. They are creaturely powers and therefore good but open to corruption. Granted, the moral and political character of the type of social space characteristic of the practice of the worship of God in Jesus' name has not always been acknowledged, to say nothing of being the object of approval or rejoicing. Nonetheless, as Wayne Meeks's research in the "social world of the Apostle Paul" tends to show, even the earliest urban Christian congregations were politically and morally structured social spaces.[17]

Two things follow of importance concerning the subject matter of theological study. On one side, study focused through questions about congregations involves theological analysis of congregations as communities of discipleship, witness, and redemptive transformation of personal identities. Central to that study is analysis of how scripture is used as "Word of God" within the communities' common life to evoke, nurture, and correct discipleship, witness, and new life. A crucial moment in that study is normative: Are some uses inappropriate to the texts themselves, and on what grounds? Are some uses suggested by the texts but not in fact practiced? Biblical studies oriented to theological questions about the nature and criteria of adequacy of congregations' common life are central to study of congregations as characterized by distinctive social space.

On the other side, attention to congregations involves the use of the human sciences to study them as distinctive social forms. If a Christian congregation is not only an intersubjective community but an interrelated set of practices, then it is materially rooted, as we have seen all practices are. Theological study focused on congregations is not just accidentally related to the things studied by sociologists, anthropologists, economists, and social psychologists; it inherently involves such matters.

The two sorts of inquiry, theological and social scientific, involve different methods. A purely sociological or anthropological study of a Christian congregation or of "the church" that purports to give a full account of what a congregation is, how and why it functions as it does, and when and why it succeeds or fails, would meet severe objections in most theological schools. All that it says may be true, but, the objection would go, its claim to give a full account of a congregation's "reality" is reductionist. It ignores the dimensions of the congregation that come to light when one thinks of its relation to God and "reduces" it to what can be studied empirically or phenomenologically. On the other hand, a purely theological study of a congregation or of "the church" that ignores its social space and social form ought to be subject to equally vigorous objection in theological schooling. A purely theological account may do full justice to those dimensions of a congregation that come to light when one considers it in its God-relatedness, but would ignore the dimensions that come to light when one considers its historical, social, and cultural location. Adequate attention to congregations necessarily involves a dialectic between the methods appropriate to both theological and social-scientific study. Neither can be "translated" into or simply identified with the other as though they were interchangeable ways of saying the same things.[18]

SUMMARY

Our proposal is that what makes a theological school theological is its overarching end of coming to understand God more truly. Because of the nature of God, however, that cannot be done directly. A variety of other matters have historically been made the direct objects of study in trust that studying them would lead indirectly to truer understanding of God. Our proposal is that what makes a theological school theological is that it seeks to understand God more truly by focusing study of these matters through questions about Christian congregations. In this chapter we have refined that proposal somewhat by exploring what constitutes a congregation. Congregations, we suggested, are constituted by enactments of a more broadly practiced public worship of God.

Exploration of how theological schooling should focus its inquiries has, in turn, highlighted subject matters that must be dealt with in theological schooling. Inasmuch as congregations are *self-defining* as groups gathering to worship God in Jesus' name, schooling focused by questions about them must attend to ecclesiological topics. For example, it must address such matters as whether faithfulness to that self-identification is a necessary condition for a group's counting as a Christian congregation, and whether groups that do not claim to worship in Jesus' name may nonetheless be said to know God and God's redemptive presence.

Inasmuch as congregations are constituted by a practice that is inherently *self-critical,* theological schooling attending to congregations must deal with both the topic of what the norms are for that critique and with the truth of the practice. To address the norms of congregational faithfulness is to do constructive dogmatic theology and moral theology. To engage in the critique itself is to do theology of culture, and to undertake "prophetic" judgment of congregations' common life.

Inasmuch as congregations are constituted by a *public* practice, theological schooling attending to congregations must therefore attend to "secular" wisdom about how the personal identities of persons engaged in public action are changed, and how the arrangements of power in a society are rearranged. And it must attend to the languages that are the medium of public discourse in congregations' host cultures.

Inasmuch as congregations are constituted by enactments of a more broadly *practiced worship,* theological schooling focused through questions about congregations must attend to their setting in time both diachronical and synchronical. That is, its attention to congregations must be both historical, placing them in the larger contexts of traditions through time, and globalized, placing them in the larger context of contemporaneous cross-cultural enactments of the same practice of worship.

Inasmuch as congregations are themselves *social spaces* with *social forms,* theological schooling focused through questions about them must attend critically to the scripture whose use creates the social space; and it must attend to the disciplines of the human sciences that provide understanding of the social forms that make congregations moral and political realities in their own right.

The proposal that has been partially elaborated in this chapter is that a theological school is a community of persons trying to understand God more truly by focusing its study of various subject matters within the horizon of questions about Christian congregations. I have suggested a way in which to understand what constitutes a Christian congregation and a way in which to identify one when it presents itself. That allowed me to show why various subject matters that ought to be studied by a theological school (e.g., Bible, Christian history, theology, psychology and sociology of religion, etc.) are best studied in their theological significance (i.e., as means to understanding God) by studying them in their relation to the common life of actual congregations. Exactly what it means to "focus study of various subject matters within the horizon of questions about Christian congregations" has *not* been explained and remains to be discussed in the following chapters. However, enough of what this proposal means by "Christian congregations" has been clarified now for us to return to the topic of a theological school itself. If the road to the universally relevant is through the concrete, then we must now ask what constitutes a theological school, what sort of social space and social form it may be, and how it is related to particular and equally concrete congregations. We turn to these questions in the next chapter. That will provide the context for turning finally in the last two chapters to what makes the school's curriculum a course of study rather than a clutch of courses, what it can do to and for its students, to and for congregations, and to and for traditions of academic research.

Notes

1. See *Building Effective Ministry: Theory and Practice in the Local Church*, ed. Carl S. Dudley (San Francisco: Harper & Row, 1983).

2. James F. Hopewell, *Congregation: Stories and Structures* (Philadelphia: Fortress Press, 1987).

3. Joseph C. Hough, Jr., and Barbara G. Wheeler, eds., *Beyond Clericalism*.

4. Cf. esp. John B. Cobb, Jr., "Ministry to the World: A New Professional Paradigm," in *Beyond Clericalism*, pp. 23–31.

5. Cf. esp. John B. Cobb, Jr., "Ministry to the World," and Marjorie Hewitt Suchocki, "Friends in the Family," in *Beyond Clericalism*, pp. 23–31 and 49–61.

6. Cf. esp. Letty Russell, "Which Congregations?" and Beverly W. Harrison, "Toward a Christian Feminist Hermeneutic for Demystifying Class Reality in Local Congregations," in *Beyond Clericalism*, pp. 31–37 and 137–151.

7. Hopewell, *Congregation*, pp. 12–13.

8. This description and following discussion grew out of my contributions to *Beyond Clericalism*, pp. 11–23, 37–49.

9. Hopewell, *Congregation*, p. 14.

10. By no means is this a peculiarly Protestant claim; cf. Karl Rahner, "Priestly Existence," in idem, *Theological Investigations,* vol. 3 (New York: Seabury Press, 1974); and Bernard Cooke, *Ministry to Word and Sacraments* (Philadelphia: Fortress Press, 1976), esp. Part 5.

11. J. A. T. Robinson, *Liturgy Coming to Life* (Philadelphia: Westminster Press, 1964).

12. See William Placher, *Unapologetic Theology: A Christian Voice in a Pluralistic Conversation* (Louisville: Westminster/John Knox Press, 1989), esp. chs. 1 and 8; George Lindbeck, *The Nature of Doctrine* (Philadelphia: Westminster Press, 1984).

13. Hopewell, *Congregation,* p. 14.

14. Ibid., p. 13.

15. Ibid., p. 15.

16. See Cooke, *Ministry to Word and Sacraments.*

17. See Wayne A. Meeks, *The First Urban Christians: The Social World of the Apostle Paul* (New Haven, Conn.: Yale University Press, 1983).

18. For the classic statement of this point, see James M. Gustafson, *Treasure in Earthen Vessels* (New York: Harper & Row, 1961).

8

A Theological School

You have been invited to share in a thought experiment about the questions, "What makes a good theological school?" and "What makes it truly theological and makes its schooling excellent?" That which ultimately makes a theological school theological and provides the criteria of its excellence as a school is not the structure of its curriculum, nor the types of pedagogical methods it employs, nor the dynamics of its common life, nor the structure of its polity, nor even the "sacred" subject matters it studies; rather it is the nature of its overarching end and the degree to which that end governs all that comprises its common life. What makes a school truly theological and what makes its schooling excellent are interrelated because both are rooted in the school's defining end.

What is that end? Conventional wisdom assumes that the defining goal of a theological school is to educate clergy for the churches, or, more broadly, to educate leadership for the churches (whether it is lay or ordained leadership is probably irrelevant). Theological schools are usually classified as "professional" schools whose overarching purpose it is to educate persons ready to fill with competence the roles of the professional clergy. That, after all, is what the denominations found and support theological schools to do. The charters of many nondenominational schools make it clear that that is what they were founded to do. True, a theological school understood on the model of paideia would not be defined by that goal; paideia aims to shape a person's identity, not to equip the person to fulfill any particular social role. However, a theological school understood on the Berlin model would necessarily be defined by the goal of educating church leadership. Schleiermacher designed that model precisely to unite a research university's *wissenschaftlich* education with education for one of society's "necessary" professions. Theological education shaped by that model, as North American theological education is today, is by definition "professional education." It is, in Edward Farley's phrase, theological education on the "clerical paradigm."[1]

The conventional view that a theological school is "theological" *because* it educates church leadership has been roundly attacked in the current conversation about theological education. Perhaps the single most dramatic and important consequence of the conversation is that the "clerical paradigm" has been thoroughly discredited. However, it is important to be clear about just what has been discredited and why. Nobody at all has denied that theological schooling can educate people for church leadership; nor has anybody denied that church leaders should undergo theological schooling.[2] Rather, two points have been made.

The first is that it is disastrous to *define* theological schooling as the task of educating church leadership because it distorts and finally destroys theology.[3] If what makes a theological school "theological" is that it educates persons to fill the roles comprising the profession of church leadership, then "theology" becomes a name for bodies of theory that are applied by religious specialists in the practice of church leadership. Since the practice of that profession is comprised of a large number of quite different types of functions, the sorts of relevant theory will need to be diverse also. "Theology" is fragmented. It becomes a collective name for an array of types of theory whose only connection to one another is the fact that they each bear on one or another of the functions that comprise the professional role of church leaders. Furthermore, "theology" is now defined, not by reference to its ultimate subject (God), but by reference to socially defined roles. On the clerical paradigm, the course of study in theological schools becomes fragmented and, further, is no longer "theological" in any fundamental and organizing way.

The second line of critique of the "clerical paradigm" is that it simply has not worked.[4] When theological schooling is *defined* as preparation for filling the functions that make up the role of professional church leadership, graduates turn out to be incapable of nurturing and guiding congregations as worshiping communities, the health of whose common life depends on the quality of the theology that is done there. The graduates may in the short run have the relevant skills to help congregations organize themselves to engage in the several practices that comprise their common life (religious education, worship, pastoral care, social action, gathering and maintaining resources, etc.), to nurture and sustain them in those practices, and to grow as organizations. However, those skills tend to become outdated fairly quickly as cultural and social changes occur. More seriously, theological schooling defined and organized as preparation for filling a set of ministerial functions unavoidably simply omits to cultivate in future church leaders the *conceptual* capacities they need in order to understand and to engage in those functions as *theological* practices, that is, as practices requiring critical self-reflection about the truth and Christian adequacy of what is actually said and done in the congregations' current engagement in the practices that constitute them *as* Christian congregations. Educated on the clerical paradigm, church leaders end up being ill-equipped to provide the most important sort of leadership worshiping communities require.

If conventional wisdom's answer is inadequate, what should we say is the overarching goal that makes a theological school "theological"? My proposal has been that a theological school is a group of persons whose overarching end is to understand God more truly. We have been elaborating that thesis by moving crabwise. God cannot be studied directly, so understanding of God must come through a focus on something else whose study is believed to lead to better understanding of God. Our first sideways step was to refine our thesis by making it more concrete: The overarching end is to try to understand God more truly by focusing on study through the lens of questions about Christian congregations. Just what is meant by "focusing through the lens of questions about congregations" has not been explained yet. The next sidestep was to propose that congregations be understood as sets of social practices (where "practice" was defined in a somewhat technical way) governed by the worship of God. A third sideways step was to propose further that this worship is practiced very widely and publicly as discipleship in response to God's odd ways of being present.

With this elaboration in hand we can now take one more crabwise step and explore our thesis' implications about what makes a theological school theological and what makes it excellent schooling.

Hence in this chapter I will develop a proposal about what constitutes a theological school. The discussion parallels the proposal in the last chapter about what constitutes a congregation. The relation between the two, however, and in particular the meaning of the proposal that a theological school's study be focused through the lens of questions about Christian congregations, will not be developed until the next two chapters. In this chapter we will focus solely on the notion of a theological school, on what makes it a school, and on what its being specifically a theological school implies for its being a school.

In doing this it will prove useful to use the language of "practices" and "acts" that we also used to describe Christian congregations. Let us consider a theological school as a complex set of interrelated practices, in the sense of "practice" outlined in chapter 6. The set will include practices of teaching and learning, practices of research, practices of governance of the school's common life, practices having to do with maintenance of the school's resources, practices in which persons are selected for the student body and for the faculty, and practices in which students move through and then are deemed to have completed a course of study.

My proposal is that what unifies this set of practices, making them genuinely "theological" practices and providing criteria of excellence, is that they are all done in service of one end: To understand God more truly by focusing on study about, against, and for Christian congregations.

The point of describing a theological school in terms of practices is to stress that the search for true understanding of God is not a free-floating "educational process" that is relatively independent of a material base and independent of arrangements of social, economic, and political power. Rather, understanding God is the end to which are ordered practices that, as we have seen in chapter 6, themselves inescapably have material bases. Furthermore, they are practices that are inherently institutionalized to some degree, that entail some structural and lasting arrangement of various sorts of social power. As a set of more or less coherent cooperative activities, a school has a social space marked by intersubjectivity. However, that social space is necessarily defined, as was that of congregations, by a social form that is itself moral and political. The school is itself a *polis*, or at any rate a crossroads hamlet. The persons who share in its intersubjectivity have different roles to play, different responsibilities, different types and degrees of authority, different degrees of status and power. Moreover, the school as an institutionalized set of practices is itself a center of (usually very minor) economic, social, and political power in a larger host society. It enjoys some particular social location within that society, and at least in that immediate vicinity fills some social roles in which it exercises what social power it has. "Theological education" is not a process that is only accidentally and externally related to social realities. It is not merely "contained" or "embodied" in institutions, a ghost in administrative machinery. Nor is it simply "housed" in certain neighborhoods and "contexted" in certain social "matrices," like a chemical reaction in a test tube. "Theological education" is an aspect of a theological school, abstracted from the school's concrete practices which are inherently materially based, institutionalized, and socially situated.

In short, as we were at pains to show in chapters 1 and 2, theological schooling is always concrete. It will be seriously misunderstood if it is analyzed in a way that leads us to treat it as something free-floating, abstracted from the factors that make it concrete. The advantage of using the language of "practices" and "actions" is that it highlights that concreteness and keeps it central to reflection on theological schooling.

WHAT MAKES THE SCHOOL "THEOLOGICAL"

What makes a theological school "theological"? We can elaborate our thesis now: (A theological school is a group of people who engage in a set of social practices whose overarching end is to understand God more truly.) The practices are very diverse. They are not only practices of teaching and learning, but also practices of raising funds and maintaining the school's resources; not only practices of governing various aspects of the school's common life, but also practices of various kinds of research; practices not only of assessing students and when they should be deemed to have completed their courses of study, but also of assessing faculty and judging when they should be promoted and when terminated; and so on. These practices are related to one another in very complicated and often very confusing ways. However, they all are ultimately ordered to the same end: the understanding of God. That is what makes the set of them theological. They all somehow, at one remove or another, have to do with the *logos* of *theos,* the understanding of God.

What does that involve? It will be especially helpful in unpacking what that involves to use the analysis of "understanding" we sketched in chapter 6. There we stressed that coming to understand something generally involves disciplined and critical deepening of certain abilities which are guided by interests that are themselves socioculturally situated. Our concern here is with understanding God, and the same three factors will be involved.

Conceptual Growth

A theological school is a community of persons trying to deepen certain abilities or capacities specifically in regard to God. They are engaged in a kind of growth. What sort of growth? The growth this community seeks is growth in its abilities or capacities to apprehend God's presence. God is not to hand. God is not immediately available to be understood. Indeed, we cannot hope to comprehend God. At best we can hope to apprehend God's presence precisely in the odd ways in which God is present.

In one sense of the term, we can say that this community is engaged in *conceptual* growth. Consider Charles Wood's characterization of concepts: "Concepts are instruments of understanding, opening up the possibility of new sorts of discernment and response. Generally speaking, a concept is a particular ability or capacity (or complex thereof), ordinarily related to language."[5]

Concepts are "instruments of understanding." Coming to understand something is a matter of enriching one's repertoire of relevant concepts. One comes to understand by learning concepts, by conceptual growth. But what sort of growth is "conceptual growth"? What are concepts, that they can "grow" in us or that we can "grow" in respect to them? In chapter 6, in my discussion of "understanding,"[6] I argued the view that to learn a concept is to acquire a capacity or capacities to do something or a capacity or capacities to act in a certain way; I shall follow that advice here.

Four features of what it is to learn a concept were stressed: We show whether we have learned the relevant concepts or not, whether we understand or not, by our actions relative to what we seek to understand. For example, I show I understand or fail to understand the sign "Keep off the grass" by my behavior, both in regard to where I walk or ride my bicycle and in regard to my talk when questioned about the sign and my behavior; I may even show my understanding by getting *onto* the grass, depending on what I say when the inconsistency between my act and the sign is remarked. Learning a concept involves, furthermore, undergoing a relevant discipline. Moreover, learning a concept is usually a matter of degree. We understand "more or less" and understanding can often "deepen" by acquiring additional capacities through relevant disciplines. Finally, learning some concepts is more existentially involving than is learning other concepts. That is, the discipline involved in learning some concepts shapes our very identities as persons, whereas the discipline through which other concepts are learned does not. Consider the difference between acquiring the abilities involved in playing chess and the abilities involved in faithful friendship; acquiring the concept "faithful" shapes one's personal identity in a way that acquiring the concept "checkmate" does not.

The point to be made, then, is that as a community of persons that seeks to understand God truly, a theological school is a community seeking to learn concepts, that is, to grow in abilities and capacities relative to God. Doing so will involve certain disciplines. It may sometimes involve shaping learners' personal identities. Acquiring the relevant abilities and capacities will always be a matter of degree. Whether or to what degree they have understood, that is, have acquired the relevant abilities, will be shown by relevant things they say or, in some cases, by the ways in which they act. As the discussion in chapter 6 suggested, none of this is unique to theological schools and the learning that goes on there. Coming to understand anything in any context involves this sort of disciplined growing in abilities and capacities. However, it is helpful to see a theological school as a community of persons engaged in acquiring particular abilities and capacities.

What sorts of abilities and capacities? Concepts are instruments of understanding "opening up the possibility of new sorts of discernment and response." In seeking to understand God more truly, then, a theological school seeks to help persons acquire abilities and capacities that make possible new sorts of *discernment* and *response* regarding God. What sorts of concepts are these?

First of all, "God" itself. From Søren Kierkegaard comes the dark but intriguing remark that "God is not a name but a concept."[7] "God" is not in the ordinary sense either a common or a proper name.[8] We use "dog" as a common name either to denote a type of mammal, a class of items in the universe, or one individual of that class ("the dog"). We may use "Muffin" as the proper name to denote a unique individual of the class. But we cannot use "God" to denote either a class of items in the universe or any individual instance of the class. Nor can we use "God" as the proper name of a unique item in the universe. God simply isn't to hand that way in the universe. God is not an item on the inventory list of the cosmos. "God" is not correctly used as a name.

Rather, coming to understand God involves two things. It involves receiving capacities to attend to and apprehend God as and when God will be present; it involves, that is, receiving capacities to *discern* God's presence. At the same time it involves receiving capacities to *respond* to that presence by understanding everything else, other persons, our shared natural and social contexts, and especially ourselves in distinctive ways, namely, in relation to God.

To understand God more truly is thus to undergo rich and complex conceptual growth, growth in a rich mix of capacities to discern and respond in various ways to God and to everything else as related to God. Consider some examples: Understanding God involves growth in one's grasp of the concept "glory," the capacity to discern the power inherent in God's presence; but that is inseparable from, though not the same as, growth in one's grasp of the concept "awe," a capacity to respond appropriately to that power. Correlatively, understanding God involves growth in one's grasp of the concept "contingency," the capacity to discern one's own, and everything else's, radical dependence on God's power; but that is inseparable from, though not the same thing as, growth in one's grasp of the concept "thanks," a capacity to respond appropriately to that contingency. Or: Understanding God involves growth in one's grasp of the concept "wrath," the capacity to discern the judgment inherent in God's presence; but that is inseparable from, though not the same as, growth in one's grasp of the concept "guilt," a capacity to respond appropriately to that judgment. Correlatively, understanding God involves growth in one's grasp of the concept "fault," the capacity to discern one's own, and everything else's, brokenness and deformity before God; but that is inseparable from, though not the same thing as, growth in one's grasp of the concept "repentance," a capacity to respond appropriately to that fault.

Or: Understanding God involves growth in one's grasp of the concept "grace," the capacity to discern the healing and liberation from fault inherent in God's presence; but that is inseparable from, though not the same thing as, growth in one's grasp of the concept "joy," a capacity to respond appropriately to that healing and liberation. Correlatively, understanding God involves growth in one's grasp of the concept "saved," the capacity to discern one's own, and everything else's, healing and liberation from fault; but that is inseparable from, though not the same as, growth in one's grasp of the concept "free," a capacity to respond appropriately to that salvation. To understand God truly involves learning an indefinitely large network of concepts that open up the possibility of new sorts of discernment and response. To seek to understand God more truly is to undergo growth in an enormously rich array of interrelated abilities and capacities in regard to ourselves, other persons, and our shared natural and social contexts, all as related to God.

A concept is an instrument of understanding, "a particular ability or capacity (or complex thereof), ordinarily related to language." The discernment and response to God and ourselves that certain concepts open up are always mediated. They are ordinarily mediated by language. That is, the concepts that open up the possibility of discernment and response to God are abilities and capacities ordinarily related to language. However, the qualification "ordinarily" is very important. It is difficult to be very specific or clear about this, for it is a suggestion that raises enormously complex problems; but it is possible in some cases that the facilities relevantly associated with particular conceptual competencies are musical, painterly, graphic, or mutely behavioral facilities rather than verbal facility. Or perhaps we should say that "language" needs to be understood broadly as any medium of communication, not only speaking or writing. What is important is that use of some specific, concrete facility mediates the opening up of the possibility of new discernment and response to God.

In Christian communities discernment and response to God is mediated in a variety of ways—by ritual action, normative patterns of behavior, exemplary persons, appropriate images and music, and above all written and spoken words. That is to say: in Christian communities, persons' conceptual competencies to discern and respond to God are abilities and capacities related to the facility to participate in ritual action, to behave according to norms, to attend to exemplary persons, to make and rightly to see appropriate images (very often of exemplary persons), to make and rightly to hear appropriate kinds of music, and so forth. However, the rituals, norms, and criteria of exemplariness and appropriateness are finally rooted in texts comprising the communities' scripture. More exactly, they are rooted in those texts as they have been conventionally *used* over long periods of time within the communities' common life; they are rooted in scripture-in-tradition.[9]

Some of those texts are narratives, but the greater part of them are laws, oracles, letters, and nonnarrative poetry. However, central among the traditional ways in which these texts have been used in the communities' common life has been the placement of nonnarrative materials within the context of the narratives, the interpretation of the significance of the nonnarrative materials by their attachment to important moments in the narratives. Thus legal texts from Deuteronomy, Exodus, and Leviticus are located in the context of narratives about God's convenant relationship with Israel and are construed as explanations of the practical implications of who Israel is in relation to God. Prophets' oracles are located in the context of narratives describing how God is related to Israel, and who Israel is—and is failing to be—in relation to God, and construed as announcements of promise and not simply as predictions of doom. New Testament letters are put into the context of synoptic Gospel narratives about Jesus and construed as comment on those narratives drawing practical implications regarding who the church is and what appropriate response to God's presence is. Nonnarrative Psalms are placed in the context of narratives about Jesus and are construed as expressions of his relation to God and God's relation to him. The narratives, for their part, are traditionally used as descriptions of who God is and who the people of Israel are in relation to God, who Jesus is and who the church is in relation to Jesus.[10] Ultimately, then, in Christian communities persons' conceptual competencies to discern and respond to God are abilities and capacities related to facility in using scriptural narratives as descriptions of God, Jesus, themselves, and the world in all their interrelations.

This has important implications regarding the concepts that are instruments of Christians' understanding of God (grace and joy; saved and free; wrath and guilt; fault and repentance; glory and awe; contingency and thanks; and the like, including the concept "God" itself). The relevant abilities and capacities need to be disciplined in quite particular ways. Many of these concepts (all of them, some theologians have argued) are given distinctive shape and content by scriptural narratives used as descriptions of who God is and who Jesus is in relation to God. The structure and movement of these narratives tend to shape the ways in which communities of Christians discern God's presence and respond to it in thought and word, affect and action. Thus, for example, what they learn to discern as the graciousness of God's presence is determined by stories about God's liberation of Israel from Egypt at the exodus, by Hosea's prophetic likening of God's relation to Israel to a lover's forgiving love for a faithless spouse, by Isaiah's prophetic celebration of God's return of Israel to its homeland from Babylonian exile, and most decisively by narratives about Jesus' crucifixion and resurrection.

It is not as though there were something like a generic concept of grace of which Christians simply use a variant. The situation is more particularist than that. There is a range of concepts of God's grace, wrath, glory, and the like, of human joy, guilt, awe, and the like, that are characteristically and particularly (though not necessarily uniquely) Christian. One does not grow conceptually in the ways needed to discern and respond to God simply by acquiring abilities and capacities related to "grace," "wrath," and "glory," and the like, as they are generally used in ordinary language in one's society or as they may be generally used in the various world religions. Christianly speaking, one grows conceptually by having one's abilities and capacities in relation to language—and therewith to ritual action, normative patterns of behavior, exemplary persons, music, art, etc.—disciplined by just *these* biblical narratives. To be sure, one brings concepts learned in one's host society and culture *to* this disciplining. Moreover, knowing other religious traditions and key concepts in them that are like—sometimes very like—key Christian concepts is enormously helpful in clarifying the Christian concepts (and vice versa). Characteristically Christian conceptual capacities may or may not overlap, one by one, in one way or another, with concepts other groups have. However, nothing but confusion is generated by assuming that they are simply variations of generic concepts.

As a community aiming to understand God more truly, then, a theological school is a community engaged in conceptual growth. That is growth in certain abilities and capacities—in regard to a variety of matters, but centrally in regard to language—that mediate discernment and response to God. What needs to be stressed is that such conceptual growth is a matter of degree. It is not growth from "no concept" to "having a concept." After all, one enters into the process already in possession of a rich array of conceptual capacities. The growth is more a matter of redefining, deepening, complexifying, noticing distinctions but also noticing overlaps in concepts called for in differing contexts, among concepts already learned.

This growth is a matter of degree in two ways. First of all it is a matter of degree how deeply scriptural narratives discipline one's capacities in regard to how one speaks and acts, how one takes oneself and one's neighbors and the shared world, all in relation to God. Borrowing a suggestion by George Lindbeck, we might say that it is a matter of the degree to which one's speech and action are Christianly "grammatical."[11]

The conceptual growth in which a theological school is engaged is a matter of degree in a second way. Some concepts, we noted in reflections on "understanding" in chapter 6, are more existentially significant than others. Learning them usually involves some shaping of one's life, some forming of one's personal identity. The concept "love," in contradistinction to the concept "infatuation," is an obvious example. Infatuations simply happen to people. One learns the concept, that is, the capacities involved, by having it happen to one. It may throw one's emotional life into turmoil for a while. But learning the concept "infatuation" does not of itself tend to deepen people. Learning the concept "love," however, learning the abilities and capacities needed to love someone over an extended period of time through a variety of circumstances, involves shaping, often deepening and changing, one's very identity.

As we noted earlier, persons appear to have the ability to undergo this sort of shaping in an "as if" mode. It is as though they can imagine what it would be like for them to undergo such a shaping of their own identities, imagine what it would be like to be "that sort of person" so vividly that they can grow conceptually in the requisite ways but entirely in the "pretend" mode. They do not simply grow in their abilities to talk about the concept in question; but neither do they appropriate it in such a way that learning it actually shapes their own personal identities. Either way, whether authentically or in an "as if" mode, growth in regard to some concepts can be a matter of degree, namely, the degree to which the growth also involves an actual or imaginable change in the learner's personal identity.

Guiding Interests

We are developing the suggestion that what makes a theological school "theological" is that it is a group of people who engage in a set of social practices whose overarching end is to understand God truly by exploring what is involved in trying to *understand* God. So far we have elaborated the claim that understanding God Christianly involves conceptual growth. Conceptual growth is growth in certain abilities and capacities to discern and respond to God and is disciplined by scriptural narratives. However, as we noted in the discussion of understanding in chapter 6, our abilities and capacities are always guided by certain interests. In regard to understanding God, what kinds of interests? What interests drive a theological school's effort more truly to understand God?

Descriptively speaking, they are an enormous variety. Persons come into a theological school with interests ranging from mild curiosity about God, through the passion to save one's own soul, to an intense longing to right injustices with God's help, to (very rarely!) a wholly self-indifferent intensity of adoration of God for God's own sake. However, God is not an item on the inventory list of the universe and cannot be understood the way such items may be. To understand God is, at best, to have the capacities and abilities needed to apprehend God as (or: "if and when") God is present. These include capacities for loyalty and trust, for living out of another's promises, for joy in another's reality for its own sake. In short, they include above all capacities for faith, hope, and love. These are abilities and capacities that must be guided by interests in *God's* own peculiar ways of being present, rather than be guided by interests in God's solving our problems or saving us from our oppression. Those are the normative (as opposed to descriptive) interests that must drive a theological school's effort to understand God.

As we have seen, such capacities are existentially very demanding, whether acquired authentically or "as if." Acquiring them normally involves deep shaping of persons' lives. This means that either the interests people bring to theological schooling will undergo significant change, or not much specifically theological schooling will occur. Detached interests requiring no existentially significant conceptual growth will be under pressure to give way to existentially shaping conceptual growth. Interests in God as useful to achieving personal wholeness, even of the most "spiritual" sort, and interests in God as necessary for social justice and emancipation, even the most urgent cases, will be under pressure to surrender pride of place to apparently "irrelevant" interests in God that take the form of joy in and celebration of the odd ways God is present, for their own sake.

The capacities needed to apprehend God must be guided by interests in God's peculiar ways of being present and by God's idiosyncratic reality, not by persons' interests in realizing or fulfilling themselves; but the shaping and transforming of persons' identities this involves will in fact also bring with them movement toward fulfillment of their humanity. The conceptual growth, that is, growth in the relevant capacities, needed to apprehend God must be guided by interests in God rather than interests in God's solving persons' problems or liberating them from their bondage; but that does not exclude such interests. To the contrary, precisely *because* of the idiosyncratic reality of God and God's peculiar way of being present, interests in liberation from oppression, realization of our full humanity, and the righting of injustice are mandated as an integral part of interests in God. They are not simply inferences or inevitable consequences of interests in God for God's own sake; they are an inherent and integral part of proper interests in God. They are interests relevant to understanding God, however, because of *how* God is present to be apprehended and not because they are morally admirable and compelling interests—although they are certainly that also—that persons bring with them *to* the effort as a theological school to understand God truly.

Situated Interests

Like any effort to understand, a theological school's effort to understand God is a matter of conceptual growth guided by certain interests that may themselves be transformed in the process, and like any effort to understand, those guiding interests are themselves socioculturally situated. What does that imply regarding a theological school?

Consider the school as a community of persons. The persons who make up this community each have distinctive personal identities deeply shaped by the social, political, and economic location of their families of origin and the communities in which they were nurtured and educated. In particular they will, by the accidents of personal history, if by nothing else, have been located on one side or the other of social and economic conflicts that have an extended history and are broadly systemic to their society. As we pointed out earlier, this situatedness inevitably will shape their understanding of themselves, their neighbors, larger social realities, and, among other matters, God.

Beyond that, a theological school will as such be itself a microculture. It will itself have its own ethos rooted in its unique history and intellectual and cultural traditions and in the ways in which economic and political power are distributed and managed within its common life. Different members of the community will have different locations within this society. Sometimes the distinctions among locations will be distinctly and formally drawn: staff vs. professional academics; students vs. both of the above; tenured vs. nontenured faculty; some or all of the above vs. the administration, and so forth. Sometimes the distinctions will be wholly informal and implicit but nonetheless socially significant within that tiny culture.

The fact that the interests guiding a theological school's efforts to understand God are socially and culturally situated has two main consequences for all efforts to understand God. It means, first, that the understanding of God that persons in a theological school come to have is always concrete. Its concreteness is in large part a function of the community's shared sociocultural location. This community is not alone in seeking to understand God. Innumerable other individuals and communities of persons are also seeking to understand God. In every case, the understanding is concrete. Indeed, the deeper the understanding is, the more concrete it is. For, as we have just seen, the capacities and abilities involved in apprehending God's presence are existentially significant. Acquiring them involves shaping of persons' identities. The identities being shaped are precisely personal identities constituted in large part by their sociocultural situatedness. *That,* in all its intersubjectivity and sociality and relative freedom, is what is quite concretely shaped. This concreteness inevitably means differentiation among various communities' (in this case, theological schools, but the point is not limited to schools) understanding of God. There is an inescapable pluralism of understandings of God. It threatens to make various "understandings" of God both mutually exclusive and mutually unintelligible.

The second consequence of the situatedness of a theological school's guiding interests is this: It means that any given concrete understanding of God is open to the suspicion of being ideological. That is, it is open to the suspicion of being biased in a way that not only reflects persons' sociocultural situatedness (that was the point of the previous paragraph), but beyond that *obscures* the ways in which they benefit from social and cultural privilege. An understanding of God characteristically is ideological in this way when it suggests that the injustice from which some suffer and others benefit is not evil at all but rather is divinely sanctioned. The fact that interest in God's idiosyncratic reality and peculiar ways of being present are situated means, in short, that the conceptual growth they guide is always open to the suspicion of being in bad faith, of being more of an interest in using God for our own purposes than an interest in apprehending God for the sake of apprehending God.

Concreteness and the suspicion of ideology are the main consequences of the situatedness of the interests guiding a theological school's efforts to understand God; but the fact that these socioculturally situated interests guide efforts to understand precisely *God* brings countervailing consequences. God is not on the inventory list of the universe, but social, political and economic powers and their arrangements are, and so are our locations within them. Those powers, capable of indefinitely various arrangements and interrelationships, are part and parcel of our concrete finitude. They are inherent in what it means for *us* to be items on the universe's inventory list. In traditional theological terminology, concrete finitude was called "creatureliness." To say that God is not on the cosmic inventory list, while we are, is a wholly negative remark; but to say we are on that list as "creatures" is to say that for all the differences between us and God, God is positively related to us: Creator to creatures. That is one of the peculiar ways in which God is present to us. To be concretely finite is no predicament we should wish to escape, no bondage from which to yearn a liberation; it is simply not to be God.

In our creatureliness our apprehension of God is always concrete, and so always situated and so always partial, but never exclusive. If our efforts to understand God are guided by interests in God's peculiar ways of being present for their own sake, then apprehending God present as Creator requires the capacity to be in constant intellectually empathic conversation with others in their concrete—and therewith creaturely—understandings of God. That the guiding interests are interests in God for God's sake means that the inescapable pluralism of our understandings of God bring with them a mandate to enter into others' understanding and share ours with them. That countervails what would otherwise be the tendency of our situatedness not simply to pluralize, but to fracture our efforts to understand God into mutually exclusive, mutually unintelligible "understandings."

We saw that the situatedness of interests guiding a theological school's efforts to understand God makes that understanding not only concrete but also open to the suspicion of being ideological. The fact that these socially located interests guide efforts to understand precisely God brings a second consequence that countervails, though can not completely eliminate, the suspicion of ideology. Theologically speaking, ideology is a form of idolatry. It is false worship because it is worship of something that *is* an item in the cosmos. To say that God is not an item in the cosmos is a wholly negative remark; but to say, in traditional theological terminology, that one of the peculiar ways God is present to that cosmos is as the Holy One is to say something positive. Indeed, it is to make two interconnected remarks: God's presence both relativizes the importance of everything in the cosmos and judges everything in the cosmos that absolutizes itself. As the Holy One, God alone is sacred and deserving of worship. To treat any item in the universe, including status quo power arrangements and "understandings" of God, as in some way "absolute" or inherently "sacred" is idolatry. In short, the presence of God means criticism and unmasking of ideology. Any effort to understand God truly that is guided by an interest in the peculiar ways in which God is present involves acquiring capacities for critique of falsity, including the falsity of ideology. For all of their being situated, interests guiding the effort to understand God have consequences that work to countervail the tendencies of situatedness to distort understanding.

We have been elaborating what is involved in saying that a theological school is a community of persons trying to understand God truly. The general point has been that to understand God involves developing a range of capacities and abilities to apprehend God. Three points emerged: (a) Cultivating these abilities is a kind of conceptual growth that requires disciplining. (b) These abilities are guided by interests in God's peculiar ways of being present, interests in them for their own sake rather than for their moral, therapeutic, or redemptive consequences. Above all, these abilities are guided by interest in truth and require rigorous testing as to their truthfulness. (c) Because these interests are socioculturally situated they are diversely concrete, threatening to fragment "understandings" of God, and they are open to the suspicion of ideological bias; but because they are interests in *God* the capacities they guide also require cultivation of capacities for conversation with other concrete understandings and capacities for critique of ideological self-deceptions.

We need now to turn from reflections on the overarching goal of a theological school (i.e., to understand God truly) which makes it "theological," to explore the implications of that goal for what makes a school the particularly concrete thing it is. The question will be, does having the goal to understand God entail particular things for a school's institutional reality? Before we do, however, we ought to raise a question about the applicability of this proposal to theological schools located on different roads at their intersection with the Berlin Turnpike.

In chapter 2 we traced four different Christian traditions regarding what it is to understand God: understanding God by, respectively, the way of contemplation, the way of discursive reasoning, the way of the affections, and the way of action. Does the proposal sketched here about a theological school's understanding God tend to privilege some of these four over the others? Not necessarily.

Admittedly, by stressing the relation between understanding and abilities, this proposal seems to favor the way of action interrelated with the way of discursive reasoning. After all, abilities and capacities are abilities and capacities to *do* certain things. And it is in relation to the doing that one makes reasoned judgments about what is appropriate to do.

But note: This does not of itself exclude either contemplative understanding or affective understanding of God. Everything depends on what sorts of "doing" are in question. *That* has not been predetermined by construing "understanding God" in terms of cultivating abilities and capacities in relation to God. Conventional contrasts between action and "passive," "inward" contemplation are ruled out by our concepts of action and practice. Without further qualification, the capacities cultivated in theological schooling could just as well be capacities for "doing" contemplation or capacities for specific affections as they could be capacities for intentional bodily action and discursive reasoning.

What this chapter's construal of "understanding God" does require is that the capacities are capacities for what is in principle *public* action. These capacities are not primarily private phenomena, present to subjects' inwardness and secondarily and only accidentally related to outward and public behavior. Rather, they are dispositions for public actions—perhaps contemplative practices, perhaps discursive reasoning employing a publicly shared language, perhaps physical expressions of emotions employing culturally conventional facial expressions or bodily movement, perhaps intentional bodily action (as we have noted, just which of these public actions has not been specified). Of course, most such public action can be suppressed or distorted. We can disguise our feelings, contemplate motionlessly and silently, reason voicelessly, act indirectly and misleadingly or not at all. Nonetheless, these are all suppressions or distortions of enactments of certain capacities. They are not the failure of private phenomena to find adequate public expressions, nor are they private "causes" failing to have their usual public "effects." The capacities and abilities for apprehending God are precisely dispositions for certain *public* actions and cannot be defined independently of those actions.

WHAT MAKES THE SCHOOL "CONCRETE"

I have been explicating what a theological school is in parallel with the way I explicated what a Christian congregation is. Just as a congregation may be seen as a set of social practices, so a theological school is best seen in its concrete particularity if it too is taken as a set of social practices. What constitutes a Christian congregation, we urged, is the practice of the public worship of God in Jesus' name. All the other practices that comprise the common life of a congregation are governed by and ordered to this broadly understood worship. So too, we have urged, all the practices comprising a theological school are governed by and ordered to one overarching end: to understand God truly. That is what unifies it.

There is an important dissimilarity between the two, however. The worship that unifies a congregation is a practice; but the aim to understand God truly that unifies a theological school is not itself a practice. It is a goal to which a number of quite different types of practices are ordered. We can distinguish at least four types.

There are practices of teaching and learning through which conceptual growth takes place. Some concern abilities and capacities that are normally acquired, as in classical paideia, through the practice of critical and dialectical discussion of texts. Others concern abilities and capacities normally acquired, as in classical *Wissenschaft,* through the practice of supervised research. Some concern abilities and capacities normally acquired by reflective participation in practices that comprise other quite different institutions, such as hospitals, congregations, agencies providing assistance to the disadvantaged, and the like. All these practices of teaching and learning are constitutive of a *school*, but no one of them alone is.

Secondly, these practices of teaching and learning each require distinctive sorts of social space. Familiar examples are the seminar, the lecture, the conference about a research project, the practicum concerning a "field placement," solitude in which to read, reflect, and write. Accordingly, a theological school will also embrace practices by which these social spaces are created and maintained. These include practices concerning the regular scheduling of the community's time and conventions governing the patterns of relationship, mutual expectations, and responsibilities between students and teachers. Practices of teaching and learning and the practices that maintain the social spaces that learning and teaching create all require a variety of kinds of material support. Persons need to be housed and fed. Collections of books and research materials need to be housed and kept available. Salaries have to be paid. Clearly a third type of practice comprising a theological school consists of practices by which the school's material resources are maintained.

Manifestly, all of this requires governance. Hence, fourth, a theological school will embrace practices that give it social form. It will have a polity. It will institutionalize practices by which to select who participates in teaching and learning and by which to hold them accountable for the relative excellence with which they engage in those practices. It will institutionalize practices by which the routines and conventions of its social spaces are administered. And it will institutionalize practices by which its resources are gathered, maintained, expended responsibly, and replenished.

What makes a theological school concrete is the fact that the practices that comprise it are not only institutionalized but have material bases and sociocultural location. In our reflection on the notion of a social practice in chapter 6 we noted that all practices are inherently and inescapably concrete in this way, that is, institutionalized, materially based, and socioculturally located. It is not simply the case that, as we noted above, the persons engaged in a theological school's quest to understand God truly are driven by interests that are located socially and culturally. It is also the case that the school *as a school* is concrete in this way. We must ask, therefore, what implications the school's being "theological," that is, having the overarching end to understand God, has for the institutionalization, material bases, and social and cultural locatedness that make it concrete.

Power Inside

A theological school has some sort of polity, some institutionalized way of governing its affairs. Obviously, if its excellence in schooling depends on all its practices being governed by its overarching goal to understand God truly, then that end must govern the school's governance practice also. This is not to suggest that some one governance pattern, or some small set of such patterns, is manifestly dictated by adopting the goal to understand God.

Historically there have been a variety of polities in theological schools in North America. Protestant "freestanding" seminaries are often officially governed by a board of trustees. They are trustees of a corporation that legally owns the school. Some of these boards are entirely free of ecclesiastical control and appoint their own successors. In other cases there are various checks and balances between boards of trustees and governing bodies of denominations with which the schools are associated. Typically, the board of trustees of a school of this type appoints a president of the school, who is charged not only with articulating a vision of how this particular school in all its concreteness, given its theological and cultural history, its present social location and responsibilities mandated by charter and trustees, can best pursue its overarching goal, but also with finding ways to keep that vision so vividly alive that it shapes how the school actually enacts the practices that comprise its common life. Furthermore, the president is charged with administering the school according to broad policies established by the board and, in concert with the board, with fund-raising, maintaining the school's property, and the like. There is a great deal of variation among schools of this type regarding the role, responsibilities, and authority of faculty in the governance of the school. The variety ranges from cases in which faculty elect some members of the board of trustees from among their number, to cases in which faculty as a group is formally charged with certain responsibilities (say, nominating new faculty, or establishing policies governing the academic program of the school), to cases in which faculty effectively have neither responsibility, authority, nor power in the school's polity.

There is another type of school which is legally wholly owned and operated by a church judicatory. Roman Catholic diocesan schools and schools operated by religious orders are most often of this type. Protestant schools of this type have not been unknown. If they have boards of trustees, their responsibilities and authority are usually limited to fund-raising and management of the school's physical resources.

A few theological schools are organic parts of universities. Their polity is simply part of the polity of the university as a whole. Typically, the university's board of trustees, or its functional equivalent, appoints a dean as the chief executive officer of the theological school. With the deans of other schools in the university, the dean is accountable to the university's president. Characteristically, faculty play a fairly large role in the governance of such schools' academic affairs and common life. In all cases in which faculty are formally charged with certain responsibilities and have specified authority and power in the school's polity, there is a good bit of difference regarding the relative roles of tenured and nontenured faculty. In some cases faculty roles are entirely reserved for tenured faculty, in others all faculty take part equally.

The issue is not whether one or another of these polities, or some other not yet devised, is in closer accord with the overarching goal that makes a theological school *theological,* namely, to understand God truly. Rather, the question is this: Does the school's overarching goal to understand God truly have any implications for the way the school is governed by *any* of these polities? Repeatedly we have seen that the effort to understand God (or anything else) must be self-critical. That is a criterion of excellence in schooling. Any polity must be so designed as to hold practices of teaching and learning accountable in this regard. However, the obverse of this is that the effort to understand God must be a genuine effort. A test of its genuineness is, in part, its freedom to embrace differences of judgment and even the freedom to be mistaken. That too is a criterion of excellence in schooling. Accordingly, it is a criterion that any polity by which a school is governed must be designed to meet.

Clearly, the issue we are discussing is the one usually characterized as "academic freedom." That is a perfectly accurate and proper characterization. As we saw in chapter 4, academic freedom is a central Enlightenment idea and was institutionalized in the design of the University of Berlin. The slogans were "freedom to teach" and "freedom to learn," polemically resisting the imposition of constraints by either church or state. Insofar as North American theological schools are also located somewhere on the Berlin Turnpike they have adopted a model of excellent schooling that gives academic freedom pride of place. For that reason, theological school faculties vigorously resist what they perceive to be impositions of constraints on freedom to teach and freedom to learn, whether the constraints are ecclesiastically imposed or otherwise.

However, entirely proper as it is, the phrase "academic freedom" may be misleading as a name for the freedom at issue here, the freedom theological schools' governance must not reduce or circumscribe. As an Enlightenment idea, "academic freedom" is usually associated with a rationale that depends on a particular view of human nature. Why is the academy to be free? Because the academy is the realm of rational inquiry and reason is autonomous. To restrict freedom of rational inquiry is a self-contradiction. If it is restricted, it is not free; and if it is not free, it is not rational. The near identity of rationality and autonomy, and of autonomy and freedom, is the keystone of a distinctively Enlightenment view of human nature. It is a powerful body of philosophical theory that has fought nobly in the philosophical wars of the past two centuries. But we are not obliged to tie our discussion to it or to its refutation.

It is enough to point out that there is a *theological* rationale for this freedom. The freedom in question is entailed in the overarching goal that makes a theological school theological: the effort to understand God truly. God alone is God. God is apprehended as one who brooks no idolatry, who claims faithfulness to God *over* faithfulness to our theological traditions and personal theological opinions. Accordingly, our objective to understand God truly requires of us that we cultivate capacities for self-criticism. As we saw in chapter 2, North American theological schools are located on various "Roads" and "Streets," all of which in one way or another have historically taken paideia as the model of excellent schooling. In paideia we are formed in such a way that we come to have certain *habitus*, certain settled dispositions to act in characteristic ways. Among those *habitus* that must be cultivated in a theological school is the capacity for critique and self-critique. That, in turn, implies the freedom to differ in understanding and to understand mistakenly.

The rationale for academic freedom need not be a view of human nature; it may be put theologically as a matter of faithfulness to God. If the defining goal of a theological school is to understand God truly, then as a matter of faithfulness to God the freedom of a theological school's effort to understand must not be constrained by the way in which it is governed as a political and social reality in its own right.

There is a demurrer often entered to this line of thought by some who claim basically to agree with it otherwise. Many theological schools are openly and clearly defined as agencies of particular Christian denominations. They are understood both from the side of the denominations and from within the schools to have as their chief responsibility the education of clergy for the denominations that sponsor them. Do these denominations not have the right, indeed the responsibility, to insist that the schools' efforts to understand God yield understanding that is consonant with the traditions of the denominations sponsoring the schools?

There are two issues here, one rooted in the fact that what we are discussing are *schools* and the other in the fact that what we are discussing are *theological* schools. Central to their being schools are their practices of teaching and learning. On both models of excellent schooling symbolized respectively by *paideia* and by Berlin, teaching can only be done indirectly. Simply to transfer directly from the teacher to the student a single line of thought is not teaching but indoctrination. The function of commitment to particular theological traditions in theological schools, whether or not symbolized by required subscription to a confessional statement, cannot imply that schooling there may only consist of directly communicating a single "authorized" line of thought on any given topic. That would mean that there is no room for serious critical questioning and assessing. Where questions are not

open, capacities for critical and rigorous reflection cannot be cultivated. Where capacities for critical and rigorous reflection are not
cultivated, no schooling is being done, theological or otherwise. But
where questions are open, there is room for differences of judgment,
including what may turn out to be erroneous judgments. Whatever a
school's commitment to a particular theological tradition may mean,
therefore, insofar as it is a *school,* it cannot entail restrictions on the
freedom of teachers and learners to differ and be in error.

That brings us to the issue rooted in these schools being "theological" schools. A school's commitment to a particular theological
tradition, sometimes symbolized by required subscription to a confessional statement, might be taken to mean a commitment to specifiable
boundaries to what questions may be explored and what range of
answers to those questions may be critically examined. That, I suggest,
would be theologically a misunderstanding of what the commitment
means. Rather than imposing boundaries to inquiry, such commitment
is better seen as the identification of a *center* and *location* to inquiry. A
given theological school may in fact be explicitly committed to a
particular theological tradition or "position." The tradition or position
is valued as a true construal of the Christian thing. That commitment is
part of what makes the school the particular concrete reality that it is.
Theologically speaking, it is part of its creaturely finitude. That is its
concrete location for theological schooling. That descriptive truth may
be symbolized by the requirement of faculty subscription to a
confessional statement. However, that commitment also symbolizes
something *normative:* a commitment to value understanding God truly
more highly than it values anything else, including presumably its
theological tradition and its faculty members' personal theological
positions. Since God can be understood Christianly only indirectly
through study of the Christian thing, this school is committed to trying
to understand God *starting* with critically reflective study of the
particular construal of the Christian thing represented by this tradition.
This is the center from which inquiry will proceed here. However, that
commitment need set no boundaries to the array of other particular
theological traditions and positions it may study as part of the way to
truer understanding of God, nor boundaries to the range of critical
questions that may be asked of any and all construals of the Christian

thing. Even when its polity requires faculty to sign a confessional statement, such a school may in full self-consistency encourage freedom to teach and freedom to learn. Generally speaking, the degree to which a school's polity allows efforts to understand God to differ and even "err" is the degree to which is genuinely an "effort"; and that is a mark of the school's excellence.

Power Outside

As a set of more or less institutionalized practices, a theological school is itself a center of social, economic, and political power, however small, in its immediate neighborhood and social setting. The excellence of its schooling, we said, depends on how far all the practices that comprise the school are governed by the central end of the school to understand God truly. Clearly, then, that end ought also to govern how the school uses its social power in its immediate vicinity.

The school has immediate social, economic, and political location. Every such location is a living community whose relative social health depends in part on roles played in its common life by local institutions that are symbolically powerful, stable, and long-lasting. It is always an open question what role a theological school plays in nurturing the social health of the neighborhood. So too, in every such location there are questions about the justice of the ways in which social, economic, and political power are distributed and how that distribution affects the people who live there. It is always an open question what the school will do to draw attention to those injustices and how it will use the economic, social, and political power it has there, however modest, in concert with others to right such injustice. A decision about these questions will inescapably be made. It will either be made inadvertently and be entirely implicit and probably unrecognized in the school's way of relating to its social context, or it will be made as a matter of deliberate policy. Only when the decision is made as a matter of deliberate policy can the school's ways of relating to its immediate situation truly be governed by its overarching end, be open to self-criticism, and become an integral part of the effort to understand God truly.

It will not do to resist this suggestion on the grounds that a school is not a social agency, that its defining end is to understand God, not to be an agent of change in its immediate neighborhood. Indeed, its defining end is to understand God. Its excellence as a theological school is not measured by its effectiveness as an agent of social change. However, many of the practices comprising the school involve transactions with its immediate social setting. Supplies and services are purchased. Resident students participate in neighborhood organizations. Some school practices may be open to the surrounding community.

These transactions constitute social locatedness. And they teach both the school's neighbors and its students. The ways in which these transactions are conducted inevitably work to symbolize to the school's neighbors that its local purpose is to underwrite the status quo, or, alternatively, that the school functions in and through its transactions with its neighborhood to raise and address questions of local justice.

At the same time, the school's transactions with its neighborhood inescapably teach certain concepts to its own members, that is, teach certain capacities and abilities about how to lead an institution in its relationships with its immediate social context. The practices that involve these transactions cannot be neatly separated from the practices through which are taught and learned concepts bearing on understanding God. The question of relative excellence in schooling does not turn on whether the school as a set of institutionalized practices is an effective agent of social change but on whether all of its practices *including* those that involve transactions with its immediate social setting cohere in regard to the concepts, that is, the abilities and capacities, those practices teach.

Institutionalized Self-critique

There is a third way in which a theological school's overarching goal shapes it in its concreteness. Not only must that goal shape the institutionalized polity that helps make it concrete by requiring structural guarantees of freedom to disagree in the effort to understand God. Not only must the overarching goal shape the transactions that constitute its concrete location in some social setting so that they cohere with the abilities and capacities it teaches as instruments for understanding God. The overarching goal to understand God must also shape the ways in which all the school's practices are institutionalized so that self-criticism is an institutionalized feature of those practices.

Precisely because a theological school is an institutionalized set of practices, it will have within itself some particular structure of social and political power. Inevitably, in such a structure some people have privileges and access to resources that others do not. Among the interests driving the school's governance will be interests rooted in this structure and concerned to preserve it and the privileges it gives some persons. Precisely because a theological school engages in transactions of material goods and services, including police and fire protection, with the particular community in which it is set, its location there is concrete. Among the interests driving these transactions will be interests to preserve the features of the arrangements of social, economic, and political power in that community from which the school benefits. Thus a theological school, precisely as a concrete social reality in its own right, is vulnerable to ideological distortions arising from within itself in regard to its governance and externally in regard to its social location. That is, there are strong tendencies to be uncritical of the status quo both within the school itself and in its immediate social setting; indeed, there are strong tendencies to preserve arrangements just as they are and to obscure ways in which they may be morally dubious.

It is inadequate to urge the sanguine view that while such ideological blinders are certainly deplorable they are relatively harmless to a theological school's pursuit of its central goal to understand God. Such a view is plausible only on the assumption that the school's practices of teaching and learning through which it seeks to understand God are relatively disengaged from its practices of governance and self-maintenance. It assumes that "theological education" is some sort of activity or process that simply "goes on" within one or another type of institutional structure, housed by the institution but relatively free-floating within it. That is a picture that serves only to obscure or mystify the inescapable *concreteness* of "theological education."

A major concern of this book is to take that concreteness seriously and see how doing so might shape our understanding of any given theological school. To that end I have stressed how understanding is

189

always guided by materially based interests. Understanding is itself "concrete." On the one hand, far from being evil, that is simply a function of our finite creatureliness. On the other hand, it is open to being distorted in self-serving and oppressive ways which are forms of idolatry. The overwhelming evidence is that we consistently dwell in that opening.

In the case of a theological school this means that both the social location of the school itself and the locations of various persons within the school, taken as a small society in its own right, leave the effort to understand God open to ideological distortion. Practices of teaching and learning are not different in kind from practices of governance and self-maintenance, as though one type were "concrete" and the other not, one type "institutionalized" and the other not. In a theological school they are inseparable. Some interests driving a school's practices of governance and self-maintenance will tend to distort ideologically the practices through which it seeks to understand God.

Conversely, the school's overarching goal to understand God *truly* requires that such ideological distortion be identified and corrected. There is of course, no way to guarantee adequate self-critique. Some systematic theological perspectives may tend to stress this issue more than do others, but there is no one correct theological stance that is not open to being used in ideologically obscuring and oppressive ways. It is not theological theory but a community's traditional practices that matter here. What is called for is an ethos, a tradition of social practices that are self-consciously vigilant in self-examination in these regards. Given the concreteness of all social practices, this means that openness to and occasions for self-critique of its own ideological distortions must be built into the ways in which all the school's practices are institutionalized. Because persons have different locations within a school's internal arrangements of power and status, there will be a variety of interests and a variety of perceptions regarding whose interests are being served. What is needed are formal arrangements that enable the parties to this internal pluralism to check and balance one another. Just as there is no one correct form of polity implied in a theological school's overarching goal, so there is no one correct institutional mechanism to accomplish internal ideology critique. That it must somehow be accomplished is nonetheless emphatically implied in the goal to understand God truly when those who seek to understand are a concrete community of embodied agents. The degree to which it is accomplished is another mark of a theological school's excellence.

A UTOPIAN PROPOSAL

What makes a theological school theological and what makes its schooling excellent? We've conducted a thought experiment in response to those questions and in this chapter it has yielded some elements of a utopian proposal about a theological school. A theological school is a set of social practices. It is concrete in that its practices are institutionalized, are guided by interests that have material bases, and are located in a larger host society. This constitutes the school a small *polis* in its own right, a crossroads hamlet with its own social spaces and its own social forms. Its criteria of excellence as a concrete social reality, I have suggested, are rooted in the same thing that makes it theological: the overarching goal of all its practices to understand God truly.

Hence a utopian picture of a theological school would include the following elements. A theological school consists of a number of social practices, central to which are practices of teaching and learning. That is what constitutes it as a *school*. The teaching and learning yield conceptual growth. To understand something is to have acquired the requisite concepts. Hence the way to understand something is through conceptual growth. It is growth in certain abilities and capacities in regard to certain media, especially language. This growth is a matter of degree, and comes through certain disciplines. What makes the school a *theological* school is that its practices of teaching and learning yield growth in abilities and capacities to discern and respond to God in the particular and odd ways in which God is present when and if God is present. The relevant practices of teaching and learning include critical and dialectical study of texts, supervised research, and reflective involvement in the practices that constitute other institutions like hospitals, congregations and social service agencies. They create their own distinctive social spaces and the social spaces require social forms. These practices of teaching and learning are central to a complex set of other practices, such as practices of collecting and maintaining resources for the school, practices of managing its common life, practices by which students are admitted and new faculty selected, and so forth. Practices of teaching and learning are "central" in that all other practices are ordered to their well-being, protecting their social space and maintaining their social forms. But what constitutes the set of practices as a theological school is that *all* these practices are ordered to and guided by one end, the effort to understand God truly, which is not itself a practice in its own right but rather the overarching goal of the entire set of practices comprising the school.

This generates two sets of marks of excellence in theological schooling. The first set is this: It is excellent to the extent that the conceptual growth is guided by an interest in God for God's own sake. It is excellent to the extent that precisely because it is guided by that interest, it is self-critically concerned with the truthfulness of its discernment and response to God. It is excellent to the extent that precisely because it is guided by interest in God for God's own sake, it honors the inevitable pluralism of understandings of God by serious engagement in conversation with differing understandings. It is excellent to the extent that, precisely because its guiding interest is in God for God's own sake, it is self-critical of ideological distortions of its own efforts to understand God.

A second set of marks of excellence in theological schooling comes into view when we turn to reflect on the *concreteness* of a theological school: Its concreteness consists in part in its having institutionalized practices of governance, and its schooling is excellent to the extent that its polity leaves room so that the effort to understand God can be genuine by being free to err. Its concreteness in part consists of its transactions with its immediate host community, and its schooling is excellent to the extent that its transactions are deliberately and self-critically shaped in such a way that what they symbolize to the immediate neighborhood and what they teach members of the school community itself are consonant with the concepts taught and learned in its central practices. Its concreteness in part consists of its own internal arrangements of power and status, and its schooling is excellent to the extent that built into those institutionalized arrangements are mechanisms fostering ideology critique within the school.

In this chapter I have made a proposal about what constitutes a theological *school* and what the implications are for its excellence as a school from the fact that it is specifically a *theological* school. I have said nothing about Christian congregations, on which we spent a good bit of energy in the last chapter. It is time now to bring the two discussions together. I shall do that in the next two chapters on a theological school's course of study, what its content should be and why, how it can be at once unified and adequate to the pluralism of the Christian thing, and how it may be at once "academically disciplined" and "professional" schooling.

Notes

1. Farley, *Theologia,* pp. 87–88.

2. One apparent exception to this is *Christian Identity and Theological Education* by Joseph C. Hough, Jr., and John B. Cobb., Jr. (Chico, Calif.: Scholars Press, 1985), who make a point of stressing that theological education must have as its end or *telos* the education of ministers (pp. 4–5). However, it becomes clear that they too reject the "clerical paradigm" insofar as that is a way of defining, not theological education as a type of education, but theological education as *theological.* They too reject the conventional view that what makes theological schooling theological is that it prepares church leaders, implying that "theology" is to be defined as the theory required by the practice of the profession of church leadership.

3. See Farley, *Theologia,* pp. 127–135.

4. See Wood, *Vision and Discernment,* ch. 5.

5. Wood, *The Formation of Christian Understanding,* p. 35.

6. See above, chapter 6, pp. 125–127.

7. Søren Kierkegaard, *Philosophical Fragments,* 2nd ed., tr. David F. Swenson and Howard V. Hong (Princeton, N.J.: Princeton University Press, 1962), p. 51.

8. In my view Kierkegaard overstates the point. There does seem to be something like an extended sense of "proper name" that fits the way "God" is

used in Christian discourse as a place-holder for the One whose identity is best described, so Christians believe, by cycles of biblical stories about God relating to the world as its creator, God relating to humankind through the history of Israel, and God relating to persons in the life, death, and resurrection appearances of Jesus.

9. See David Tracy's development of the phrase "scripture-in-tradition" in "On Reading Scripture Theologically," in *Theology and Dialogue,* ed. Bruce Marshall (Notre Dame, Ind.: University of Notre Dame Press, 1990), pp. 35–69.

10. See James Barr, *The Scope and Authority of the Bible* (Philadelphia: Westminster Press, 1981).

11. Cf. George Lindbeck, *The Nature of Doctrine.*

9

A Theological School's Course of Study

Thus far we have addressed only the third of the three central issues about theological schooling that we identified in chapter 5: How to keep discussion of theological schooling as concrete as possible. We have done that through a sketch of the practices that constitute an individual school and make it the concrete particular reality it is, and through a sketch of the practices that constitute any individual Christian congregation and make it the concrete particular reality it is. We now turn to the first two of the central issues we identified in chapter 5: How to unify a theological school's course of study; and, how to keep the course of study adequate to the pluralism of ways in which the Christian thing exists in actual practice. We can address those two issues by exploring how the practices constituting, respectively, a theological school and a Christian congregation relate to each other.

We noted in chapter 2 that differences on this point are one of the theological factors that pluralize rather than unite theological schools. Some have seen a theological school to *be* a Christian congregation; some have seen a theological school as distinct from but interrelated with congregations in ways analogous to the relation in the Reformed tradition between the congregation and its clergy; others have seen a theological school as related, not to congregations, but to a cadre of active clergy for whom it provides "in-service" or "extension" education.

THEOLOGICAL SCHOOL AND CONGREGATION

The sketch in the last two chapters of what constitutes a theological school and what constitutes a Christian congregation allows us to see how they are distinct in principle and yet nonetheless intersect in ways that are central to both. That will allow us to explain more exactly how a theological school's study can be *focused* "through the lens" or "within the horizon" of questions about congregations. That, in turn, will allow us to show how theological schooling can be a unified course of study that is nonetheless adequate to the irreducible pluralism of ways in which the Christian thing is actually construed.

A theological school and a congregation are distinct *in principle*. The rhetoric of practice brings this out. Each is a complex set of interrelated practices. However, for each there is an overarching goal that governs the practices, defining the set as the *kind* of set it is. These goals, I have argued, are different: The central practices of Christian congregations are ordered to the end of worshiping God; the central practices of a theological school are ordered to the goal of understanding God truly. Because the set of practices constituting each of them is defined by different ends, a theological school and a congregation are in principle distinct institutions of practice.

This might appear to rule out one traditional view, namely, that a theological school *is* a Christian congregation. It does rule that out as a *conceptual* identity. However, it does not rule out that the group of persons cooperatively engaged in the practices constituting a theological school might *also* at other times cooperatively engage in the practices constituting a Christian congregation, and vice versa.

The practical difference this makes is important. Each set of practices is, we have repeatedly noted, inherently institutionalized. The institutional structure that gives vertebrate and sometimes all-too-rigid form to the central practice of a school is not going to be the same as that which informs the central practice of a congregation. The well-being of neither is enhanced when one institutional arrangement is made to do service for both sets of practice. Either the doxological core of what makes a congregation will be subordinated to information communication (preaching as lecturing: "What John Calvin thought about this text was . . . "), to moralizing, and to posturing ("See, this is how to perform the liturgy with real ritual expertise"). This is a major cause of the thinness of much worship that does go on in theological schools. Or the quest for understanding that lies at the core of a school will be marginalized, trivialized ("Academics are all right for those so inclined, but are finally fairly irrelevant to the life of a congregation"), and unduly constrained. This is a major cause of *de facto* restrictions of academic freedom in theological schools.

To stress that theological schools and congregations are distinct institutions of practice is clearly consistent with each of the other traditional pictures of the sort of "community" a theological school is and how it is related to the community of the church. It coheres, for example, with the view that the school relates to churches in a way analogous to the traditional relation between clergy and congregations in the Reformed tradition. And it is coherent with the view that the school is a service agency in support of a cadre of clergy already engaged in ministry.

Now precisely because they are fundamentally distinct, a theological school and congregations can also genuinely *intersect* or overlap as sets of practices. Both, for example, engage in practices to raise money and maintain property. The point of intersection of central importance to us in this book, however, is the interest both theological school and church have *to understand God truly*.

We should pause for a moment to address an important question. Does this thesis mean that one has to be personally and existentially involved in the common life of a congregation in order to be capable of engaging fruitfully in the practices comprising a theological school? That is, need one be a "believer" or a "person of faith" to undertake theological schooling, on the description of a theological school sketched here? No. Clearly, if a theological school is going to focus its study through the lens of questions about congregations as the way to truer understanding of God, it is dependent on there being congregations to study and refer to. It does not follow, however, that the persons involved in the practices constituting a theological school must also be existentially engaged in the practices constituting a worshiping congregation.

From the side of a theological school, the possibility is always open *in principle* that persons who come to understand God will choose not to worship God. The most that can be asked is that persons involved in the practices that constitute a theological school also be thoughtfully involved in the practices that constitute a congregation as participant observers. There is, however, more than one way to be "thoughtfully involved" in practices. Failure to engage existentially in the central practice of a congregation may well make it more difficult to understand God because participation in the common life of a congregation is a common way to be capacitated, that is, to acquire the requisite concepts, for apprehending God. However, there is also the possibility of acquiring those capacities, or at least many of them, in an imaginative "as if" mode. If it were not so, it would be impossible to grasp in any degree the allegedly "true understandings" of God that one may take to be, not just partially mistaken, but wholly false. A theological school may require that Christian congregations exist, but it does not require students' existential engagement in the practices of a congregation in order for the school to pursue its central project.

Conversely, a Christian congregation neither requires that a theological school exist nor that the members of the congregation be engaged in the central practices of a theological school. In may be that the relation of congregation to a theological school is like the relation some Anglicans say obtains between the churches and a bishop: Churches do not need a bishop for their being *(esse)* but they do need a bishop for their well-being *(bene esse)*. I shall argue below that while a theological school is not of the *esse* of congregations, it is of congregations' *bene esse*.

The fact that the practices comprising a theological school and Christian congregations intersect in their common interest to understand God brings out a further point about the relation between the two. It allows us to sharpen the fundamental difference between the two in regard to theology in particular. To "try to understand God more truly" is "to do theology" in the broadest sense. However, theology is not some one thing. It embraces a number of different practices.

What defines an inquiry as "theological" is its guiding *goal* to understand God simply for the sake of understanding God. What defines the inquiry as "theology" is its guiding goal, not the distinctive "methods" it employs (although it will be poor theology if it employs inappropriate methods), nor the distinctive subjectivity of the persons engaged in the inquiry (although it may be pretty thin theology if the inquirers are not personally "formed" by faith, hope, and love). To adopt this view is to set aside two alternative pictures of theology that are widespread. Both of them see theology as some one thing having a universal structure and movement. One is the view that what defines an inquiry as "theology" is that it employs *the* distinctive methods or disciplines required by its peculiar object or subject matter. Looked at that way, the essential content of revelation, or perhaps the very nature of God (whatever is the ultimate "subject matter" or "object" of the inquiry) dictates certain methods and movements of thought which, if followed, denominate the inquiry as "theology." Also set aside is the view that what defines an inquiry as theology is a distinctive subjectivity or consciousness that the person who is engaged in theology is attempting to bring to reflective and self-critical expression. On this second view, insofar as persons have apprehended God through the medium of Christian myths, symbols, and rites, their subjectivity will be shaped by a distinctive dynamic and structure which then dictates the proper movement and structure of theological study. Both of these views bring with them the corollary that Christian theology is some one enterprise with an essential structure that is fundamentally invariant cross-culturally and historically. By contrast, the picture of theology sketched here implies that "theology" is not some one enterprise and may have no single core "essential structure."

This brings us back to our point: the differences and relation between a theological school and Christian congregations in regard to doing theology. I urged in chapter 7 that Christian congregations be viewed as complex sets of practices ordered to the enactment of worship of God in Jesus' name. I also stressed that doing theology is inherent and not just optional in that set of practices. In a congregation, however, practices of theology are secondary to the worship that is primary and constitutes the congregation as a Christian congregation. Practices of theology are required by the congregation's enactment of worship and are in its service. In particular, I pointed out, worship requires a congregation to engage in constructive and critical theological practices. Because worship is a response in ever-new situations to God's peculiar way of being present, especially in the ministry, crucifixion, and resurrection appearances of Jesus of Nazareth, it constantly requires fresh formulations of what it is it is responding *to*. That is, it requires constructive theology. For the same reason, worship constantly requires critical self-reflection testing whether what is said and done in worship, broadly understood, is faithful to that to which it is responding: critical theology.

More often than not theology is practiced in the common life of congregations in a piecemeal and ad hoc way. It is done ad hoc whenever any type of action or form of speech in any of the congregation's practices becomes problematical. This will happen, for example, when the social and cultural context of its practices changes and seems novel and puzzling. When questions arise, such as, "Should we be doing and saying these things under these circumstances? What should we be doing and how should we express ourselves?" some judgments have to be made on the spot. In the course of making them, formulations of "Who we are" and "Who it is we are trying to be faithful to" will be devised, reexamined, and perhaps revised. Usually, of course, this sort of thing happens both quickly and informally. Nonetheless, to do it is to do theology in an ad hoc way. Theology may also be done within the common life of a congregation in a more sustained, methodical, and orderly way. When it is done in this way, attention focuses not so much on addressing particular quandaries about how to speak and act faithfully but rather on questions of coherence—coherence among various formulations of who and what God is, who we are and what our shared world is in relation to God, and coherence between all of these and beliefs widely shared in the congregation's host culture. In any case, whether done ad hoc or in a more sustained and methodical way, doing theology is inherent in the practices constituting a Christian congregation; but it is inherent as secondary, done in the service of the central practice of worship.

Particular persons may be given responsibility for doing theology within the common life of Christian congregations, or for seeing to it that it is done. In the first five centuries it was often bishops who held this responsibility (consider how much of what is now called "patristic theology" was written by bishops: Gregory of Nyssa, Basil, Athanasius, Augustine). In the Reformed branch of the Reformation, responsibility was often assigned to the ordained minister or "teaching elder" of a congregation (hence in that tradition clergy were expected to be above all "learned ministers," which meant that they had the resources of information and conceptual capacities that empowered them to fill this role).

The possibility this creates for theological disagreement and controversy within the life of a congregation is obvious. Accordingly, means have been devised by which to settle theological disputes. In the Roman Catholic tradition the ancient practice is preserved of making bishops responsible for doing theology; and then that tradition is developed to make bishops, and preeminently the Bishop of Rome, responsible also for discerning and authoritatively declaring the correct or "orthodox" theological judgments. Thus the practice of doing theology authoritatively is institutionalized in a teaching office, the magisterium. In other traditions the practice of doing theology authoritatively is institutionalized in the powers of constitutionally legitimated representative denominational assemblies elected to govern the church. In other traditions it is institutionalized as a responsibility of the governing board of particular congregations. In other traditions it is hardly institutionalized at all, being worked out through informal consensus processes.

However, what needs to be stressed is that even though certain persons may be made responsible for doing theology, or seeing to it that it is done, or even for declaring authoritatively what the correct theological judgment is regarding particular issues, a great many other people in Christian congregations are in fact doing theology. Insofar as people who make up a congregation are serious enough to be critically self-reflective about their own lives as acts of discipleship, they are doing theology, at least in an ad hoc and piecemeal way. The more clearly it is understood that ministry or, in the broad sense of the word we have adopted, that worship is the work of *all* the people (the *laos,* the laity), the more explicit will their doing theology be. Moreover, the more theologically educated the people are, the more self-critical will their doing theology be. The conclusion that follows, of course, is that it is critically important for the well-being, the *bene esse,* of congregations that the persons who do their theology be capacitated to do it as well as possible. This is true not only of those made responsible for doing theology, not to mention those responsible for declaring authoritatively the correct theological judgment about particular issues, but it is also true of everyone who commits to enact a more broadly shared practice of the worship of God in Jesus' name.

In contrast to the congregation, among whose practices doing theology is inherent but secondary, in a theological school doing theology is primary and central among its constituting practices. Whereas theology is necessarily done "properly" in congregations in the service of their "worship," that is, their response to the odd ways in which God makes Godself present, it is done not only "properly" but also "educationally" in a theological school. That is, it is done both in the interest of actually making theological judgments ("proper" sense) and in the interest of cultivating persons' capacities for making sound theological judgments. Of the interconnected pair "making judgments/cultivating judgment," the accent falls in a theological course of study on "cultivating judgment." This is the force of characterizing a theological school, not simply as a group of people whose overarching goal is to understand God, but as a group of people whose overarching goal is to *try* to understand God *more truly* simply for the sake of understanding God. The accent on "try. . . more truly" is an accent on cultivating more nuanced and perceptive capacities for judgment.

FOCUSING THEOLOGICAL STUDY

If what makes a school "theological" is its effort to understand God, albeit indirectly by studying something else whose study is supposed to lead to understanding God; and if what makes it "Christian" is that in order to understand God it studies "the Christian thing," then where is a school concretely to find the Christian thing? My proposal has been that it is to be found in a wide variety of Christian congregations. The Christian thing is to be encountered in concrete actuality *in and as Christian congregations*. Perhaps not only there; but at very least there. However, that proposal needs to be elaborated.

We have used G. K. Chesterton's expression "the Christian thing" to name a complex set: scriptures in various traditions of interpretation and use, God as described in those traditions, Jesus as described in those traditions, theological doctrines in various traditions of interpretation and use, patterns of worship, "social action," structures of polity, moral codes, exemplary persons, and so forth. These matters constitute the Christian thing insofar as they are held together and interrelated in complex ways in certain practices in which people actually engage, communally and individually, and engage in such a way that their identities are significantly shaped. One major place where the practices (as well, to be sure, as major and demonic distortions of them) may be encountered is the common life of Christian congregations. That is why the effort to understand God Christianly, which must in the nature of the case proceed indirectly, might best proceed indirectly by way of study of the Christian thing in and as Christian congregations.

That procedure would provide both a large array of subject matters for theological schooling to study and a way to focus study on the theological significance of those subject matters.

Indeed, this procedure would largely retain the range of subject matters or content conventionally found in theological schools' curricula. Every course ever found in a theological curriculum could be justified by this proposal. Recall the array of possible objects of inquiry implied in our discussion of Christian congregations in chapter 7.

1. That a congregation's defining practice of worship is a *response* "in Jesus' name" implies study of that *to* which it is a response: Just how is God understood to be "present" is Jesus' ministry, crucifixion, and resurrection appearances; what understanding of God follows from this; who is Jesus; what are the sources and the warrants of these characterizations of Jesus and of God (scripture, tradition, history of doctrine); what understanding of these sources makes them not only sources but also authoritative for these understandings of God and Jesus?

2. That a congregation is constituted by enacting a more *broadly* and *ecumenically* practiced worship that generates a distinctive social *space* implies study of what that space is and how it is formed: What are the varieties of the shape and content of the common lives of Christian congregations now, cross-culturally and globally (synchronic inquiry); how do congregations characteristically define who they are and what their larger social and natural contexts are; how do they characteristically define what they ought to be doing as congregations; how have they defined who they are and what they ought to do historically (diachronic study); how is the social form of their common life nurtured and corrected in liturgy, pastoral caring, preaching, education, maintenance of property, service to neighbors; what is the role of scripture in all this, the role of traditions of theology, and the role of traditions of worship?

3. That a congregation is constituted by *publicly* enacting a more universally practiced worship that generates a distinctive social *form* implies study of that public form: What are the social, cultural, and political locations of congregations of Christians and how do those locations shape congregations' social form today (synchronic inquiry); what have been the characteristic social, cultural, and political locations of congregations historically and how have those locations shaped congregations' social forms (diachronic study); in what ways do congregations engage in the public arena as one type of institutionalized center of power among others?

4. That a congregation is comprised of a set of practices that necessarily include critical self-reflection implies study of its mechanisms and criteria for self-criticism: How do congregations govern, criticize, and reform themselves; by what criteria; subject to what influences from their host societies; in the light of what historical and cultural changes in their settings?

Thus, the very nature of congregations directs inquiry into a large array of types of subject matters: Texts, patterns of communal and individual life, traditions of thought and of ritual practice, moral codes, and so forth. Each of these can be the subject of perfectly legitimate scholarly inquiry taken by itself. Moreover, study of each of them may involve the use of any or several of a variety of well-established types of inquiry: sociological, anthropological, psychological, philosophical, or—the dominant mode of inquiry in theological schooling today—historical. Left at that, the study would lack theological significance. What makes these objects of inquiry theologically significant is that together they constitute the Christian thing whose study is believed to lead to truer understandings of *God*. They constitute the Christian thing insofar as they are held together in various patterns of interrelationship with one another in certain practices. How shall study of these subject matters be so focused that it attends to them in their theological significance?

My proposal is that exactly the same thing that implies the array of subject matters for theological schooling also implies the way to focus study of that subject matter: The complexity and pluralism of Christian congregations solicit three broad types of questions.[1] These questions are solicited by congregations' own self-descriptions. We may call pursuit of each type of question a different type of theological inquiry as long as that does not suggest either that they are like links or successive moments in a single extended inquiry or that they are somehow variations or aspects of some postulated "theology as such." The three questions can serve as horizons within which to conduct rigorous inquiry into any of the array of subject matters implied by the nature of congregations, disciplined by any relevant scholarly method, in such a way that attention is focused on the theological significance of what is studied:

a. Explicitly and implicitly in the practices that comprise this Christian congregation, how does it construe the Christian thing and how is it like and unlike the construal implicit and explicit in the practices constituting these other contemporaneous and historically distant, and very different, congregations? More generally, what different overall construals of the Christian thing are there, and on what issues do the fundamental differences among them turn? Thus far the inquiry is descriptive, analytic, and comparative of congregations' implicit and explicit self-descriptions. It solicits a further normative question: In conversation with these others, what overall construal of the Christian thing seems most adequate to you the inquirer, and on what bases? Call this combination of descriptive and normative inquiry *constructive theology*.

b. Given its construal of the Christian thing, what types of speech and action in the practices constituting this congregation are faithful enactments of its self-described identity and what are not? How would these judgments differ were its self-description changed to be like that implicit in the construals of the Christian thing by other congregations (and vice versa), each very different from the other? Thus far the inquiry is descriptive, analytic, and comparative. However it solicits a further normative question: What types of speech and action in the practices constituting the array of Christian congregations seem to you the inquirer to be, in their cultural content, faithful, and what ones unfaithful, to the Christian thing? Call this combination of descriptive and normative inquiry *critical practical theology*. It embraces both what is often called "practical theology" and "moral theology."

c. What criteria are there in this congregation's construal of the Christian thing by which to assess whether the Christian thing is true?

what about distinctive community, embodying faith

How would the criteria differ were this congregation to adopt the construals of the Christian thing that are explicit and implicit in the practices constituting other congregations that are very different from one another? Thus far the inquiry is descriptive, analytic, and comparative. It solicits a normative question: How do you the inquirer assess the truth of the Christian thing, in what construal of it, and by what criteria? Call this combination of descriptive and normative inquiry *apologetic theology*.

Clearly, the proposal that a theological school's study be focused through the lens of questions about congregations does not mean that somehow congregations become the sole or even the central subject of disciplined inquiry. To the contrary, all the traditional subject matters remain in place, including, of course, study of particular congregations. Rather, the proposal is that study of every subject matter that is selected for study (using whatever academic disciplines are appropriate) be shaped and guided by an interest in the question: What is that subject matter's bearing on, or role in, the practices that constitute actual enactments, in specific concrete circumstances, of various construals of the Christian thing in and as Christian congregations?

In this way a theological school's study would be *against* and *for* Christian congregations, and only for that reason also in a way would be *about* them. It will be "against" congregations in that its study will be inherently *critical*. It will constantly bring to light the ambiguity of what Christian congregations "are" and the incoherence of what they *say* they are responding to in their worship. It will persistently disclose congregations' faithlessness to who they themselves say they are, and the scandal of the roles they actually play in North American social and cultural life. It will consistently probe the softness and question the dubiousness of congregations' claim to witness to truth. The picture of a theological school developed here implies that inherent in the defining interest of a theological school is a certain distancing and even alienation from Christian congregations.

At the same time, and without modifications of the "againstness," a theological school's study may be "for" Christian congregations because it is the place where people can be helped to acquire the capacities for theological judgment that, as we saw, congregations inherently need in their common life. By engaging people in the effort to understand God by focusing study of various subject matters within the horizon of questions about Christian congregations, a theological school may help them cultivate capacities both for what Charles Wood[2] calls "vision," that is, formulating comprehensive, synoptic accounts of the Christian thing as a whole, and what he calls "discernment," that is, insight into the meaning, faithfulness, and truth of particular acts in the practice of worship (in the broad sense of worship that we have adopted for this discussion). As we have seen, having persons with such capacities in its midst is critical to a congregation's well-being. A theological school can be for congregations' *bene esse,* even though it is not of their *esse.*

In being "against" and "for" congregations, a theological school's study would also be in a certain way "about" them. Not that Christian congregations become its central, let alone its sole, subject matter. Rather it would be "about" congregations in the sense that everything it *does* study is studied with regard to that subject's relation to, or role in, the Christian thing as *that* is present in and as the common life of different types of congregations. In this way we appropriate the truth of H. Richard Niebuhr's contention in *The Purpose of the Church and Its Ministry* that a theological school should be seen as an "intellectual center of the Church's life,"[3] but with the major reservation that a theological school can be that only if it is not *defined* by being that. By being at once against and for congregations a theological school can be an intellectual center for them. However, it cannot be for them without being inherently against them too. Theological schools ought not to disguise their distancing from congregations, and congregations ought not to be dismayed at signs of it. Indeed, what ought to dismay would be the absence of distancing tensions in a theological school's relationship with congregations. For a theological school cannot simply be "for" congregations. It cannot be a useful intellectual center for congregations if it is defined as a center for research and development to promote church growth. Nor did Niebuhr suggest that it could. A theological school can be "for" congregations only by also being "against" them.

A theological school can be about them in being both for and against congregations but not if it is *defined* by an interest in being "about" them. It is "about" congregations only contingently and, as it were, accidentally. A Christian theological school is *defined*, we have repeatedly stressed, by its interest in truly understanding God by focusing study on the Christian thing; but as a matter of contingent fact it happens that the Christian thing is most concretely available for study in and as Christian congregations. Hence a theological school does focus study on congregations, but is not defined by an interest in doing so.

There is a parallel here with a paradox about clergy education that we noted in chapter 5. Competent church leadership requires theological schooling; but a theological school will not adequately educate church leadership if its *defining* goal or interest is to educate future church leadership. So too, congregations may require theological schools as their intellectual centers, but a theological school cannot be an adequate intellectual center "for" Christian congregations if its defining interest is to be an intellectual center for congregations.

UNITY AND PLURALISM

We can now see how the two remaining issues on our agenda can each be addressed without undercutting the other. We noted in chapter 5 that two major issues have arisen from the current discussions of the nature and purpose of theological education: (a) the unity of a theological course of study and (b) its adequacy to the pluralism of the Christian thing. Not only does the pluralism in question characterize past and present construals of the Christian thing and their respective social and cultural locations; it also characterizes particular theological schools, the practices that constitute them, and their respective social and cultural locations. Within individual schools, it may characterize groups of faculty and students and *their* various social and cultural locations.

We noted how difficult it is to resolve both issues at the same time. It looks as though the bases on which fragmentation of the course of study might be overcome all explicitly or implicitly deny the reality or importance of "apparent" pluralism in the Christian thing. On the other hand, to make a theological course of study adequate to pluralism is to acknowledge *within the course of study* not only that there are differences among various construals of the Christian thing but also that tensions and the possibility of conflict are inherent in the very practices constituting the school and, in particular, inherent in its course of study. Consequently, we need to be clear about what *sort* of unity, what model of integral oneness, we are adopting when we discuss these issues. Otherwise, adequacy to pluralism will necessarily work against unification of the course of study, and vice versa.

Strictly speaking, a theological school's course of study is its curriculum. "Curriculum" is a metaphor. It is literally a running course. Used metaphorically, curriculum ought to designate something singular, a unified movement of study. In North American higher education a curriculum is usually divided into discrete units or courses. This permits us to quantify the educational process by ascribing value units, or credits, to each course. A given number of course credits is the quantifiable criterion to determine whether a course of study has been completed at such a level of competence as to have earned an academic degree. No one of the courses is itself the course of study. Each course may have an internal integrity, some rationale governing the selection of subject matter and choice of appropriate methods or disciplines. That does not guarantee that any given set of these courses has any rationale or internal integrity. The ever-present danger is that a given number of such courses adds up only to a clutch of courses and not a course of study.

When there is a deep dissatisfaction with a school's course of study, theological educators characteristically undertake a reform of its curriculum. The conventional way to analyze the faulty curriculum is to ask either or both of two sets of questions. The first set addresses the issue of the unity of the curriculum: Which courses are so central to an adequate theological schooling that they ought to be a core that all students take? And in what order should they take them? The other set of questions addresses the issue of pluralism in the curriculum: Granted that students represent a variety of life-worlds and Christian traditions, and granted that many of them will become leaders in congregations situated in a variety of social contexts, what range and variety of courses should there be? How much freedom should individual students have to fabricate their own course of study out of the array provided by the curriculum?

These conventional questions, however, do not address the fundamental issue, and frequently lead to a revised curriculum that still yields only a clutch of courses. The basic issue is indeed how to unify a clutch of courses into a course of study that honors and is adequate to genuine pluralism of construals of the Christian thing and to profound pluralism of the social situations in which the Christian thing is practiced. However, that will not be achieved merely by rearranging the courses already present into a new sequence, restricting the number of courses to a core, enlarging the number of courses, or increasing or decreasing students' freedom of course selection.

Rather than attempting to resolve our two issues by concentrating on questions about content (Which courses ought we to include in the curriculum?), structure (Which courses ought to be considered central and which more peripheral?), and movement (Which courses ought to be in the beginning, middle, and end of the course of study?), it would be more fruitful to concentrate on the question of the overarching goal of the course of study and the interests it generates to guide inquiry.

My proposal has become increasingly more defined: The overarching goal of a Christian theological school is to understand God more truly by way of study of the Christian thing in and as Christian congregations. That goal generates an interest in studying all that goes to make up congregations as enactments of the Christian thing; and congregations, in turn, invite three types of questions to focus and guide study of all that goes to constitute the Christian thing in and as congregations:

1. How is the Christian thing construed in practice here—just *what is it?* What would we have committed ourselves to were we to become existentially engaged in it? How, and for what reasons, is it different from other available construals of the Christian thing? Descriptively, what construal seems the most apt one, and why?

2. What would count as *faithful* enactments of it in its current social and cultural location? How do different construals of the Christian thing correlate with different judgments about faithfulness in speech and action?

3. Is the Christian thing as construed here *true?* On what grounds is this decided? How would the grounds and the judgment about truth vary as construals of the Christian thing vary?

This yields a combined resolution for both the issue about recovering unity in a fragmented course of study and the issue about making the course of study more adequate to the deep pluralism of the Christian thing.

On the unity side, the proposal here is, quite simply, that a theological course of study would be unified if every course in it were deliberately and explicitly designed to address centrally one of the three questions about the Christian thing in and as Christian congregations (What is it? Is it faithful to its own identity? Is what it claims true?). Since the three questions in their interdependence simply refract the overarching and unifying interest of a theological school, they would thereby unify a course of study.

Theological schools' courses of study tend to become fragmented when they consist of clutches of courses each of which is, at best, an internally well-ordered and coherent intellectual world of its own but has little or, at worst, no clear and intellectually significant external relationship with other courses. Even when the courses in a single field, say New Testament, are significantly related to one another, they will together still notoriously tend to be a self-contained intellectual world having little intellectually significant relations with courses outside their own field. In large part this fragmentation is the result of the types of interests governing courses, one by one. Assuming it is internally ordered and coherent, each course has such a governing interest, implicitly if not explicitly. Indeed, a course is internally ordered and coherent precisely to the extent that its design is governed by some central interest. The interest may be to convey to students a certain range of information, or to cultivate in students certain capacities for research, or to "form" students in certain ways, or to advance the instructor's research agenda, and so forth. These are all perfectly legitimate interests. However, when the courses comprising a curriculum are ordered to a large and incoherent range of interests, it follows that the curriculum itself will be a clutch of courses rather than a course of study. The suggestion here is that the dominant interest unifying every course in a theological curriculum ought to be the interest guiding one of the three sorts of theology (constructive, critical practical, or apologetic), that is, interest reflected in one of the three ranges of questions congregations invite about their construals of the

Christian thing (What is it? Is it faithful? Is it true?). Naturally, that does not mean that the courses comprising a curriculum will all tend to give the same *answers* to these questions. The unity of the course of study does not rest on agreement in judgment. It only means that the unity of a theological course of study would be grounded in the fact that in all its parts it raises and addresses the same three interconnected types of questions which are themselves simply three refractions of the one overarching goal to understand God more truly.

On the pluralism side, the proposal here is, quite simply, that a theological course of study would be much more adequate to the "pluralism of pluralisms" characterizing the Christian thing if every course in it were deliberately and explicitly designed to address one of the three questions invited by Christian congregations *and* the array of types of congregations were broad and rich. The proposal that study of various subject matters be focused through the lens of questions about congregations introduces pluralism into the heart of the course of study.

The proposal has been that study of the conventional variety of subject matters (scripture, doctrine, sociology of the congregation, etc.) be kept tied to questions about their bearing on particular construals of the Christian thing in and as *different* types of Christian congregations. The richness of the variety is what is crucial. If the congregations are genuinely different from one another, the study will be made more adequate to pluralism precisely as it is being unified. The differences in the actual practices of speech and action between one congregation's construal of the Christian thing and other congregations' construals of the Christian thing are not only a function of their belonging to diverse "theological traditions," although that is certainly an important aspect of the difference. It is also a function of differences in the congregations' social and cultural and ethnic locations. Moreover, the differences among congregations' construals of the Christian thing is also partly a function of different sorts of pluralism *within* each of them in regard to their members' location not only according to class and ethnicity but also according to gender.

The differences among their construals of the Christian thing are simply . . . differences. A background conviction to this book has consistently been that there is no one underlying "essence" of Christianity that can be explicitly defined and to which these differing construals can be reduced as mere variations. Another background conviction has been that there is no one underlying pre-conceptual (in the quasi-technical sense of "concept" we sketched in chapter 6) religious experience of which differing construals of the Christian thing are simply alternative "symbolic expressions" or "thematizations." Rather, we have insisted that congregations' differing construals are genuinely and profoundly pluralistic. They bear important family resemblances to one another. They are plural responses to the odd ways in which God has been and promises yet to be present, especially in Jesus' name. They share a number of things, notably scripture and practices of worship, that they use in identity-shaping ways. But the theological, historical, cultural, social, and gender-generated pluralisms are as profound as the commonalities.

Thus, if a theological course of study focused inquiry into its various subject matters within the horizon of questions about the bearing and role of those subject matters on the practices constituting a rich diversity of types of congregations, and did not abstract from the diversity or claim somehow to go "behind" it, it could be more adequate to pluralism in the Christian thing without threatening to fragment the course of study.

This proposal clearly rejects three other ways to remedy curricular fragmentation. It clearly rejects proposals to solve the problem by designing sequences of courses in which some courses are the required prerequisites for admission to others. Within certain "fields" this may be a useful move. Regarding the course of study as a whole, however, this is too rigid to be practicable except in schools with relatively small and very homogeneous student bodies. However, if the student body is that homogeneous, it is doubtful whether the school is adequately addressing genuine pluralism. The more pluralized the student body becomes in regard to age, previous experience, earlier education, sex, race, social location, and vocational self-understanding, the less workable is a single, prescribed sequence of courses.

This proposal also rejects the suggestion that fragmentation is a consequence of the disciplinary variety that has crept into theological schooling, and can be solved by minimizing the importance of schooling in the various disciplines. On the contrary, the various disciplines at their most rigorous are required by the complexity of concrete congregations. What is needed is not to soft-pedal them but to harness a diversity of academic disciplines to a single interest by employing them within the horizon of a single set of interdependent questions.

Finally, this proposal clearly is different in principle from the view that fragmentation is rooted in the course of study's inadequacy to the integral structure and movement of its proper subject matter. No, it is not the subject matter that makes theological schooling either "theological" or unified; rather, it is its overarching interest to understand God, an interest refracted in three interdependent questions that may order each course's inquiry and unify them all into a single course of study.

IS THIS PROPOSAL COHERENT?

A little reflection might raise questions about whether this proposal really holds together. I have proposed that fragmentation in a theological course of study could be overcome if each of its constituent courses were unified by a controlling interest in one of the three questions Christian congregations invite about their construals of the Christian thing (What is it? Is it faithful? Is it true?), and that the course of study could be more adequate to the pluralism of the Christian thing if the construals of the Christian thing that are studied comparatively are the construals of very different congregations. However, we might ask whether these three types of questions about congregations do not in fact fragment a course of study, and in at least two ways. Do they not, in the first place, reintroduce the distinction between "theoretical" and "practical" (or "academic" and "professional") which, once adopted as a way to organize the world of a theological school, ends up alienating the "theoretical" or "academic" and making it functionally irrelevant to the "practical" or "professional"? And, in the second place, does not the introduction of a distinction among three questions guiding theological schooling simply fragment the so-called theoretical or "academic" inquiries themselves into self-contained and unrelated enterprises? No, none of the above—not if we keep clear what we are proposing.

The proposal consistently employs a conceptual scheme in which the conceptual disjunctions "theory/practice," "academic/professional," "reflection/action" simply have no work to do. We characterized "understanding," not in terms of formulating true "theory" nor in terms of the results of disciplined academic "research," but in terms of acquiring competencies to *do* certain things, capacities for certain types of *action*. We characterized congregations (about whom these three types of questions guide "understanding") as sets of practices; and we characterized "practices" as patterns of intentional bodied action. Inquiry guided by our three questions, then, entails acquiring capacities for and active engagement in (even if only in an "as if" mode) activities comprising the concrete reality of congregations.

If we think of "theory" as the forming of generalizations or synoptic judgments and think of "practice" as requiring judgments about particular cases, then inquiry guided by these three types of questions will always require capacities for doing both. As Charles Wood points out in *Vision and Discernment,*[4] inquiry always involves both capacities for "envisioning" (making synoptic judgments) and capacities for "discernment" (making judgments about particular cases). No matter what the question, vision and discernment are exercised directly in regard to concrete practices of Christian congregations. The proposal that the unifying interest governing theological schooling factors into three types of questions does not subtly reintroduce into the discussion of theological schools the stultifying "theory/practice" divide.

Nor does it reintroduce a fragmentation of the subject matter of a theological school's course of study. The reason it does not is that the three questions are logically interdependent. No one of them can be pursued without exploring the other two also.

Consider the array of questions that arise when we ask, "How do we best understand this particular congregation as 'the Christian thing' *in concreto?*" As the Christian thing concretely present, a congregation is a complex of practices comprised of bodily and mental acts regarding ourselves, our neighbors, our shared social and physical contexts, and God. In order to answer the question, "What is this construal of the Christian thing, how do we best describe it?" we have to discover what concepts, what capacities for action, we need to acquire in regard to the congregation in order to enter into *its* grasp of itself, its social and physical worlds, and God. We have to ask what sorts of comprehensive, synoptic pictures of the Christian thing appropriately characterize this congregation (entailing capacities for "vision"). For example, what is this congregation fundamentally: The local outpost of an international institution for the preservation of an intellectual, moral, and aesthetic tradition? An agency for social change? A community of mutual support and solace for the psychologically wounded and spiritually broken? Something else altogether? If more than one of these, in what sort of combination? We have to ask what the most adequate characterizations are of particular practices and action by the congregations in particular settings (entailing capacities for "discernment"). For example, how shall we characterize this congregation's "healing service," especially in relation to its clergy's prayers in hospital rooms? And we have to do all this in a comparative mode, contrasting this congregation's construal of the Christian thing with other, very different congregations' construals.

To offer answers to this array of questions is to make constructive theological proposals. Some will be comprehensive and highly structured: This is how this congregation's construal of the Christian thing is best characterized concretely as a whole in contradistinction to other congregations' construals. Others will be more particular: This is how best to characterize this congregation's construal of who Jesus is; this how best to understand "faith"; this how best to understand "creation," and so forth.

However, exploration of these questions must rest in part on the results of the exploration of two other questions. It will have to rest in part on the results of exploration into how faithful congregations' social space and social form are to the congregations' self-described identities. For when we set out to ask how to characterize "it" we need to be clear how far the concrete "its" in question are, *on their own criteria,* authentic or inauthentic, faithful or faithless, as the Christian thing. Also, exploration of how best to characterize particular Christian congregations' construals of the Christian thing will have to rest in part on the results of exploration of whether their practices involve truth claims and, if so, whether they are true and under what circumstances. For when we set out to characterize a congregation we need to be clear, among other things, whether what we are trying to understand does itself make and logically require certain particular fact claims ("Jesus of Nazareth was crucified and raised from the dead"; "God had called Abram to leave Ur and promised him certain territories in Canaan") and certain universal truth claims about reality in general ("All of 'nature' is radically contingent on God for its reality"; "All historical events are governed by God's providential rule").

Or consider the array of questions that arise when we ask, "Are these congregations being faithful to their self-described self-identities in their current forms of speech and action?" To ask this second type of question is to raise a variety of issues: "Are the forms of speech and action in question a traditional legacy from an earlier social and cultural setting? If so, were they faithful then? If conditions have changed significantly, are they faithful now, even if they were faithful in the past? Have social, cultural, and intellectual conditions changed in ways that introduce issues not addressed at all by these congregations' current forms of speech and action? If so, is that itself a type of faithlessness?" Clearly, this array of questions cannot be explored without identification of some criteria of "faithfulness." Since that is precisely what inquiry guided by the first set of questions provides, clearly exploration of congregations' "faithfulness" to their own identities depends on the results of exploration of how best to characterize them, just as we saw the latter inquiry requires the former. Just as clearly, since an important type of faithfulness is faithfulness to the truth, exploration of congregations' "faithfulness" is dependent on the results of exploration of their truth-claiming, just as we saw the latter is on the former.

Or consider the array of questions that arise when we ask, "Is the Christian thing, concretely present in and as these congregations, true?" To characterize some congregations' construal of the Christian thing is not yet to establish the truth of the Christian thing *as* construed. Stackhouse in *Apologia*[5] rightly stresses the importance of the "truth" question. Nor is exploration of congregations' faithfulness in concrete cases necessarily the same thing as demonstrating the truth of the Christian thing. It is at least a logical possibility that a belief or action may be both authentically or faithfully Christian and false. One condition under which this would be the case, for example, would be if the entire Christian thing were false.

Criteria of truth must be relevant to the sort of inquiry one is engaged in; criteria of truth in historical inquiry are of little relevance in physics. The types of criteria that are relevant are largely internal to the interests that define a given inquiry. It may be that what is normatively Christian includes or implies criteria *beyond* the criteria of faithful "Christianness" by which the truth of Christian theological formulations may be assessed.

Accordingly, to ask about the truth of theological proposals is in part to raise questions about the "logic" of the types of speech and action that comprise the Christian thing. In this way it raises questions about its rationality, its ways of meaning, and the character of its various claims to truth in order to identify the criteria the Christian thing itself entails as relevant for assessing its truth. Among these is the conviction that the Christian thing can illumine our lives in all situations. Hence part of the critical task of assessing the truth of theological formulations is to ask how those formulations help us to understand our lives in historically novel contexts. Another part of the inquiry into the "logic" of the types of speech and action that comprise the Christian thing is to ask about the relations between apparently particular claims about unique historical events and persons, on the one hand, and universal claims about reality as a whole. None of this, of course, will demonstrate the truth of any aspect of the Christian thing, or of the thing itself, by knockdown argument. The apologetic task is to test for truth, not necessarily to vanquish opponents.

Already it is clear, however, that inquiry into the truth of the Christian thing depends in part on the results of inquiry into how any particular construal of it is best characterized, for we cannot really ask whether something is true unless we understand it in the first place. And when part of the inquiry into truth involves asking how the Christian thing helps us understand our lives in novel contexts, it clearly depends on the results of inquiry into which forms of speech and action in the novel situation are genuinely "faithful" ways to live the Christian thing.

Thus, rather than fragmenting a theological course of study, the three basic theological questions can serve to unify it precisely when it is focused on a genuine pluralism of concrete Christian congregations. We have argued that the unity of theological schooling arises from its having a single overarching goal. That goal is defined by its interest to understand God by focusing study on the Christian thing. The Christian thing is concretely available for study *in* and *as* Christian congregations. It is the self-description of those congregations that demands they be studied along three lines of questioning. The threeness of the types of questions does not so much fracture as *refract* the unifying overarching interest that guides the inquiry. Taken together in their interdependence the three questions provide a single framework or horizon within which a multitude of inquiries can be unified into a single course of study.

THE CONTENT OF THE COURSE OF STUDY

According to this proposal the fact that Christian congregations are sets of practices both defines an array of subject matters to be studied in theological schooling and provides the way to unify the course of studies in a fashion adequate to the pluralism of the Christian thing. However, not everything that might justifiably be treated as subject matter in theological study can be selected for study. There are simply too many possibilities. To get down to cases, just which types of congregations ought to be selected as the variety of construals of the Christian thing by reference to which the course of study can be unified and made adequate to pluralism? And just which aspects of them shall be studied, and by what methods? Just which possible courses dealing with these subjects and methods should be included in the course of study? (New Testament courses? Yes. Qumran studies? Well, maybe. Greek, in order to read New Testament texts as carefully as possible? Yes. The social and cultural setting of Hispanic churches in whose common life the New Testament functions importantly? Perhaps. Spanish? Hmmm.)

It is clear that the proposal to focus theological study of the components of the Christian thing through the lens of questions about a variety of Christian congregations does not itself give us a basis for answering this question. The proposal does not imply any particular organization of the courses making up a course of study. The three theological questions may unify the course of study, but in their interdependence they cannot define three "areas" or "fields" into which a curriculum could be organized. Every possible subject matter might fruitfully be studied by inquiry guided by each of the three questions. Hence subject matters cannot be neatly parceled out among the three types of questions. Nor can the three questions be the basis on which to decide the sequence or movement of a theological course of study, that is, which subjects should be studied first, which second, and the like. The interdependence of the three questions rules that out; no one of them is "prior" to the other two.

Moreover, the proposal has explicitly ruled out two frequently suggested bases for the organization and movement of a course of study. The proposal has rejected the supposition that there is some one underlying essential structure to Christianity, on the grounds that such a supposition requires denial of the depth and importance of the pluralism of Christianity. Therefore we cannot adopt the suggestion that the structure and movement of a theological course of study should simply reflect the essential structure of Christianity. The proposal has also rejected the "clerical paradigm," the suggestion that the defining goal of theological schooling is the education of church leadership. Therefore we cannot adopt the suggestion that the structure and movement of a course of study be dictated by the skills and capacities needed to fill ministerial functions.

How, then, shall the organization and the movement of a course of study be decided? At this point our discussion of the institutionalization and polity of a theological school in chapter 8 comes to bear on the discussion of a theological school's course of study in this chapter. Decisions about the organization and movement of a theological course of study are, I suggest, largely a matter of prudent judgment by the theological school itself.

To put it that way is to stress respects in which a theological school is self-regulating. Some of its institutionalized practices, such as its polity, are practices of self-examination, self-criticism, self-regulation and self-change. Individual persons can be self-reflective and thus by entering, in a sense, into a relationship with themselves, effect changes in their own practices; so, by analogy, can schools in their own fashion. Theological schools do so through practices of self-governing that, as I argued in chapter 8, must be qualified in certain respects by the fact that they are *theological* schools. Thus, just as the range of possible subject matters, unity, and adequacy to pluralism of its course of study are decided by a theological school's relationship to congregations, so selection, organization, and movement of a course of study are decided by the school's relation to itself.

It is in regard to a school's own identity and ethos that its governance practices can have the most important implications for its course of study. Theological schools are concrete and quite singular social realities. Each stands in some historical tradition (at the junction of the Berlin Turnpike and Augsburg Road or the road to Trent; Azusa Street or Canterbury Road, etc.) which shapes its distinctive identity and ethos. That concrete, singular identity is one of the major contingencies shaping the course of study. It is the context within which a school will make decisions about the specific content of its course of study. Granted, its concrete identity is an historical given; nonetheless, a theological school is not simply the creature of its heritage. It actively reshapes its identity all the time. As it does so, it may change some of the contingencies that determine the content and shape of its course of study. This is a dimension of its self-governance that is of major importance for the school and is usually of minor visibility. More often than not these changes in identity and ethos come about incrementally and slowly. (Indeed, fascinating histories might be written of major changes in the identities of both denominational and university-related theological schools that came about over the past thirty years not by grand vision and masterful decision but through the accumulated impact of individual decisions about particular proposed courses, programs for this and centers for that.)

At bottom, changes in a school's concrete identity come by decisions it makes, deliberately or inadvertently, about three factors we noted in chapter 2 that distinguish schools from one another: Whether to construe what the Christian thing is all about in some one way, and if so, how; what sort of community a theological school ought to be; how best to go about understanding God. Judgments a school at least implicitly makes about these three questions deeply shape its identity and will almost certainly be reflected in the decisions it makes about the content and movement of its course of study.

One entirely legitimate exercise of a theological school's governance practices is to decide to own and honor its inherited identity rather than merely to perpetuate it tacitly and passively. That will mean that the ethos of its common life as a school will tend to privilege certain answers to the questions about construal of the Christian thing, community, and understanding God. Through the exercise of its governance practices it will have decided to be a distinctively Pentecostal pietist theological school, for example, or a distinctively Roman Catholic school. That is certain to shape the school's decisions about which subject matters to stress relatively more than others in its course of study, which courses to include in what sequence. A school located on the Geneva Road might be expected to include more courses on Reformation history than a school on the road to Canterbury. A school whose concrete identity is that of a church-like community tending to understand God by way of contemplation is likely to include more course work in spirituality, especially ascetical theology, than is a school whose ethos is that of a cadre of clergy tending to understand God by the activist way.

From the point of view of this proposal, there would be no cause for alarm in such decisions. In the nature of the case every school has *some* concrete identity and ethos, and in the nature of the case that identity will be one of the contingencies shaping decisions about the content of the course of study. It is not a goal of this proposal to develop criteria by which to judge that some theological schools' identities are theologically more equal than others. What this proposal does highlight in this regard is that by virtue of their being "self-related," theological schools have the capacity within historically imposed limits to *decide* about their concrete identities. In that way they may to some considerable extent shape some of the contingencies on which the content of their courses of study will depend.

The one constraint this proposal does lay on decisions about the content of the course of study is that it be focused by rigorous and sympathetic study of a *pluralism* of types of Christian congregation. Even when a school explicitly and firmly adopts one construal of the Christian thing as its own, it should study it in comparison with others. That a theological school inescapably has some concrete identity and ethos does not mean that it schools by focusing study only on congregations whose own identities bear the strongest family resemblances to the school's identity. To the contrary, the proposal urges that the best way to affirm any school's theological identity is through study focused on as a wide theological and social-cultural diversity of Christian congregations as possible.

A quite different, but entirely legitimate exercise of a theological school's governance practices is to decide to embrace within its ethos several contrasting answers to each of the questions about how to construe the Christian thing, how to go about understanding God, what sort of community to be. This is the decision made when schools with quite diverse identities merge or "affiliate" or "cluster." It is, presumably, the decision inherent in university-related theological schools' efforts to become more genuinely "interconfessional." This decision becomes the context within which such schools will make judgments about which courses to include in their courses of study and in what sequences (if any!). This interconfessional identity is obviously quite a different context from that created by a school's decision to ground its identity and ethos in only one answer to each of our three questions. That is, by deciding to embrace several different answers to these three questions a theological school changes some of the major contingencies shaping the content of its course of study. It is no part of this proposal to declare this type of decision either more or less theologically legitimate.

It is central to this proposal, however, to stress that when a school makes such a decision to be "open," "interconfessional," or whatever, it should not delude itself into claiming that it merely provides a "theologically neutral arena" and "level playing field" for free theological inquiry and exchange of opinion. It too has a very concrete identity and ethos. It has some specific historical location, probably more extensively on the Berlin Turnpike than on the Athens Highway. It has some particular location in its social and cultural setting. It is ordered to some distinctive arrangement of power and status. It is only realistic to suppose that as a result it will not give equal weight to all of the answers to our three questions that it seeks to embrace. Just how a plurality of ways to construe the Christian thing, ways to go about understanding God, and ways to be in community will be related to one another is finally an internal political matter settled through the school's governance practices. The exact configuration of these matters will play a decisive role in shaping its distinctive identity and ethos and therewith shaping the content of its course of study. Here too the particular ways in which any given school is self-governing carry important implications for the actual content of its course of study.

Notes

1. This structure of three basic theological questions has historical roots in Schleiermacher's organization of theology and, more proximately, is very similar to Charles Wood's way of organizing theology in *Vision and Discernment*. Unlike Wood's scheme, this one does not make a point of separating "moral theology" as a distinct inquiry in its own right; here it is a mode of "critical practical theology." More significant, perhaps, is the fact that my proposal does not call for the synoptic, synthetic inquiry Wood terms "systematic theology." Cf. Wood, *Vision and Discernment*, ch 3.

2. Ibid., ch. 4.

3. Niebuhr et al., *The Purpose of the Church and Its Ministry*, p. 107. Recently James Gustafson has argued anew for this picture of theological schools in "Reflections on the Literature on Theological Education Published Between 1955–1985," *Theological Education*, vol. 24 (Supplement II, 1988).

4. Wood, *Vision and Discernment*, ch. 4.

5. Stackhouse, *Apologia*, Part 3, esp. ch. 9.

10

Between Athens
and Berlin

What picture of excellent schooling does this proposal imply? Does it tend toward paideia as its model of schooling, for which we let "Athens" be the emblem in chapter 3? The proposal's stress on cultivating persons' conceptual growth, on shaping their identities, suggests that it does. Or does it tend toward the model for which we let "Berlin" be the emblem in chapter 4, with its combination of professional education and research-university *Wissenschaft*? The proposal's stress on keeping inquiry rigorous and on cultivating persons' capacities for critical inquiry by use of all relevant scholarly disciplines might suggest that it does. The contrast between the two models described in chapters 3 and 4 suggested that they cannot finally be synthesized. It was pointed out that for historical reasons theological schools in North America can disavow neither model and have to negotiate between them. Rather than favoring one model, does this proposal imply some distinctive way to negotiate between them? I think it does. We can bring this out by examining its implications for two issues that most strongly bring out the differences between "Athens" and "Berlin": (a) What role various academic disciplines have in theological schooling, and (b) what the schooling is intended to do to and for its learners.

A THEOLOGICAL SCHOOL AND THE DISCIPLINES

The model of excellent theological schooling symbolized by the inclusion of a faculty of theology in the University of Berlin tied "practical" education for a socially necessary profession (the clergy) to the "theoretical" education of a research university on the grounds that future clergy would be best equipped for their ministerial functions if they acquired capacities for rigorous critical research. That way they would be best prepared in an ongoing manner, on the one hand, to understand the cultural setting in which they ministered and possible new developments in it, and, on the other hand, to distinguish the essence of Christianity from its various historically conditioned forms and to reformulate it for every new cultural context of ministry. Schooling on this model can be said to aim at "shaping" persons after a fashion. However, what is "formed" is not the person as an agent in a shared public world, but "reason." Put simply, "reason" names the capacities needed to solve problems by asking and finding how to answer the right questions. It is "formed" by acquiring "disciplines" that keep its question-asking and question-answering rigorously self-critical.

By contrast this book urges that the overarching end or goal of theological schooling is to understand God; and "to understand" is to come to have certain conceptual capacities, *habitus,* that is, dispositions and competencies to *act,* that enable us to apprehend God and refer all things including ourselves to God. That is quite clearly in accord with schooling on the model of paideia. What is the relation between cultivating those dispositions and competencies, on one hand, and the academic disciplines that constitute the research university on the other?

The proposal here, in concert with a number of other commentators on theological education,[1] is that academic disciplines should be embraced by a theological school's course of study, although only in such a way that they do not define or organize the course of study. The question is whether this is rather like embracing a boa constrictor. Can the academic disciplines that define the modern research university, heir to Berlin, be embraced by a paideia-like schooling, heir to Athens, without the latter being crushed or, indeed, swallowed without a trace?

First we need to be clear why it is necessary for theological schooling to embrace relevant academic disciplines. Then we shall take the full measure of how difficult it will be to do so. Finally we shall take note of reasons to think that it is nonetheless possible to do.

There is a theological reason why it is necessary to embrace academic disciplines in a theological school's effort to understand God. God cannot be apprehended directly. Understanding of God comes indirectly by focus on something else whose study is thought to capacitate us for apprehending God. My proposal has been that the focus be the Christian thing in and as congregations. This is to make theological inquiry a *positive* inquiry in Schleiermacher's sense, that is, an inquiry into something that is concretely "given" and available for study. Furthermore, the proposal is that Christian congregations be looked at as sets of practices whose governing center is the enactment of a more broadly practiced public worship of God. This means that a theological school should engage not only in positive inquiry but in an inquiry that is inherently and inescapably a *practical* inquiry. Understanding God is rooted in practices; so are both misunderstanding God and bad faith. Furthermore, these practices are materially based and socially located. That is what makes them *concretely* "positive" or given.

Accordingly, study focused on these practices must include inquiry not only into what the practices are that constitute a congregation, what their history has been, how they are to be evaluated, but also into their social and cultural locations. All of this generates the subject matter of the theological course of study. Although the ultimate point of studying this subject matter is to understand God, the more proximate point is simply to understand the subject matter truly. That requires rigorous and orderly methods of inquiry. That is, it requires a variety of types of relevant academic disciplines in order to accomplish the study's theological goals.

What is an academic discipline? For our purposes we may adopt Stephen Toulmin's description of a discipline as a "communal tradition of procedures and techniques for dealing with theoretical and practical problems."[2] On this description an inquiry is a "discipline" when it involves an ongoing community of inquirers whose work is a "practice" (in the sense described in chapter 6) disciplined by a common tradition of methods to be employed, a common language of technical terms and heuristic models, a body of accepted theory, and consensus about what counts as relevant data and a strong argument. Notice how this description of a discipline stresses its communal character: a

229

discipline involves among other things a shared language and agreed-on conventions governing practices of inquiry. All of this is a matter of degree. Physics is a discipline, and so is neurology. Astrophysics is too, but with weaker communal agreement about what counts as a strong argument. History is a discipline, but perhaps with so weak a consensus about methods and heuristic models as to be closer to being a family of subdisciplines. Some inquiries may be nondisciplinable, as are, Toulmin thinks, ethics and philosophy.

What disciplines need to be embraced by a theological course of study? The answer must be: Those disciplines mandated by the sorts of interests we have in congregations. Our guiding and overarching interest lies in the ways in which congregations in their concrete reality are construals of the Christian thing, that is, it lies in the ways they go about worshiping God and therein apprehending God's presence. Given our goal to understand God, we want to ask three types of theological questions about congregations (What are these construals? In practice are they faithful to their self-identified norms? Are they true?). As we saw in the last chapter, interest in congregations as construals of the Christian thing generates a large array of possible subject matters for study, and the three types of theological questions can focus that study on the theological significance of those subjects. The process of answering the three questions needs to be as rigorously critical as possible. The critical rigor depends on the inquiry being disciplined in appropriate ways. Hence the academic disciplines that must be embraced by theological schooling are those dictated by our effort to question the Christian thing in three ways as it is available in and as congregations.

The effort to characterize construals of the Christian thing in the particular cultural and social locations that make them concrete will involve several disciplines: (a) those of the intellectual historian and textual critic (to grasp what the congregation says it is responding *to* in its worship and why); and (b) those of the cultural anthropologist and the ethnographer[3] and certain kinds of philosophical work[4] (to grasp how the congregation shapes its social space by its uses of scripture, by its uses of traditions of worship and patterns of education and mutual nurture, and by the "logic" of its discourse); and (c) those of the sociologist and social historian (to grasp how the congregation's location in its host society and culture helps shape concretely its distinctive construal of the Christian thing).

The effort to assess a congregation's faithfulness to its own self-described identity in relation to God will involve the disciplines of the intellectual historian and the textual critic (to grasp what are the congregation's self-adopted criteria of faithfulness in its uses of and allusions to scripture and the history of Christian thought, its references to Jesus, and its descriptions of its own relationship to God); and the disciplines of the human sciences (to grasp descriptively just what the congregation's dominant forms of speech and action are and what they signify in the context of the congregation's host society and culture).

The effort to assess the truth of the Christian thing as construed by a particular congregation will involve the disciplines of the textual critic and intellectual historian (to grasp the criteria of truth to which the congregation's construal of the Christian thing implicitly or explicitly appeals) and philosophical inquiry (to assess to cogency of the truth claims).

For theological reasons, all these disciplines, and probably more, are needed to make rigorous a theological school's pursuit of its threefold questioning of the subject matter it studies. A theological course of study must cultivate capacities to understand the practices comprising Christian congregations in several disciplined ways. It does not simply cultivate conceptual capacities in relation to congregations. Rather, it cultivates specifically philosophically and historically and sociologically and psychologically and anthropologically *disciplined* capacities to understand Christian congregations, *in the interest* (N.B.!) of acquiring capacities to apprehend God Christianly.

This qualification makes all the difference. It may be that exactly the same array of disciplined capacities is cultivated in a research university in a course of study focused on the phenomena of Christian congregations. The overarching goal of schooling in that context would be simply the cultivation of these capacities for disciplined inquiry for their own sakes. That they are focused on congregations would be accidental. So far as the defining interest of a research university is concerned, they might just as well be focused on any other set of institutionalized practices. In contrast, what makes a theological school *theological* is that its overarching and defining goal is to understand God, and it appropriates the cultivation of capacities for variously disciplined inquiry to *that* end.

This is not a matter of theological schooling taking in something alien. Embracing these disciplines does not create any problem of a threat to the broadly theological "integrity" of theological inquiry. None of these disciplines is inherently "theological" or "non-theological." I have urged that theology is no one inquiry. In the sense of "discipline" we have adopted, theology is no more a single discipline than Toulmin thinks philosophy is. What defines an inquiry as properly theological is neither its immediate and proximate subject matter (which in any case cannot be God) nor the distinctive method of inquiry it employs. Rather, what defines an inquiry as theological is its goal of understanding God more truly. There is no reason in principle why these disciplines cannot be appropriated and employed in the interest of pursuing that goal.

While there may be no reason in principle why a great variety of disciplines could not be embraced by theological schooling without threatening its integrity, there will be great difficulty doing so in practice. There is every reason not to underestimate this difficulty. The difficulty is that, while not the cause of the fragmentation of theological schools' courses of study, the differences among the disciplines have come to be a major force to preserve the fragmentation.

Fragmentation of theological schools' courses of study is currently legitimated and masked by the venerable and apparently rational fourfold pattern of organization of the course of study. The fourfold pattern was not generated by the differences among the disciplines theological schools had embraced. Rather, it was developed as a way to organize the courses of a curriculum in a pattern that reflects what the "clerical paradigm" took to be the overarching goal of theological schooling: the education of clergy. By the seventeenth century, pietist Protestantism had come to look on theological schooling as a movement from revealed sources (scripture), through the extraction and systematization from the sources of their doctrinal content (theology), to clarifying doctrine and making it more precise through the history of theological controversy (church history), to application of the doctrine in ministerial practices.[5]

This movement was the basis on which the courses making up a theological curriculum could be organized in a fourfold way. The fourfold pattern can be traced historically to the influence of Karl R. Hagenbach's *Encykopädie und Methodologie der theologischen Wissenschaften*, first published in 1833.[6] It tends to divide the courses that make up the curriculum into four "areas" or "fields": biblical, theological, historical, and practical. There are variations in the pattern. For example, the historical and theological areas may be combined into an area described as "Interpretation of Christianity" while the older "practical" field is divided into two, one dealing with "Church and Culture" (sociological, psychological, and philosophical studies of church phenomena in American culture) and the other dealing with the practice of ministry construed as the application of social scientific and psychological theory to clergy responsibilities. Or the traditional fourfold pattern may be retained by a fifth "area" to house "Christianity and" inquiries ("Christianity and Society," "Christianity and the Arts," etc.).

It is important to note that these areas or fields are not defined by distinctive methods of inquiry or "disciplines," but by subject matter. They are not fields of some *one* discipline, say history. Within a given area several different disciplines may be employed. The number of areas is defined by the number of types of subject matter that are deemed to be essential to a well-rounded theological education. The function of areas is to divide the curriculum's courses into the academic equivalent of food groups, daily selection from each of which is essential to a healthy theological diet. Each student is to have some study in each area.

The four curricular areas have become holding pens for groups of "academic specializations." Edward Farley points out that academic specializations do not correspond to curricular areas. They are partly defined by their subject matter. Specializations have relatively *narrow* subject matter. They are usually subdivisions of areas. Within the area of biblical studies there are the specializations of "Hebrew Bible" and "New Testament"; and within them there can be further specializations, such as "Gospel studies" in contradistinction to "Pauline studies." Research in the Gospels, in turn, becomes even more specialized as groups of scholars concentrate on using a distinctive method: rhetorical criticism vs. redaction criticism, and the like. So specializations, partly defined by subject matter, are also partly defined by specific disciplines.

This brings us to the way in which various academic disciplines can serve to *preserve* the fragmentation of theological courses of study. Academic specializations tend to be partly defined by the use of a distinctive discipline. Disciplines, in the sense of the term we are borrowing from Toulmin, have a strong communal dimension. They consist of practices that are communally shared. The social practices involved in academic specializations tend to be institutionalized (often informally) outside of theological schools in what are often referred to as academic guilds. These are institutionalizations of the groups engaged in these practices of research on national and even international bases. They become the arbiters of excellence in the specialization. Status and social and political power within the guilds thus shape inquiry as deeply as do status and power within a theological school.

The possible tension between the two institutionalized sets of practices, that of the guilds and that of the theological schools, has powerful consequences for a theological school. It may easily come to be the case in a theological school that the objectives governing, say, inquiry into Old Testament historical narratives, may be more deeply shaped by interests currently central to the relevant guild than by the horizon of three questions that refracts the interest defining the theological school, namely, to understand God truly. More generally, disciplines tend to develop an agenda of their own as sets of practices with interests rooted in the social location of these practices (e.g., in universities). They tend, in short, to take on a life of their own, having the power to order and govern the courses comprising a course of study. In this context, commitment to the specialization and its central discipline may lead to a commitment to preserving one's own area in the fourfold curriculum, thereby preserving the curricular fragmentation that the fourfold pattern of curricular organization has come to represent. For that reason, in the present state of inquiry in theological schooling it may be difficult for theological schools to embrace the disciplines without threat to the theological integrity of their theological task.

Clearly, *theology* as the effort to understand God better by focusing study on Christian congregations is not itself an area (not a discrete subject matter), certainly not an academic specialization, and not at all *a* discipline. It is no one thing. It is certainly not to be equated with "systematic theology." It is rather the work of the entire theological school (and is too important to leave to the systematic theologians alone). It is, in Stephen Toulmin's phrase, "field encompassing." Hence the courses that make up a theological school's course of study must not only draw on information and insights from a variety of fields or areas of subject matter but must also employ the methods, forms of argument and accepted types of evidence, regnant theory, and technical language that constitute the several disciplines. However, if it is genuinely to be a *theological* course of study its use of these disciplines must be governed by the overarching end of theological inquiry: To understand God by focusing study within the horizon of questions about congregations.

While the communal character of the disciplines may tend to make it difficult for a theological school to embrace them without threat to the school's integrity, another feature of academic disciplines makes such embrace entirely possible. What makes it possible is the fact that disciplines are themselves defined not by their subject matter but by their interests in the subject matter. Those interests (What is the historical provenance and origin of this text or practice? What is the internal logic or "grammar" of that way of speaking, of that emotion or this passion, of that type of action? What is the social location of this group and its characteristic points of view? etc.) can be subordinated to and appropriated by the interests governing a theological course of study (How and why do these congregations understand themselves, their neighbors, and their shared worlds in relation to God under these specific circumstances?).

In order to appropriate the relevant disciplines for its course of study a theological school needs to find ways in which to countervail the disciplines' tendency to take on lives of their own. A theological school must find ways to insist that its own interests set the agenda guiding inquiry that uses the several disciplines. This is a point at which attention to the concrete reality of a theological school is of utmost importance. A theological school is a self-governing institutionalized set of practices. Nothing would be accomplished by recommending that a school disassociate itself from the disciplines, except loss of capacities for rigorous self-criticism in inquiry. Theologically speaking, that would be an act of faithlessness. Not much more would be accomplished by attacking the academic guilds in which disciplines' communal practices are institutionalized. Given that they are constituted by such practices, if they lacked the guilds, the disciplines would nevertheless necessarily have some sort of institutionalized social space and form which would pose the same type of problem to theological schools that the guilds do now. Consequently, far more to the point would be the deliberate development and institutionalization of practices within and among theological schools that would make prominent the theological school's own particular agenda of interests in congregations, encourage inquiry governed by that agenda, and reward such inquiry in its processes of promotion and assigning of scholarly status and esteem.

If a Christian theological school succeeded in doing that, it would have negotiated between "Athens" and "Berlin" in a distinctive way. With regard to its overarching goal it would side more with Athens than Berlin. The goal is to form persons with the *habitus* that capacitate them as agents in a shared public world to apprehend God Christianly, rather than to form only their "reason" with capacities for disciplined critical and self-critical inquiry. As in paideia, *habitus* that capacitate people to apprehend God are formed only indirectly by study of something else. However, the *range* of things studied and the type of *critical thinking* employed are appropriated from "Berlin." Classically, paideia focused study on texts and, while it cultivated capacities to test the cogency of arguments critically, it was uncritical of received or traditional authorities to which arguments might appeal. A theological school according to this utopian proposal would appropriate from "Berlin" an openness to take as its subject of study *all* components of the Christian thing concretely present in and as congregations, their social and institutional forms as well as their texts and their forms and contents. It would also appropriate from "Berlin" its disciplines of critical and self-critical inquiry that assume nothing is exempt from critical testing. However, it would appropriate these aspects of the "Berlin" model of excellent schooling by abstracting them from the institutional structures that make them the concrete practices they are in research universities. Thus, in its concrete reality such a theological school would no more consist of the institutionalized practices constituting an actual school modeled on "Berlin" than it would consist of the institutionalized practices constituting an actual school modeled on "Athens." It would simply be itself.

A THEOLOGICAL SCHOOL AND ITS LEARNERS

Central to the practices that comprise a theological school are practices of teaching and learning. They are institutionalized in the roles of "teacher" (faculty) and "students" and the structure of the status and power relationships between those roles. Nonetheless, the distinction "faculty/student body" is not identical with the distinction "teaching/ learning." It is a commonplace that in the practices of teaching and learning, faculty often learn and students often teach. Our concern here is with a school's relationship to *all* who learn. What does a theological school's practices of teaching and learning do to and for these people? Is what it does more in accord with paideia than with *wissenschaftlich* "professional" schooling, more modeled on "Athens" or on "Berlin"?

A theological school does two things in particular to its learners. What it centrally tries to do for people is to cultivate and nurture in them a range of capacities and abilities in relation to understanding God. A theological school cultivates conceptual capacities in the sense of "conceptual" we discussed in chapter 6. They are capacities and abilities to act in certain characteristic ways in relation to God, and to ourselves, other persons, and the social and natural contexts of our lives insofar as all of these are related to God. To have these abilities is at least to some degree to understand God and all things in relation to God. Put another way, to have these conceptual abilities is to be capacitated to apprehend God "Christianly." Recall the distinction drawn in chapter 8 between "doing theology" in the proper sense and doing it "educationally." Congregations necessarily do theology in the proper sense; doing theology is inherent in the practices constituting a congregation. A theological school also necessarily does theology in the proper sense, and for the reason that it is inherent in the defining goal of such a school. However, it also is the case that a theological school does theology in an educational way. That is, by doing theology a theological school aims to cultivate particular capacities for theological reflection and for theological critique.

Does the fact that this proposal pictures theological schooling as a kind of "formation" of people mean that it implicitly adopts the model of theological schooling as paideia? I think not. Granted, there are important formal resemblances. Our proposal suggests that theological schooling, paideia-like, helps capacitate persons with *habitus*. Like classical paideia, it does this indirectly, by focusing study on something else. Unlike the capacities cultivated by schooling on the Berlin model, these *habitus* are not limited to capacities for engaging in critical inquiry. Rather, as in classical paideia, what is cultivated are dispositions to act in the public realm in certain ways. Moreover, the *habitus* cultivated in paideia necessarily include ones that are existentially shaping. Acquiring them helps shape and change one's very identity.

However, active engagement in the practices comprising a Christian congregation will do that too. Indeed, as we saw in chapter 3, that is what gives an air of plausibility to looking on the practices of Christian worship as engagement in a "Christian" type of paideia. By contrast, recall that we have made a major point of the fact that engagement in the practices of theological schooling focused by study of Christian congregations requires no more than an "as if" acquisition of the conceptual capacities constituting Christian identity. Theological schooling involves conceptual capacities that are existentially forming, but perhaps in a subjunctive mood, "condition contrary to [personal] fact." In that way, the picture of theological schooling sketched here is finally not a picture of paideia. Some of the practices of a congregation may be like paideia, but theological schooling in the end is not.

Underlying that difference is another having to do with view of human personhood. The concept of paideia entails postulation of something like an ahistorical and universally self-identical essential self—a substantial soul (Plato) or consciousness-as-such. In contrast the picture of a theological school outlined here logically requires nothing of the sort. While it doubtless overlaps with the paideia model of schooling, it is finally like it only in superficial ways.

Is this utopian proposal then more like the Berlin model in what it calls for a theological school to do for learners? After all, we have said in addition to "forming" persons' conceptual capacities to apprehend God Christianly, a theological school may capacitate people specifically for leadership roles in Christian congregations. Granted, while it has the capacity to do this, it does not necessarily do so. A constant theme in this proposal is that the unifying and defining goal of a theological school is its interest to understand God for the sake of understanding God and *not* for any other purpose such as preparing leadership for Christian congregations. Nonetheless, a school's practices of teaching and learning are in fact the best way to prepare church leadership. Does that align this proposal with the Berlin model and its call to theological schooling to be "professional" education of church leaders? I think not.

To explain this we need to explore the idea of church leadership. We have already tended to associate it with ministry. This is not wrong, but it could easily mislead us into equating the two. "Ministry" is frequently used as a generic characterization of what I have called "public worship of God in the broad sense" or discipleship. To minister is to be in the service of the One to whom the congregation is responding in worship. It is the entire congregation and not only its leaders that engages in ministry. However, there are a variety of activities embraced in the practice of the public worship of God. Each of them requires leadership, sometimes of more than one type. Precisely because it is leadership in relation to the worship of God, it calls for well-developed capacities for theological judgment. These are the capacities cultivated by participation in the practices comprising a theological school.

The *variety* of types of leadership calling for capacities for theological judgment needs to be stressed. For all of their diversity they all require capacities for doing theology ad hoc, and in some cases capacities for doing it in a sustained and methodical way. Consider some examples. Central to the entire practice of the public worship of God, we have insisted, is the activity of reminding, indeed confronting the congregation with Who and what it is they are responding to. Someone must be made responsible for preparing and delivering the word, and someone made responsible for presiding at the sacrament. Carrying out this leadership responsibility requires a variety of abilities and capacities. Crucial is the capacity for ad hoc self-critique of the Christian adequacy and truth of sermons and homilies as well as of liturgical forms while they are being prepared and enacted. It also requires capacities for sustained and methodical reflection on the theological standards that are likely to be largely implicit in the ad hoc critique.

The practice of the public worship of God, in the broad sense adopted here, also embraces pastoral care of persons in various sorts of trouble through acts of reconciliation, healing, guiding, and sustaining.[7] These acts ultimately aim to help persons deal with questions about the meaning and worth of their lives by helping them not only to understand their troubles in a fresh way in the light of God's presence but also actively to live through their troubles in the context of God's presence. A variety of capacities are needed in order to provide such care. They are in some respects quite different from the capacities needed for leadership in word and sacrament. Pastoral caring requires not only those capacities that make someone "empathetic," "sensitive," and "perceptive" about other persons. It also requires some grasp of a range of theological concepts that are existentially shaping—for example, hope, and how it is different from optimism; joy, and how it is different from euphoria; grief, and how it is different from depression; acceptance, and how it is different from resignation; anger, and how it is different from self-hatred; self-regard, and how it is different from egotism. Moreover, like leadership in proclamation, leadership in pastoral caring requires capacities to make ad hoc theological judgments in the midst of pastoral care-giving. They are judgments about the Christian adequacy of what is pastorally said and done given the particularities of that individual situation.

The public worship of God also embraces acts done in the public realm in solidarity with those who suffer because of unjust social, economic, and political arrangements that are systemic in the society. This is perhaps less obvious. However, if the normative instance of the odd way God has been and promises yet to be "present" is the ministry, crucifixion, and resurrection appearances of Jesus of Nazareth; and if what is central to Jesus' mission was the proclamation of the imminence of God's "kingly" rule breaking the powers that bind and deform creaturely life; and if what is significant about the crucifixion and resurrection appearances of Jesus is that in that very peculiar way and form God's "kingly" rule has been inaugurated in history, though not yet realized; and if public worship of God in the broad sense is faithful discipleship to God's mission in Jesus; *then* faithfulness itself requires that the practice of the worship of God include witness to and celebration of God's redemptive work in the public realm on behalf of those who suffer bondage to injustice.

Granted, there is room for considerable disagreement about the Christianly appropriate mode of this action. It ranges from the view that such action should only take the form of a "witness of presence," when necessary going no further in action than civil disobedience; to the view that it may take the form of active intervention in the political life of society, on rare occasions going as far as active involvement in violent revolution. On any view, however, these activities require leadership that has ranges of theological capacities and abilities that are different in many respects from the capacities needed for leadership in proclamation or in pastoral caring.

This leadership also requires that these abilities be governed by other capacities. These latter are capacities for ad hoc judgment of the Christian adequacy of the forms of speech and action being employed, and capacities to weigh in a sustained and methodical way the truth and "Christianness" of the theological criteria used in the ad hoc assessments.

The public worship of God also embraces activities that are specifically educational. These are activities in which the communal identity of congregation and the personal identities of its members are shaped in ways appropriate as responses to God's presence in Jesus of Nazareth. Central to this "forming" are the various ways in which biblical writings are used in the community's common life. They are used in informational ways so that their content is learned, their historical backgrounds understood, the histories of various types of communities that use them is known, and the relation to various traditions of Christian thought and practice is grasped. Ultimately, however, the informational education in a congregation is ordered to another more identity-shaping type of education. In this type of education persons are helped to see God's odd way of being present in Jesus as the context of their own lives. It is a context in whose light they come to see themselves and their shared public world in unexpected and fresh ways. These educational activities call for leadership capacitated by still different ranges of abilities—knowledgeability about the relevant information, pedagogical skills, understanding of the conceptual capacities of persons of different ages and of what they are capable of acquiring conceptually, etc.

Beyond that, leadership in educational activities in a congregation requires capacities for theological judgment. Here most of all, these must be capacities not only for ad hoc theological judgments in the midst of educational activity about what is being said and done, but also capacities for sustained and methodical theological reflection, both constructive and critical, on the theological formulations being used as norms of Christian adequacy and truth in the ad hoc theological judgments made in all of the activities comprising the congregation's common life.

Thus in many and various ways the leadership required by the activities embraced in a congregation's practice of the public worship of God demands capacities for theological judgment that are conceptual capacities which may be acquired in a theological school. However, this is not really what the Berlin model calls for. Recall that Schleiermacher's proposal justifying theological schooling in the new University of Berlin had two poles. Insofar as it is excellent schooling, it had to be *wissenschaftlich;* insofar as it is genuinely theological, it had to be "professional" schooling preparing leadership for a "necessary practice." True, my proposal includes features that formally resemble each of those poles. However, the resemblances have such different contexts and bases that they can hardly be considered to be so much as a modification of the Berlin model.

The relationship between a theological school and the *wissenschaftlich* disciplines was discussed in the previous section. There the argument was that for theological reasons theological inquiry needs to be as critical and self-critical as possible and therefore must make use of rigorously critical conventions of inquiry, that is, *Wissenschaft*. However, the argument went, unlike the Berlin model, this proposal does not set up the cultivation of capacities for critical inquiry as the defining goal of schooling. Cultivation of those capacities is secondary and instrumental to pursuit of theological schooling's own proper goal. To that distinction between this proposal and the Berlin model another must now be added.

The Berlin model introduces an important modification of the traditional picture of the movement of theological schooling. As was pointed out in the last chapter, whereas ancient theological schooling was a movement from revealed sources (scripture) to personal appropriation, in seventeenth-century Europe it became a movement from revealed source to formulation of doctrine contained in the revealed source (systematic theology) and clarified through the history of doctrinal conflict in the church (church history) to application of that doctrine in the tasks of church leadership (practical theology). The view of theology that Schleiermacher assumed in his argument for the inclusion of a theology faculty in the new University of Berlin implied a modification of that movement. Theology was for him a movement from descriptive accounts of what Christianity has been and now is as actually given (i.e., as a "positive religion") to the development of a *theory* about what is the "essence" that makes all those different versions of Christianity nonetheless one thing (i.e., their shared "Christianness"), to the formulation of the implicit rules governing practices, and leadership of those practices, that are genuinely "Christian." So theological schooling was to have a movement from sources (history of Christianity or historical theology, including scripture) to a theoretical moment (philosophical theology) to the application of the theory to practice (practical theology). This is why *Wissenschaft* was so important. It meant, quite particularly, the disciplines of the academic *historian* to make sure the first moment was rigorously done, and the disciplines of the academic *philosopher* to make sure that the second, theoretical moment was rigorously done.

Schleiermacher's three-step movement did not affect the future of theological schooling very much at the organizational level. Theological schools tended to preserve the fourfold organization of the curriculum rooted in the earlier four-step movement of schooling. However, Schleiermacher's proposal did profoundly affect the *movement* of subsequent theological schooling. Where once it had been a movement from revealed wisdom to changed personal identity through personal appropriation of the wisdom, and then it had been a movement from revealed truth to the application of that truth to life, especially the life of church leadership, now it became a movement from theory *about* "positively" given Christian phenomena to application of that theory in practice. In this, theological schooling was of a piece with research university schooling generally. It was a movement from data to formulations of theory (here university responsibility ended) which might then be applied to solve various problems (here applied science and engineering of all sorts begin). Schleiermacher argued that in the case of medical, law, and theology faculties the University of Berlin ought to make an exception at just this point. Here the university ought to combine research with its application *for sociological reasons:* These are the three professions that are necessary for society's health (presumably civil or mechanical engineering were not "socially necessary" in the same way). Hence these three were to be "professional schools" incorporated in a research university, although admittedly anomalous there.

In this context "theory" means a type of description that is highly general and very powerful. It is highly general in that it applies to wide ranges of phenomena that might appear to be quite different from one another. It is very powerful in that it generates a large number of explanations of otherwise puzzling matters, or a large number of solutions to practical problems, or large numbers of predictions that turn out to be correct. Theory, in this sense of the term, is ordered to practice. Thereafter doing theology, which had been seen as "sapiential," the cultivation and exercise of the wisdom that is inherent in faith, came to be seen as a type of theorizing which could subsequently be applied to solve problems in Christian life and thought. That is central to the Berlin model of excellent theological schooling.

This is a major point at which this utopian proposal does not comport with the Berlin model. While it implies the appropriation of the academic disciplines that keep schooling *wissenschaftlich,* this proposal rejects the Berlin model's picture of doing theology as a type of "theory construction" and its picture of theological schooling as a movement from theory to application. The proposal roots theology in engagement with a set of practices. "Theology" covers a wide variety of activities all of which are required in one way or another by the effort to access critically a certain array of practices. It simply is not a type of academic theorizing in the sense of "theory" symbolized by "Berlin." Moreover, the proposal entails no particular pattern of movement for theological schooling and implicitly rejects the Berlin model's movement from theory to application (if there is no "theory," there can be no movement "to" application!). If anything, the proposal is closer to the earliest picture of the movement, the appropriation of wisdom inherent in practices for which faith, hope, and love are the *habitus.*

What about the "professional" pole of the Berlin model? Does not our claim that a theological school is of the *bene esse* of congregations because it can prepare church leadership imply that we have adopted at least this half of the Berlin model? No, for at least two reasons. For one thing, I have argued for the "theological school paradox": It is precisely by being schooled in a way that is governed by an apparently nonutilitarian (read: "useless") overarching goal (that is, to understand God simply for the sake of understanding God) that persons can best be prepared to provide church leadership. Consequently a school that can prepare such leadership cannot be defined by the goal to educate leadership for the churches—which is exactly what the Berlin model does do. This too is a fundamental difference in principle between the Berlin model and the proposal sketched here.

A second difference between the two regarding the "professional" character of a theological school arises from the nature of "leadership" in congregations. It is not clear that church leadership is best characterized as professional leadership in the sense of professional assumed by the Berlin model. Profession and professional are sociological concepts. The "sociology of professions" is a recognized subfield in the field of sociology. However, profession is used in different ways by different sociologists. Jackson W. Carroll has surveyed this variety and helpfully analyzed its implications for characterizing church leadership.[8]

There seem to be six elements commonly thought to constitute a profession, but different writers interrelate them and weight them variously.[9] A profession is:

(1) a full-time occupation (vs. the part-time amateur);

(2) set aside from others by various signs and symbols (vs. the laity) and identified with peers (often in and by an organization with power to enforce a common ethos and ethic, to impose standards for education for the occupation, to control entry into

the occupation and thereby control its market, to be self-governing).

Leadership for the activities comprising the common life of a congregation does not necessarily incorporate these two elements of a profession. "Set aside from others" raises the topic of ordination. Not all church leadership is ordained. What the theological rationale is for ordination and just which leadership roles should be ordained is a controversial issue that has no implications for this book and to which this book, in turn, has nothing to contribute. What is clear is that theological schooling does not qualify persons for leadership responsibilities that are to be "set apart" simply because they have received that kind of schooling. If they are set aside by ordination, it is for other reasons. The nature and purpose of ordination does not define the nature and purpose of a theological school. In any case, neither ordained nor nonordained church leadership is necessarily "full time." It may be that for historical and cultural reasons ordained leadership will in fact continue to be largely a full-time occupation in most congregations in North America. If so, that is a contingent fact and not inherent either in the concept "leadership in a congregation" nor in the concept "ordained."

Furthermore, a profession is:

(3) marked by a sense of calling, which means that the occupation and all of its requirements are treated as an enduring set of normative and behavioral expectations;

(4) marked by a service orientation, which places the needs of the client(s) above self-interest.

Leadership in a congregation does incorporate these two elements of a profession. "Call" is not limited to the ordained. From the perspective of Christian congregations it is not even limited to "leaders." Theologically speaking, to be a member of the congregation is to be called to ministry. Different kinds of leadership roles and responsibilities give different specific content to "service." Most important, the relation of leader to the congregation is not in any of its varieties the same as the relation of a "professional" to a "client." The service is always an exercise or enactment of *habitus,* or capacities and abilities for theological judgment. Indeed, this theologically formed service orientation is central to the set of normative and behavior expectations that go with having a call. However, incorporation of these two elements alone is probably not enough to classify congregational leadership as "professional."

Finally, a profession:

(5) is marked by possession of esoteric but useful knowledge and skills based on specialized training that is usually long and difficult; and

(6) enjoys autonomy in the exercise of its knowledge and skills, restrained only by the profession's ethics.

This is the point at which the deepest difference occurs between our proposal and the Berlin model of "professional" schooling. There are two issues: "What counts as 'competence' in congregational leadership?" and "How can competence be valued without introducing theologically unacceptable divisions between clergy (the competent) and laity?"

Theologically, it is important to stress that it is the entire congregation that engages in ministry in the public worship of God. Various kinds of leadership in regard to that ministry are exercised by persons who stand in parity with everybody else so far as their shared ministry is concerned. Hence a profession's stress on "autonomy" and its view of those served as "clients" are both inappropriate in congregational leadership. Nonetheless, leadership requires competence. Our stress that leadership does require highly developed theological conceptual capacities, capacities for theological judgment, underscores that point.

Sociologically, it is important to note the sorts of "esoteric but useful knowledge and skills" that our society values as the basis of true professionalism. Under the all-pervasive cultural influence of modern science and technology, our society values knowledge rooted in scientifically based theory that is translated into skills for solving individual and social human problems. These are knowledge and skills that involve the distinctively modern type of rationality that social theorists call "technical rationality." That is the sense of "rationality" taken for granted by the Berlin model of excellent schooling. If congregational leadership were "professional" in that sense it would be scientifically based and would rely on technical rationality.

Some sociologists deny that clergy are a profession on the grounds that clergy do not rely on technical rationality, have no skills based on a distinctive body of scientific theory, and therefore have no socially useful role to play. The line of thought could easily be shifted from ordained clergy to congregational leaders. Conversely, some theologians in effect deny that church leadership is a profession precisely because it *ought* not to employ technical rationality. Technical rationality is a quite different mode of rationality from the sort of wisdom that is rooted in faith, hope, and love for God. Any effort to produce scientifically based knowledge and skills regarding *theologia* would simply objectify and deform it and thereby misunderstand it. To think of church leadership as a profession is to require that education for it be training in a set of scientifically based skills. Others go further. They distinguish between authority based on expertise and authority based on personal relationship with God.[10] The former would be a profession relying on technical rationality to rationalize the holy that is a-rational, which sounds like a fruitless undertaking; the latter would be a "sacramental person" mediating God's presence.

Surely, however, it is a mistake to divorce competency for leadership in a congregation's common life from rational competencies. There is strong theological reason to challenge narrowing of "rationality" to "technical rationality." Rationality names the array of capacities required to understand critically and self-critically, in the sense of "understand" outlined in chapter 6. That array certainly includes capacities for various sorts of "problem-solving," which seem to be the capacities valued by technical rationality. But rationality goes beyond that, including a richer range of capacities. Nonetheless, it does not exclude the capacities comprising technical rationality. Competence correlates with having the richest array of capacities-to-understand that is required by a certain set of practices. They are all rational capacities. Congregation leadership requires high competence. What counts as competence cannot be adequately characterized as "information and skills." It certainly includes that. However, competence in congregation leadership is probably more adequately characterized in a general way as "knowledge, capacities, and abilities," which mark it as eminently rational competence.

Such competence is acquired through participation in the long and difficult practices constituting a theological school. The knowledge and capacities in which this competence is based are not necessarily rooted in technical reason but are nonetheless rational. Accordingly, theological schooling that may incidentally prepare church leadership, even though like "professional education" it may be long and difficult and nurture common skills and capacities, ought not to be considered professional schooling in the Berlin model's sense of professional. Thus, our proposal no more adopts the way the Berlin model defines the professional school side of its picture of excellent theological schooling than it does the way it defines the *wissenschaftlich* side of that picture.

This honors the tradition in theological schooling that insists that whatever else it does, a theological school should prepare "learned ministers." My proposal has been that precisely because a theological school is not defined by the goal of educating church leaders it may, as a matter of contingent fact, prepare its students very well for leadership in congregations. The leadership may be either lay or ordained, full or part time. The theological course of study may equip persons particularly well for these leadership roles precisely by cultivating in them variously disciplined capacities for understanding the congregations they lead, and capacities for understanding how congregations concretely are the Christian thing in a particular construal, for understanding how to assess with both vision and discernment congregations' faithfulness to who they say they are, and for understanding how to lead them into being "truer" to themselves. What justifies calling such leadership "learned" is not necessarily that it has an unusually deep fund of arcane information and an unusually subtle grasp of esoteric theory, for it may well be that many other members of the congregations who are not in leadership roles have acquired all of that. Rather, such leaders would be learned in the distinctively modern sense of having had their capacities to understand variously *disciplined* by the several relevant academic disciplines.

If a Christian theological school succeeded in doing that, it would have negotiated between "Athens" and "Berlin" in a distinctive way, not only in regard to modern academic disciplines, but also in regard to what it does for its learners. The goal is to form persons with the *habitus* that qualify them as agents in a shared public world to apprehend God Christianly. Most broadly speaking, that is what a theological school can do for its learners. In that regard it sides perhaps more with Athens than with Berlin. However, although acquisition of some of the requisite conceptual capacities shapes the personal identity of the learner, they can be acquired through theological schooling in an "as if" mode. Since it is a mode of schooling aimed at "forming" the very identity of its learners, paideia is more like what goes on in Christian congregations than it is like the theological schooling proposed here.

More narrowly, theological schooling aims to capacitate its learners to understand Christian congregations as diverse concrete construals of the Christian thing. In doing that it can prepare its learners for leadership responsibilities in congregations. The nature of the practices making up congregations requires that their leaders be "theologically schooled" in the sense of the term developed in this proposal. Schooling modeled on both "Athens" and "Berlin" can and has done this. However, unlike most theological schools on either model, the school sketched in this proposal is not defined as a "theological" school by a goal to educate church leadership. If some (or all) of its learners end up providing leadership for congregations, that is simply a contingent fact, although the fact that they are *well* educated for such roles is a result of their having been well schooled theologically! In any case, a theological school according to this utopian proposal would reject central features of the Berlin model by denying that the capacities it cultivates in its learners are capacities for "theory" (in the "Berlin" sense of the term) which are subsequently to be "applied." Moreover, since for theological reasons congregational leadership cannot be adequately characterized in the sociological sense of the term as a "profession," a theological school in accord with this utopian proposal is not a professional school on the Berlin model and does not even contingently educate church professionals. Thus, in regard to what it does for its learners quite as much as in regard to what it does with the academic disciplines, a theological school in accord with this proposal would simply be itself, comporting no more with "Berlin" than it does with "Athens" but holding aspects of each together in what can only be described (and, if one lived in such a crossroads hamlet, experienced) as "dialectical tension."

Notes

1. See Edward Farley, *Theologia,* esp. chs. 6 and 8; idem, *The Fragility of Knowledge,* esp. ch. 3; Max L. Stackhouse, *Apologia,* ch. 9; Charles Wood, *Vision and Discernment,* esp. ch. 5.

2. Stephen Toulmin, *Human Understanding,* vol. 1; *The Collective Use and Evolution of Concepts,* p. 142.

3. As James Hopewell's pioneering work points out. See Hopewell, *Congregation: Stories and Structures.*

4. Although Toulmin doubts that it is a discipline! See note 2 above.

5. See Farley, *Theologia,* Part I, for a brief, generally accepted history of this development.

6. K. R. Hagenbach, *Encykopädie und Methodologie der theologischen Wissenschaften,* 12th ed., ed. Max Reischle (Leipzig: S. Hirzel, 1889).

7. William Clebsch and Charles R. Jaekle, *Pastoral Care in Historical Perspective* (New York: Harper & Row, 1975).

8. Jackson W. Carroll, "The Professional Model of Ministry—Is It Worth Saving?" *Theological Education* (Spring 1985), pp. 7–48. Carroll answers the question in his article's title with a "Yes"; I will answer it with a "No."

9. What follows is a rearrangement of a list Carroll (ibid., p. 10) draws

from sociologists Wilbert E. Moore and G. W. Rosenblum, *The Professions: Roles and Rules* (New York: Russell Sage Foundation, 1970), p. 5.

10. Carroll cites A. M. Carr-Saunders and P. A. Wilson, *The Professions* (Oxford University Press, 1933) and Robert Towler and Anthony P. M. Coxon, *The Fate of the Anglican Clergy: A Sociological Study* (London: Macmillan & Co., 1979).

Epilogue

This proposal has been an invitation to reflect critically on a theological school well known to you.

When one has begun one's first academic year in a North American theological school, the Fall is on its way; when the second year has begun, the Fall will almost certainly arrive. A sharp pinch is likely to be felt between assumptions and hopes with which one first entered into the school and the experienced reality of the school. One sure sign that this has begun to happen will be a shift in informal out-of-classroom conversations from talk about course work, or even from talk about other people in the school, to talk about the school itself.

It will be talk in a very specific language. It is absolutely predictable that diagnoses of what causes the pinch and suggestions of ways to correct it will be posed in the same few pairs of contrast terms:

- theory/practice—as in, "This school doesn't do enough to integrate theory and practice";
- academic/professional—as in, "This school puts so much stress on professional training that it slights academics"; alternatively, "This school may be strong academically but it provides little help in preparing for professional ministry";
- head/heart—as in, "The students and faculty here seem to assume that Christianity is mainly a matter of feelings; it's all heart and almost no head"; or vice versa;
- classroom/field—as in, "Have you noticed how hard it is to get

contextual learning here? Learning is all supposed to happen in the classroom and none in the field."

There is conventional wisdom in theological schools about these terms. Conventional wisdom has it that these pairs are largely interchangeable, as though they were simply alternative ways in which to name basically the same contrast. A major assumption in conventional wisdom is that this underlying contrast is inherent in the task of educating future clergy so that they will be ready for their ministerial functions. Furthermore, conventional wisdom has it that the two terms in each of these pairs are inversely related to one another: The more we have of one, the less we can have of the other. Consequently, conventional wisdom has it, every theological school must strike a quasi-quantitative "balance" between the poles of each pair.

Eventually one discovers that there is another piece of conventional wisdom about conversations that use these phrases to diagnose theological schooling's ills and prescribe cures: The conversations are interminable and inconclusive. One has only to participate in them for a relatively short time to begin to feel that they go in circles and get nowhere.

The proposal developed in this book is based on a hunch that discussions of theological schooling and proposals to reform it might get further if some of the assumptions and many of the terms conventionally used in the discussions were changed. The heart of the proposed reframing of the discussion is the effort to keep discussion of theological schooling as concrete as possible. The content of the proposal itself is doubtless an entirely utopian picture of a theological school. However, plausible or not, persuasive or not, sketching it is a vehicle by which to make some suggestions for critical reflection about some particular concrete theological school after the Fall.

Above all the proposal suggests that reflection on a theological school begin by distinguishing two questions and then asking how the answers to each might bear on the other question. The two questions are: What makes this school a *theological* school; what is "theological" about it? and, What makes this school the particular, concrete *school* that it is? Then the two questions impinge on each other: How does whatever it is that makes this school "theological" shape or modify its concrete reality as a school? How does what makes it the particular, concrete school it is shape or modify its being genuinely "theological"? An entire budget of questions for reflection grows out of these questions.

They suggest that it would be helpful to reflect on the following questions when we seek to understand, to criticize, and perhaps even to reform some particular theological school:

1. What marks this school as specifically "theological"?

Presumably, as the word "theological" suggests, it is theological because in some way it has to do with God and, furthermore—since God is *God*—it has to do with God for God's own sake and not in order to "use" God to some further end. "Having to do with God" is, presumably, the school's overarching goal. But just how in actual practice does this school "have to do with God"?

What answer to this question is assumed by this school's practices, especially its practices of teaching and learning? Do they, for example, assume that it is the study of distinctive subject matters that marks the school as properly "theological"? Or, do they assume that some distinctive method disciplining inquiry into those subject matters makes it properly "theological"? Does the assumption that either of these is "distinctive" to a theological school prove sound when this school's teaching-and-learning is compared with supposedly "non-theological" teaching-learning in, say, "liberal arts" studies? Are they really all that different?

Do the practices that make up this school assume that what marks them off as "theological" is the fact that together they are aimed at preparing future clergy to fill ministerial functions competently? In that case "ministerial functions" seem to define the goal of the school. Are these functions defined in a theological or in a sociologically functionalist way?

If they are defined in a sociologically functionalist way, is not the school then in practice defined in a nontheological way (i.e., without significant reference to "God") and thus in no important way any longer precisely as a "theological" school?

If they are defined in a theological way, how in actual practice is this school's goal to educate persons for "ministerial functions" related to its overarching goal in some way "to have to do with God"? If "education for ministerial functions" is in practice *definitive* of "having to do with God," is that not an idolatry of ministerial functions? Surely there are other richer ways of "having to do with God"? On the other hand, if the concrete way this school does "have to do with God" is *ordered to* education for ministerial functions, is it not then in practice using "having to do with God" for a further, ulterior purpose ("educating for ministerial functions"), thus corrupting its proper theological character ("having to do with God for God's own sake")?

More broadly, what do the practices that constitute this school seem to assume would count as genuine *corruption* of its properly "theological" character? For example, are they in any way designed to draw attention to ways in which their "doing theology" might have become idolatrous, one-sided, ideological, or false? Do its practices of teaching and learning lay stress on the cultivation of critical capacities to identify and unmask such corruption?

The answers to these questions need to be framed as concretely as possible. The suggestion developed in this proposal is that discussion can be kept concrete if we reframe conventional description and analysis of a theological school in language centered on stipulated uses of "pluralistic," "understand," "concept," "act," and "practice." Among other things, this terminology makes it possible to exhibit what is deeply questionable about the contrast pair "theory/practice" that conventional wisdom likes to use in analyzing theological schools. Is the way that we "have to do with God" really analyzable into "theory" which is then subsequently applied in "practice"? Is it not at least as true to say that "having to do with God" is first of all *itself* a set of practices that gives form to subsequent critical reflection on it? Accordingly, is it any more adequate to the way this theological school "has to do with God" to analyze *it* in terms of a contrast between "theory" and "practice"? If this terminology seems inadequate to keep discussion of theological schooling concrete, what would be more adequate terminology?

2. What makes this school the concrete, particular *school* it is?

What is the *polity* of this school? How are the practices that constitute this school interrelated? The school is constituted by a great deal more than "teaching and learning." It is a community with a common life. It engages in worship. It engages in various types of self-regulation—ordering and, if necessary, disciplining its common life, managing its personal and material resources, admitting students, monitoring their progress through a course of study, evaluating their academic work, hiring faculty and staff and evaluating their work, and so forth. That is why it is inadequate to analyze a theological *school* mainly in pedagogical terms, for example, by critique of the school's relative reliance on "classroom" teaching vs. "field" or "contextual" learning. To be sure, there is no school without teaching, and more effective teaching would make for better schooling. But pedagogy is only one element of a far more complex whole. It takes all of these practices somehow braided together to make a school. All of this is done in ways that are to some degree institutionalized as the school's polity. Just how are the practices constituting this school intertwined? Just how is that intertwining institutionalized? How are power and status distributed in this polity? Who has access to them, on what conditions, to what degree?

What *historical* traditions determine the particularity of this school's culture and ethos? For example, what tradition or tradition of construal of the Christian thing has shaped it? (In other words, does it sit on the road from Geneva or Trent or Canterbury, etc.?) Which historic construals of the Christian thing does it explicitly own? What traditional judgments about how best to go about having to do with God shape it? the contemplative way? the affective way? the way of discursive thought? the way of action? What historical pictures of the relation between the school and the church shape it? If there is more than one, do they shape different aspects of the school's common life (one shaping its teaching and learning, another its life of worship, perhaps another its common life as a community of students, faculty, and staff)?

How does this school's social and cultural *location* help make it the concrete actuality it is? From what types of social location are its students, faculty, and staff drawn? How diverse is that and what tensions does that diversity create in the school's common life? Within the micro-society and culture that this crossroads hamlet is in itself, what types of social location are characteristically assigned to faculty, to staff, to students? As an institutionalized set of practices, how is this school located in its immediate social and cultural setting? How does it characteristically interact with its immediate neighborhood? What types of social dynamics and tensions do all of these factors create, helping to shape this school's characteristic communal identity?

How does this school negotiate between two *models* of excellent schooling to which it inescapably is heir and from neither of which it can escape: "Athens," which shapes theological schooling as paideia, through which people grow conceptually in regard to God by way of teaching that communicates indirectly, and "Berlin," which shapes theological schooling as "professional education" by way of inculcating capacities for rigorously disciplined critical and self-critical inquiry?

3. How does this school's being "theological" modify its concrete reality as "school"?

Does the particular way in which this school goes about "having to do with God" constrain its polity in any way? Does it require, for example, that the school's polity explicitly include institutionalized mechanisms enabling the school critically to examine the practices making up its common life for ways in which they are deformed ideologically and idolatrously? Because it is this school's way of "having to do with precisely *God,*" does it require that the school's polity institutionalize protection for "freedom to teach and freedom to learn?"

How does this school's particular way of "having to do with God" both unify the school's practices of teaching and learning into a single course of study and make them adequate to pluralism?

Whatever it is, is it in principle capable of doing both? Can it prevent a course of studies from fragmenting into a clutch of courses? Can it do that without minimizing or denying the reality of several sorts of deep pluralisms in the Christian thing? If it is capable of being adequate to the pluralism, does it do that in a way that simply increases the fragmentation of the course by requiring more and more additions to the clutch of courses?

If what makes this school properly "theological" is *not* the same as what the school relies on to unify its course of study and keep it adequate to pluralism, what does it rely on? How is it related to whatever it is this school assumes makes it a "theological" school? Can the two really be different and the course of study nonetheless remain genuinely a "theological" course of study? If the course of study were to be genuinely "theological," would that which unifies it and makes it adequate to pluralism not necessarily have to be the *same* as that which makes the school "theological"?

Does that which not only unifies this school's practices of teaching and learning into a single course of study but makes it adequate to pluralism imply a contrast between "academic" schooling and "professional" schooling? What defines "academic" schooling that "has to do with God"? Since conceptual capacities needed to understand God include capacities that are "existentially" significant while at the same time fully as rational and as rigorously disciplined as any other capacities to understand anything else, can academic schooling be understood adequately simply as the acquisition of capacities for disciplined accumulation and mastery of data and capacities for critical and self-critical theorizing (cf. the "Berlin" model)? So too, what defines "professional" schooling? Is professional not a sociological category? If theological schooling is defined sociologically as professional schooling, has not the theological integrity of the schooling been corrupted again?

The terminology suggested by this utopian proposal makes it pointless to contrast "academic" with "professional." It proposes to terminate an interminable discussion by proposing a way to reframe the issues. This prompts yet another line for critical reflection: Are the contrast pairs conventionally used in analysis of theological schooling really interchangeable?

The contrast pair "classroom/field" has to do with pedagogy, with questions about how to teach and in what contexts so that people learn best. Does not the pair "academic/professional" normally have to do, not with pedagogy, but with the social context of the goal of the schooling, with the question whether the schooling aims at preparing people to fill specific social roles (professional) or at making them generally well-informed and capable in all circumstances of "thinking critically" (academic)?

Moreover, does not the contrast pair "theory/practice" cut across both of the other two? Does it not pertain to the relation between thought and action? Does it not mainly have to do with what it is to understand and, perhaps more deeply, with what it is to be human? Do we not have to ask about the relation between theory and practice in *both* classroom and field, in *both* profession and academy? Can it really be, as conventional discussions of theological schooling so often seem to assume, that theory lines up with academic and classroom (and, as we shall see, "head"), while practice lines up with professional and field (and, as we shall see, "heart")? If the terminology proposed here for reframing these issues itself is finally judged to be inadequate, then what would be more adequate terminology?

How do the several relevant, recognized academic disciplines function in this school's practices of teaching and learning? That the school necessarily includes those practices means, in this culture, that it must necessarily include academic disciplines. How does the fact that it is a theological school constrain the concrete ways in which the disciplines function in these practices? Do the disciplines in effect determine the content of the courses and the organization of the curriculum? Do they use any particular organization of the curriculum to justify the autonomy of their own scholarly research agendas? Do they contribute to the fragmentation of the school's course of study?

Conversely, does the specific way in which this school "has to do with God" have the effect of minimizing the role of the disciplines and their ability to nurture in learners' capacities for independent and rigorous critical thinking? Is there any way in which this school's particular way of "having to do with God" can honor and embrace academic disciplines precisely by employing them in its own interests "having to do with God"?

4. How do the factors that make this theological school the particular concrete school it is shape or modify the way in which it is properly "theological"?

How do the historical heritage, the social and cultural location, the internal culture and ethos, and the polity of the school concretely particularize the school's way of "having to do with God"? These factors determine the concrete reality of the practices that comprise the school; how do they shape its practices of teaching and learning "having to do with God"?

For example, how do they shape the particular ways in which

authority and status in teaching and learning are assigned, acknowledged, and, if necessary, enforced?

How do practices other than those of explicit teaching and learning nonetheless conceptually form persons in the micro-culture that is the school? For example, how do the practices in which this school engages in transactions with its immediate neighborhood, with the larger host society and culture, with third-world cultures, or with other religious communities all help from learners' ways of "having to do with God"?

What does this school's polity effectively teach about what it is to "have to do with God"? How is this school's overarching goal concretely enacted by the role that worship has in its common life, and by how decisions about that role are made?

How does the particular culture of this crossroads hamlet concretely determine the way it attends to the personal religious life, the emotional life, the social life of the people who make up its population?

Is it adequate to pose the central diagnostic question in relation to these matters as a question whether this school in its full social reality tends more to form persons' "heads" or their "hearts," as though if it were more a matter of heart it would then necessarily be less a matter of head, or the reverse? The persons being formed are fully as concrete, as deeply particularized by history, by social location, by being bodies as is this school. It is the entire bodied agent who is formed by this theological school's complex of practices aimed at somehow "having to do with God." Do the contrast terms conventionally used in discussions of theological schooling, such as "head/heart," really serve to illuminate the relation between this school and these persons, or do they not rather tend to obscure it by abstracting it from its social, cultural, and very physical dimensions? The terminology suggested by this proposal as a way to reframe these issues makes the head/heart contrast pointless: "Conceptual capacities" are as necessary for emotional life (heart) as they are for critical reflection (head); bodily "action" is as integral to reflection (head) as is experience (heart), even "religious experience." However, if this terminology is finally judged to be inadequate too, then what would be more adequate?

This is but the beginning of the budget of questions for critical reflection about a theological school that is generated by the interplay among these four groups of questions. In the world of North American higher education most theological schools are like crossroads hamlets. However, down the roads at whose crossings they stand comes all the most powerful cultural traffic of their host society. This makes theological schools, for all their relatively small size, very complex microcosms of their larger siblings in academe and, indeed, of their larger social and cultural worlds. If one has for any reason invested one's life for a while in such a school, and especially if one has begun to feel a pinch between expectation and experience, it is important not only to reflect critically about the school but also to reflect critically about the way in which the school is being described and analyzed. Perhaps it is only by being ironically utopian that this or any proposal can serve as an invitation to just that sort of critical reflection about a theological school well known to you.

Select Bibliography of Books Cited

Ahlstrom, Sydney E. *A Religious History of the American People.* New Haven: Yale University Press, 1972.

Brown, William Adams, and Mark A. May, et al. *The Education of American Ministers,* 4 vols. New York: Institute of Social and Religious Research, 1934.

Cannon, Katie G., et al., and the Mud Flower Collective. *God's Fierce Whimsy: Christian Feminism and Theological Education.* New York: Pilgrim Press, 1985.

Chandler, Douglas R. *Pilgrimage of Faith: A Centennial History of Wesley Theological Seminary, 1882–1982.* Edited by C. C. Goen. Cabin John, Md.: Seven Locks Press, 1984.

Clebsch, William, and Charles R. Jaekle. *Pastoral Care in Historical Perspective.* New York: Harper & Row, 1975.

Cooke, Bernard J. *Ministry to Word and Sacraments: History and Theology.* Philadelphia: Fortress Press, 1976.

Deem, Warren. *Theological Education in the 1970's: A Report of the Resources Planning Commission.* Dayton, Ohio: Association of Theological Schools, 1968.

Dudley, Carl S., ed. *Building Effective Ministry: Theory and Practice in the Local Church.* San Francisco: Harper & Row, 1983.

Fallon, Daniel. *The German University: A Heroic Ideal in Conflict with the Modern World.* Boulder, Colo.: Colorado Associated University Press, 1980.

Farley, Edward. *The Fragility of Knowledge: Theological Education in the Church and the University.* Philadelphia: Fortress Press, 1988.

———. *Theologia: The Fragmentation and Unity of Theological Education.* Philadelphia: Fortress Press, 1983.

Gambrell, Mary Latimer. *Ministerial Training in Eighteenth-Century New England*. New York: Columbia University Press, 1937.

Gustafson, James M. *Treasure in Earthen Vessels: The Church as a Human Community*. New York: Harper & Row, 1961.

Handy, Robert. *A History of Union Theological Seminary in New York*. New York: Columbia University Press, 1987.

Hopewell, James F. *Congregation: Stories and Structures*. Philadelphia: Fortress Press, 1987.

Hough, Joseph C., Jr., and Barbara G. Wheeler, eds. *Beyond Clericalism: The Congregation as a Focus for Theological Education*. Atlanta: Scholars Press, 1988.

Hough, Joseph C., Jr., and John B. Cobb, Jr. *Christian Identity and Theological Education*. Chico, Calif.: Scholars Press, 1985.

Jaeger, Werner. *Paideia: Ideals of Greek Culture*. 3 vols. Trans. Gilbert Highet. Oxford: Basil Blackwell, 1939–1963.

———. *Early Christianity and Greek Paideia*. Cambridge, Mass.: Harvard University Press, 1961.

Kelly, Robert. *Theological Education in America*. New York: George H. Doran Co., 1924.

King, Gail Buchwalter, ed. *ATS Fact Book on Theological Education for the Academic Years 1988–89 and 1989–90*. Pittsburgh: Association of Theological Schools, 1990.

Lindbeck, George A. *The Nature of Doctrine: Religion and Theology in a Postliberal Age*. Philadelphia: Westminster Press, 1984.

Lobkowicz, Nikolaus. *Theory and Practice: History of a Concept from Aristotle to Marx*. Notre Dame, Ind.: University of Notre Dame Press, 1967.

MacIntyre, Alasdair. *After Virtue: A Study in Moral Theory*. Notre Dame, Ind.: University of Notre Dame Press, 1981.

McInerny, Ralph. *St. Thomas Aquinas*. Notre Dame, Ind.: University of Notre Dame Press, 1982.

Meeks, Wayne A. *The First Urban Christians: The Social World of the Apostle Paul*. New Haven, Conn.: Yale University Press, 1983.

Niebuhr, H. Richard, et al. *The Purpose of the Church and Its Ministry: Reflections on the Aims of Theological Education*. New York: Harper & Brothers, 1956.

———, Daniel Day Williams and James M. Gustafson. *The Advancement of Theological Education: The Summary Report of a Mid-century Study*. New York: Harper & Brothers, 1957.

Paulsen, Friedrich. *The German Universities and University Study*. Trans. E. T. F. Thilly and W. W. Elang. New York: Charles Scribner's Sons, 1906.

Placher, William C. *Unapologetic Theology: A Christian Voice in a Pluralistic Conversation*. Louisville, Ky.: Westminster/John Knox Press, 1989.

Preller, Victor. *Divine Science and the Science of God: A Reformulation of Thomas Aquinas*. Princeton, N.J.: Princeton University Press, 1967.

Rahner, Karl. *Theological Investigations,* vol. 3. New York: Seabury Press, 1974.

Schreiter, Robert J. *Constructing Local Theologies*. Maryknoll, N.Y.: Orbis Books, 1985.

Schuth, Katarina, ed. *U.S. Catholic Seminaries and Their Future*. Washington, D.C.: United States Catholic Conference, 1988.

Stackhouse, Max L., et al. *Apologia: Contextualization, Globalization, and Mission in Theological Education*. Grand Rapids: Wm. B. Eerdmans Publishing Co., 1988.

Toulmin, Stephen. *Human Understanding*. Vol. 1: *The Collective Use and Evolution of Concepts*. Princeton, N.J.: Princeton University Press, 1972.

Vos, Arvin. *Aquinas, Calvin, and Contemporary Protestant Thought: A Critique of Protestant Views on the Thought of Thomas Aquinas*. Grand Rapids: Wm. B. Eerdmans Publishing Co., 1985.

Wheeler, Barbara G., and Edward Farley, eds. *Shifting Boundaries: Contextual Approaches to the Structure of Theological Education*. Louisville, Ky.: Westminster/John Knox Press, 1991.

Wilken, Robert L. *The Myth of Christian Beginnings: History's Impact on Belief.* Garden City, N.Y.: Doubleday & Co., Anchor Books, 1972.

Wolterstorff, Nicholas. *Art in Action: Toward a Christian Aesthetic*. Grand Rapids: Wm. B. Eerdmans Publishing Co., 1980.

Wood, Charles M. *The Formation of Christian Understanding: An Essay in Theological Hermeneutics*. Philadelphia: Westminster Press, 1981.

―――. *Vision and Discernment: An Orientation in Theological Study*. Atlanta: Scholars Press, 1985.

Index

academic freedom. *See* freedom, academic
action: as charity, 37; contemplation and, 35–38, 45–46; as public, 35, 37, 47; understanding God as, 45–49
action, concept of, 118–124. *See also* paideia; practices
affections, religious, 42–45
agency. *See* action, concept of
Andover Theological Seminary, 54
Aristotle, 39, 40, 45, 72
asceticism, 37–38, 46
Association of Theological Schools (ATS), 14, 18, 93
Athanasius, 201
"Athens" model of schooling, 64, 72–75, 236, 259. *See also* paideia
Augustine, 37, 38, 42, 201
authority, 87–88, 202
Azusa Street Mission, 43

Basil of Caesarea, 201
"Berlin" model of schooling; 64, 236, 259; American modifications of, 93–94; and curriculum, 88–89; historical methods and, 91–92; influence of, in U.S.A., 83; as professional, 88–97; public character of,
92; role of theory in, 95–96; teacher-student relationship in, 91–92; understanding God and, 90. *See also* research university; *Wissenschaft*.
Berlin, University of, 78–83, 86, 91
Bible. *See* narratives, biblical; scripture
bodiliness, 119–122
Bonaventure, 42, 44, 45
Brown, William Adams, 93
bureaucracy, 122

Calvin, John, 72
Cannon, Katie, 106
Carroll, Jackson W., 245
charity, 37–38
Chesterton, G. K., 32, 203
Chicago, University of, 93
Christian life. *See* understanding God
Christianity, "essence" of; 33, 213; curriculum and, 105–106, 221; Schleiermacher's views on, 88–89, 243
"Christian thing," the: in "Berlin" model, 90; congregations as focusing, 110–111, 131; construals of, 32–33, 49, 109–110, 117, 134, 186–187; curriculum and, 204–